CHARLES
WATERTON
1782–1865
Traveller and Conservationist

JULIA BLACKBURN
Foreword by GERALD DURRELL

CENTURY
LONDON SYDNEY AUCKLAND JOHANNESBURG

For Hein, Natasha and Martin Thomas

First published by The Bodley Head Ltd, London,
1989.

Published in paperback in 1991 by Century
Random Century Ltd
20 Vauxhall Bridge Road, London SW1V 2SA

Century Hutchinson Australia (Pty) Ltd
20 Alfred Street, Milsons Point, Sydney, NSW 2061,
Australia

Century Hutchinson New Zealand Ltd
9-11 Rothwell Avenue, Albany, Auckland 10, New
Zealand

Century Hutchinson South Africa (Pty) Ltd
PO Box 337, Bergvlei 2012, South Africa

Set in Sabon

Printed and bound in U.K. by The Guernsey Press,
Guernsey, Channel Islands

British Library Cataloguing in Publication Data

Blackburn, Julia
Charles Waterton. –New ed.
1. Natural History. Waterton, Charles
I. Title II. Series
508.092
ISBN 0-7126-4746-5

CONTENTS

LIST OF ILLUSTRATIONS

ACKNOWLEDGEMENTS

Because much of the Waterton material is in private collections my research has, to a considerable extent, been dependent on the kindness and indeed the hospitality of a number of individuals. Gordon Watson, Senior Keeper at the Wakefield Museum where most of Waterton's taxidermal work is housed, provided me with a network of contacts as well as giving me access to all the material at the museum. Bari Logan, Anatomy Prosector at Cambridge University and formerly Prosector to the Royal College of Surgeons, kindly made his considerable archive of letters and papers available to me. The Reverend F. J. Turner, Librarian at Stonyhurst College, was most helpful and informative and unexpectedly discovered a bundle of letters connected with Waterton's legal battle with the soap manufacturer. John Goodchild, Principal Local Studies Officer and Archivist at the Balne Lane Library, Wakefield, made his private archive collection available which included important biographical material on Edmund Waterton and on the Simpson family. Jim Daniel of Batley gave me access to his very interesting collection of Waterton family papers which includes material relating to Waterton's marriage. Sister Mary Aline, Archivist at the English Convent, Bruges, painstakingly went through the convent records with me, and helped a great deal with my research. Mrs Ann Moore of Hancox allowed me to consult the Waterton family papers which had originally been collected by her husband's grandfather, Norman Moore.

Gerald Durrell read the manuscript in its early and later stages, and gave me the encouragement of his own immense fondness for Waterton. Anthea Morton-Saner, my agent at Curtis Brown, has been immensely supportive throughout. I would also like to thank my editor Jill Black, my mother Rosalie Blackburn, Florence Pieters,

Librarian at the Artis Library, University of Amsterdam, Sandra van Beek, C. M. Bonger, and my husband, Hein Bonger.

The London Library has been the chief source for all the books and periodicals I have consulted. The most recent edition of Charles Waterton's *Wanderings in South America* is published by Century Publishing Company, and I am indebted to it for a number of references.

FOREWORD

Of all the strange birds in the wilderness down in Demerara, Charles
Waterton was surely the strangest. It is unfortunate, however, that his
extreme eccentricity has always obscured his importance as a naturalist, writer, observer and conservationist; but now, at last, we have this
important book which puts him in the right perspective.

Of course, Waterton was an eccentric and his life story reads like
something invented by Edgar Allan Poe with a certain amount of help
from Richard Jefferies, but we have always needed the eccentrics to
point the way. It was Waterton who warned the Americans, for
example, of the ultimate cost of their profligate destruction of their
forests. It was Waterton who fought against the beginnings of pollution in the Industrial Revolution. It was he who turned the grounds
of Walton Hall into a sanctuary, even maintaining trees with holes in
them in which birds could nest and building a special bank for
sandmartins. Is it also to be considered eccentric that this humane man
would have what were in those days called lunatics up to the Hall from
the local asylum and allow them to view his lake with its birds through
his telescope? Nowadays, it would be called excellent therapy. It was
Waterton who warned that if we did not mend our ways and respect
the world we live in and not ravage it, we would go to hell in a
handcart.

He was a man who did no harm to the world he lived in but
enhanced it by his presence and his care of it. Would that we could all
have a similar epitaph.

GERALD DURRELL
May 1988

ix

'He is mad in patches, full of lucid intervals'

Cervantes

INTRODUCTION

You are old, Father William, the young man said,
And your hair has become very white;
But yet you incessantly stand on your head,
Do you think, at your age, it is right?[1]

Charles Waterton in his eighties and nearing the end of his life was said to look 'like a person recently discharged from prison',[2] or, as another friend chose to describe him, 'a spider after a long winter'.[3] Often he was dressed in such shabby clothes that he could be mistaken for a vagrant or a poor farm labourer, but on formal occasions he would wear a dark blue, brass-buttoned, swallow-tailed coat that was a little too tight and almost a hundred years out of fashion, loose trousers much too short in the leg, and a top hat with a peculiar stiffness to it caused by regular immersions in a solution of bichloride of mercury, a powerful acid which he used to protect his specimens of natural history, his shoes and anything else that might get damaged by insects or the weather. His hands were surprisingly large and heavy; his hair was always cut close to his skull; he was tall, but although he did not stoop his emaciated appearance made people presume that he was small. He was double-jointed and could place his foot on his head and pick up small objects with his toes, and even until the year of his death he was able to climb high trees at a great speed. There was a gentleness and an intensity in his facial expression which for some people was disconcerting. He had a heavy Yorkshire accent and when he spoke it sounded as if he was munching walnuts at the same time.

His private territory was a park surrounded by a high stone wall; a landscape of innumerable trees, many of them so battered by the years that they looked like the dried and fragmented carcasses of ancient reptiles. Barefoot, he might clamber amongst the branches of an oak where he could sit and watch a barn owl who watched him in return. Barefoot, he paid his daily visit to the top of a high fir tree where a jackdaw had her nest. Silently he would crouch beside a bluetit sitting on her eggs: she had grown so accustomed to his presence that

1

she did not fly away, even when he stroked the feathers of her back.

In the eighteenth-century country house that was his family home the main entrance hall and the wide staircase served as a museum, crowded with specimens of natural history and with blowpipes, feathered headdresses and classical paintings, as well as Waterton's own nightmarish taxidermal creations including a thing called the Nondescript, which looked like the head and shoulders of an ageing elf with a worried expression, but was in fact moulded with great care from the hindquarters of a howler monkey. The hallway led into the front drawing room where a large telescope stared out across a wide expanse of lake water. Sometimes Waterton would swing from the carved door frame or stand on his head, and then his two sisters-in-law would praise him politely but with genuine enthusiasm, as they had done so many times before. In the adjoining dining room there was a long table where breakfast, lunch and tea were served with meticulous punctuality, and where Waterton might recently have been at work dissecting an adult male gorilla sent to him in a barrel of rum. Unfortunately the animal had been too long in the spirits and could not be added to the museum collection; only the bones were worth keeping.

Charles Waterton was odd, he was in many ways very odd, and his oddness grew more pronounced as he grew older. But during his own lifetime he was also extremely famous, not only for his eccentricities, but also for his achievements and his outspoken opinions. He was a naturalist who turned his private park in the West Riding of Yorkshire into a sanctuary for birds and animals, and in a single year more than 17,000 visitors came to see the extraordinary accumulation of wild life that had chosen to live within its boundaries. He was an explorer, and in the early part of his life he learnt how to survive in the tropical rain forests of South America, without using a gun, without wearing shoes, and without having contact with other white men for months on end. He was also a taxidermist, and his museum contained specimens of natural history that were preserved with better anatomical accuracy and skill than could be seen anywhere else in Europe at that time. Above all he was what would now be called a conservationist, and he fought passionately to protect wild nature in an age when birds, animals, trees, everything that lived and was not human was in danger of being unthinkingly and haphazardly destroyed.

Waterton's book about his travels, *Wanderings in South America* first published in 1826, was disapproved of by his more serious-minded contemporaries, because of its humorous and erratic style, but nevertheless it won him a huge reading public. It is not possible to assess how many copies were sold before the turn of the century, since he never held a copyright and it was produced by several publishers and in many editions, but one reviewer in the 1830s could confidently state, 'that delightful book is now in almost every hand in the land'.[4] It was translated into French, German and Spanish and was highly successful in America, where 'Captain Waterton', grappling with a boa constrictor and riding on the back of a crocodile, appeared on the cover of several popular magazines.[5] Theodore Roosevelt felt that the book marked 'the beginning of literature wherein field naturalists who were also men of letters, have described for us the magic and interest, the terror and the beauty of the far-off wilds, where nature gives peace to bold souls and inspires terror in the mind'.[6]

The later collections of *Essays on Natural History* (three volumes, 1838, 1844 and 1857), although not apparently so widely read, were greatly admired for their accuracy in detailed observation, as well as for the intimate and vivid way in which they were written. Dickens was 'very partial' to them;[7] so too was Charles Darwin who praised 'such discussions and observations on what the world would call trifling points of Natural History which to me appear very interesting'.[8]

Why is it then that since his death in 1865, the memory of Waterton's eccentricity has flourished, but most of the facts of his life and his way of thinking have been forgotten or apparently ignored? It could be said that his reputation was disrupted by two men: his son Edmund, and his former physician Richard Hobson. For his own complex reasons the son managed within a very short period of time to sell, to lose and to destroy almost everything that had been of value to his father. What has survived in the way of papers, journals and letters, museum specimens and even the odd nesting box in the remnants of the park, has survived in spite of this determined filial effort. The physician, Dr Hobson, was a close family friend until the occasion of a bitter quarrel which took place three years before Waterton's death. Inspired it would seem by this quarrel, he produced a book called *Charles Waterton: His Home, Habits and Handiwork. Reminiscences of an Intimate and Most Confiding Personal Association for Nearly Thirty Years* (first published 1866). It is a book written in the spirit of a curious ambivalence, with praise and derision going hand in hand, and the 'esteemed and worthy naturalist', emerging like a Don Quixote but without humanity; Alice's White Knight without even a horse to carry him through the world. Much of the information is simply false; much involves a stretching and an embroidering of the truth to make the hero appear more dramatic but also much more foolish.

Hobson's book served as the model on which Waterton's present reputation as an eccentric has been built. It was first referred to by Norman Douglas in a collection of essays published in 1925, in which he celebrates 'that mad Englishman . . . that dodo of a man . . . so unsystematic, so very permanently unsynthetic, fragmentary in every point save one: his crankiness.'[9] Edith Sitwell followed suit in her book *English Eccentrics* (1933) in which the 'care-worn' Dr Hobson can be seen watching his good friend climbing a tree 'like an adolescent gorilla'.[10] Philip Gosse and Richard Aldington in their biographies, *The Squire of Walton Hall*, 1940, and *The Strange Life of Charles Waterton*, 1949, also relied on Hobson in preference to Waterton's own writing.

This is not to deny that Waterton was an eccentric in his way of dressing and behaving, in his writing style and his defiant Catholicism —Graham Greene remarked that 'Roman Catholicism has always been a great breeder of eccentrics in England. One cannot picture a man like Charles Waterton belonging to any other faith'[11]—but the root of his oddness, at least in the eyes of many of his contemporaries, lay in his passionate love of wild nature. It was considered decidedly eccentric to enjoy owls flying through your room at night; to sit in a tree to study a bird rather than to examine it stretched out dead on a dissecting table; to pay sixpence for every live hedgehog brought to your park; to encourage weasels and other 'vermin' to breed; to declare yourself a friend of the hawk and the carrion crow; to keep old trees standing and to doctor them if a branch was broken or a fungus grew from their side. It was naive to declare that the forests of South America were places where there was no danger from savage beasts, so long as one did not offer to attack them first. It was anti-social to wage a long legal battle with a local factory owner, who, as one of the early producers of what is now called acid rain, was spilling his chemical effluents into the surrounding countryside. It was, for many people, although of course not for all, very old-fashioned and short-sighted to be horrified by the encroachment of the industrial world and to try to create at least one small and enclosed island of safety where wild creatures would find no human enemy.

CHAPTER I

Brown Rats and Black Rats

Many people who met Waterton for the first time, as well as those who knew him well, were impressed by his extreme gentleness, the inner calm of someone who had learnt to sit still, watching, endlessly watching. But there was a savagery in him as well. It erupted in bursts of fury against certain human beings, especially scientifically-minded naturalists, and it was also released in his lifelong hatred of the common brown rat or, as he called it, the 'Hanoverian Rat'. Perhaps an understanding of his attitude towards this rat can give a first clue towards an appreciation of the nature of the man, and the world he felt he inhabited.

The Watertons had been staunch Catholics for generations, and when Waterton was a child his father told him the story of how the brown rats defeated the black rats. It was a political fable, and one that was told by many Catholics in England at that time, who felt that they, like the black rats, had been turned into exiles in their own land. It was said that the brown rats landed on English soil in the year 1688, and that they were brought over the Channel on the same boat that was carrying the Protestant King William of Orange, who came to oust the Catholic James II. These brown rats were short-nosed and short-tailed, fierce, cunning and filled with self-righteous Protestant zeal, and they were merciless in their treatment of the black rats. Those whom they failed to kill were forced to live in isolated pockets of the countryside, far from the comforts of the big cities, and stripped of all power and authority.

This then was how the brown rat became known, incorrectly, as the 'Hanoverian Rat', and the many things that the English Catholics hated about their foreign King, his Church and his State, were heaped on to the countless flea-bitten shoulders of a very determined and prolific rodent. But whereas Waterton's family would have treated the story as an ironic metaphor of their predicament, Waterton himself allowed his hatred to become a complex obsession. Although he was loath to kill or to hurt any living creature, he was ruthless in his attempts to destroy the brown rat. He had a team of ratting cats, led at one time by a wild Marjay tiger cat from the forests of Guiana,[1] he concocted deadly but irresistible mixtures of porridge and treacle laced with arsenic, and he took pleasure in watching his victims die. He was once seen holding a rat by its tail and twirling it through the air, before dashing its brains out with a wild cry of 'Death to all Hanoverians!' He bricked and barricaded the floor, the walls and the underground tunnels of his house, and he devised complicated traps that would catch just this one enemy. On several occasions he proudly announced that the Hanoverians were defeated for ever, but then some new representatives of this tribe of house-haunters would creep back into his territory and the battle was on once more.

In the life of Charles Waterton, different aspects of the story of the two races of rats will return again and again. He saw himself as a black rat, marooned on the safe island of his house and his park, while all around him, beyond this boundary, the English landscape was filled with Hanoverians of one sort or another. Visitors who came through the gate and over the narrow bridge that led to the house had to agree to accept certain rules of behaviour which might have seemed odd anywhere else, and, if they objected, then they could leave. This is not to say that Waterton lived in a state of dread of the outside world, but rather that he found it extremely important for the sake of his own sense of well-being to keep it at bay. The extraordinary sanctuary that he made for birds, animals and trees was also a sanctuary for himself.

Charles Waterton was born on 3 June 1782, and he was buried on his birthday eighty-three years later. His family was aristocratic and stubbornly Catholic, and although he had four brothers and one sister, as the eldest son he took upon himself the responsibility of carrying the weight of his ancestry through into the next generation. Among his surviving papers there is a little undated piece[2] in which he explains that he would have liked to become a Jesuit priest, but determined to marry for the sake of perpetuating the family name. However, although he eventually did marry and had a son who in turn had children of his own, he was in many ways the last of a long line of Watertons. He inherited that peculiarly defiant and isolated mentality which characterized the Catholic aristocracy in England up until the mid-nineteenth century, and with his death that tradition of defiance was brought to an end. From his mother Anne Bedingfield, and from his father Thomas Waterton, he came from determined stock; there were said to be nine martyred saints in the family, and on his mother's side he was a direct descendant of Henry VIII's unbending chancellor, Sir Thomas More.

Going back as far as the records will go, the first Waterton was Reiner, the son of Norman of Normandy, who became Lord of Waterton in the county of Lancashire in the year 1159. Charles was the twenty-seventh inheritor of this title, although since the Reformation the family has not been able to use it. There was a Sir John who was Master of the Horse to Henry V, and a Sir Robert who was Governor of Pontefract Castle when Richard II was imprisoned within its walls. Watertons had fought at the Battle of Agincourt, and they were prominent among the lords who became entangled in the Wars of the Roses. Shakespeare mentions the name in *Richard II*. Waterton was reported to have said that the family library contained a first folio edition of the play with a dedication by the author, but if that was so then it must have been sold at one of the many auctions which followed so quickly on the heels of Waterton's death, as it has since disappeared without trace.

During the reign of Henry VIII, 'our royal goat' as Waterton called him, members of the family maintained their faith and as a consequence lost a number of material benefits, though they fought for Charles I at Marston Moor during the Civil War. William III, the first of the line of Hanoverian rats, pulled the net still tighter: a Roman Catholic could not sit in Parliament, could not hold a commission in the army, could not be a justice of the peace, and could not attend an English school or university. He was not allowed to keep a horse valued at more than five pounds for fear he might lead an army, and not allowed to have more than two horses drawing a carriage for fear that he might be plotting a rebellion. Up until the early eighteenth century he had to pay double land taxes on whatever land he had left, and if he refused to attend the local parish church every Sunday there was a monthly fine of twenty pounds. By the end of the eighteenth century many of these laws had been modified or had lapsed, but the remaining Catholic families who had resisted conversion were still to some extent considered outcasts by the rest of the English establishment.

At the time of Waterton's birth, his family owned the house that they lived in, Walton Hall, in the West Riding of Yorkshire and the park of almost 300 acres which encircled it; while in the nearby village of Walton they leased out a few cottages, some arable land and two farms. Their income was sufficient to run the estate, and they had certain overseas investments but they were far from being wealthy.

When he died Waterton had £585. 18s. 2d. in the bank, and the house was heavily mortgaged.

During the long years of Catholic oppression most of Waterton's relatives had moved out of England and gone to live in more congenial countries: he had uncles in southern Spain, cousins in Belgium, and there were other members of the tribe who had settled in South America, North America and New Zealand. Only this one pocket of resistance had maintained its territorial rights in the West Riding of Yorkshire, and the surviving account books from the eighteenth century[3] show that the Watertons were remarkably self-sufficient and isolated, even for those times. They had their own priest and their own doctor, and no need of the outside world, or interest in it either unless it happened to be related to them by blood or by religion. In return they expected to be left alone. The siege mentality had been acquired over the years and it was practised with great thoroughness.

There are a few brief glimpses of Waterton's parents: it is like looking through a tunnel to catch a distant image, a floating detail out of context with its surroundings. His mother was once stopped at a toll gate because she had three horses pulling her carriage; she circumvented the problem by going home and setting out again with a team of oxen yoked in front of her. When Waterton was three years old he swallowed the tiny and delicate egg of a meadow lark, and when his mother learnt what he had done she made him swallow a powerful mustard 'vomit' to empty his body of the unknown danger. She displayed a similarly dramatic response when a visitor's dog went mad, and showing all the obvious signs of rabies raced from the house, wild-eyed and foaming at the mouth. The dog was caught and destroyed before it had done any harm, but Mrs Waterton solemnly assembled the entire household and insisted that they must all drink a foul-tasting patent medicine to protect them from the effects of a bite which they had not received and from a disease for which there was no known cure. As an added precaution she arranged for her eldest son's dog to be hung. Maybe such a ritual removal of fears was not so strange in that age, but when Waterton wrote about the incident many years later, it still shocked him deeply.

All that we know directly of Thomas Waterton is that he explained the history of the rats, perpetrated one joke, and asked one question. He can also be known indirectly from a bundle of letters which he received from his formidable aunt, Mary Augustine More, and by his hasty decision to demolish the Elizabethan manor house that was Walton Hall, and replace it with something large, symmetrical and slightly Palladian.

The one joke seems too macabre to be called funny, but maybe that is to do with the thinking of another age. A fisherman caught an eel, which a heron then swallowed, complete with the hook and line. The eel slipped out of the heron's anus and was promptly caught by another heron. This incident was repeated until there was a row of fifteen birds ignominiously strung together. Thomas Waterton found the sight so remarkable that he decided to let the birds die, and then he propped them in a row against the wall of his house where they stood for many years as a topic of wonder and conversation.

Waterton senior was interested in animals and birds in as much as he rode horses, hunted, fished, and shot. When his son had finished his academic studies, he enquired, 'with a gracious though significant smile', if these studies had served any useful purpose and what he now planned to do with his life. Shortly after this brief interview Waterton left home, to go first to Spain and then to South America; when he finally came back to settle in England many years later, his father was long since dead.

The aunt who wrote to Thomas Waterton was the mother superior at the English Convent in Bruges, Belgium. There are twenty letters which date from 1779 to 1791. In the background there are fleeting references to the political developments of the French Revolution, while in the foreground there is a very forthright and tenacious lady, watching the approach of the revolutionary armies and, it would seem, rather enjoying the sense of imminent emergency and danger.

One odd and perplexing story is contained within these letters. On several occasions Mother More sent her nephew the fond greetings of his wife at the convent, and then almost in the same breath she went on to enquire after the well-being of his wife and young family in England. There is even one letter from the lady herself. She bore the name of Eusebia Pickering, and described herself as:

> your once sweet and beloved wife, and I must confess I am not a little proud of the order, as it may serve to revive your former sentiments in my regard, as for my part I remain constantly and invariably the same being. With sincere regards and esteem
>
> Sir,
> Your Obliged Humble Servant[4]

Eusebia Pickering was of Portuguese-English descent. She arrived at the convent in 1758, when she was twenty years old, accompanied by her two sisters. There is no way of knowing where or how she lived before that time, but she was the same age as Thomas Waterton, and it is possible that she had reason for considering herself to be his wife even though her 'marriage' had never been solemnized in a church. Perhaps she had been placed in the convent so that she could make no claims on the twenty-sixth Lord of Walton Hall, but it is strange that Mother More should refer to her with such regularity, and it would seem such mock solemnity, and strange too that a letter from her to her 'husband' should have been preserved.

The convent archives also contain a brief but meticulous account of the way that each member of the order confronted and dealt with the act of dying, and here there is a last brief glimpse of Eusebia, who died 'in great peace and resignation in the seventy-second year of her age and the fifty-second of her profession . . . she was naturally of good temper, till it became considerably attacked by anxiety and scruples, and reasoning fell until she had no reason left. Superiors were afraid to contradict her, fearing she might lose her senses, as some of her family had had that misfortune.'

There is one final aspect of Thomas Waterton which can be seen by looking at the house he built. He inherited Walton Hall in 1767, when he was twenty-nine years old, and his first act of possession was to remove all traces of the original building, apart from an old water gate beside the lake which was left crumbling and alone and which later served as a nesting site for so many birds. The building that he erected was, and indeed still is, solemn and imposing, much in the way that a bank or a town hall might be. The house is rectangular, the stone is grey, the windows are large, plain and sensible. There are no carvings or decorations to divert the eye, although just above the main entrance there is the family crest: a stone carving of an otter with a fat fish in its mouth. This is surmounted by the cryptic motto, 'Better kinde frende than strange kyne', which can be roughly translated as meaning that it is not always a good idea to trust one's relatives.

The building was imposing even if it was unremarkable and without ghosts, but the view from the windows was spectacular. The house stood on a small natural island close to the southern bank of the lake. Thomas Waterton replaced the original stone bridge with a delicately-curving cast-iron one, which could carry a horse and rider, but would not support even a small carriage. The lake itself covered an area of over thirty acres, and it was long and meandering, so that from the house it looked like a motionless river. In spite of the eighteenth-century fashion for landscaping, the park had been left pretty much to itself. There was a carriageway to the main gate, a grotto, an arbour and a kitchen garden by the stable buildings, but apart from these

10

intrusions it was a huge and untamed area, with a few marshy meadows and thousands of trees.

Walton Hall was situated three miles from the village of Walton, and ten miles from what was then the small market town of Wakefield. Leeds was fifteen miles to the north and Liverpool was eighty miles to the west. During the last quarter of the eighteenth century the area was already beginning to undergo dramatic changes. It has been said that 1782, coincidentally the year of Charles Waterton's birth, can be chosen to mark a point of transition from which there was a sudden upsurge in industrial output throughout the manufacturing districts of England. From that time on there was a spiralling growth of population and production, which would change the face of the land beyond all recognition within the space of a few years.

Throughout Waterton's lifetime Walton Hall was surrounded, and eventually hemmed in, by such changes. A tangled web of new coal mines, iron foundries, cotton mills and corn mills, factories and slums, was spreading out steadily and inexorably across the surrounding countryside. In the 1780s Leeds had a population of about 20,000; by the 1860s it had reached almost 200,000. Similar concentrations of human beings, their houses and their machines were accumulating all over the north of England.

It is against this background that Waterton's early childhood and later behaviour must be seen. When he was young the huge silhouettes of buzzards were a common feature over the wide heathlands near Walton village. By 1813 the last buzzard had been shot, the common lands were neatly parcelled into fields, and tall factory chimneys were sprouting up in all directions, their smoke poisoning the air. The last raven in Yorkshire was sighted, and shot, in 1820. The herons which used to build their nests in such untidy heaps were becoming increasingly scarce; swallows avoided the area and sandmartins had all but disappeared. The threat of industrial pollution and the growth of the human population was coupled with rapid improvements in firearm technology, so that it became increasingly easy to shoot huge numbers of birds and animals. When he was an old man, Waterton wrote to one of his sisters-in-law, describing a journey he had made from Walton Hall to just beyond Leeds. Once he had left his own park, his sanctuary teeming with an extraordinary profusion of wild life, he neither saw nor heard a single bird, until the moment when he was walking up the little hill which led to his friend's house, when a robin burst into brave song. Certain aspects of Waterton's character, and the patterns that his life followed, developed out of what he considered to be a sharp necessity.

CHAPTER II

Aspects of an Education

Waterton remembered his childhood in a series of anecdotes: brief, vivid, and often macabre. He made no comment, he made little attempt to describe himself, or the people who came into contact with him, he simply wrote down an accumulation of the images which haunted or impressed him when he was a child and which remained with him throughout his life, like an assortment of pebbles in a box.

There was a Scottish boy who had two thumbs on one hand; a horse which gave birth to a foal without any vestige of a tail; a tree stump where the body of a murderer had been hung long ago, and a sliver of whose wood was a certain cure for toothache. There was a huge black horse with a headless rider which was said to rise up out of the village pond on the night when death was due in some household, and the less impressive ghost of a large brown mouse which haunted the streets by night, and had often been seen by a farmer who described his fears to the young Waterton who was interested to know more about such things. There was Tiger Duff, a man who visited Waterton's first school, with a scar across his cheek which bore witness to the fact that he had been bitten by a Bengal tiger, and 'seeing me stare at his face, he most kindly allowed me to examine the scar.'[1]

Throughout his life Waterton maintained a tactile approach to the external world. He wanted to taste it, to roll in it, to get closer and closer still to everything which invited his curiosity. At the age of three he had swallowed that lark's egg and been punished by his mother; a few years later he was creeping across a roof trying to reach a starling's nest and was punished by the housekeeper. At night when the moon was full he would escape from his bedroom, cross the iron bridge and climb into the branches of an old oak tree which stood by the lake, and from there he could watch a family of foxes dance and fight beneath him. For this he was never found out, and so he was never punished.

12

Seventy years later he was still busy in the same kind of way: up in a pine tree with a rook's egg held gently in his mouth (he wanted to know if the parent bird would consider the egg in some way changed by the experience); writing to a friend trying to describe the peculiar flavour of a swallow's nest—'I have chewed a piece for a quarter of an hour but found it absolutely tasteless';[2] talking to the droves of hedgehogs he had encouraged to come and live in the safe confines of his park.

> I am a great friend of the hedgehog . . . On a summer's evening at about four o'clock, you may see my hedgehogs slowly advancing from the woods in quest of food. And if you know how to act, you may approach within two feet of them, and see them thrusting their snouts into the sward, and fetching out fat grubs . . .[3]

Until he was nine years old, Waterton was tutored at home, and allowed the freedom of the park and countryside around Walton Hall. His formal education began when he was sent to a newly-established Catholic school called Tudhoe, in the county of Durham, some fifty miles away from familiar territory. For the next four years he was there almost continuously, without even returning to Walton for the summer vacation, and he hated the place. The landscape in which he found himself had a classic beauty 'with an ample supply of weeds and hedgerow trees to insure a sufficient stock of carrion crows, jackdaws, jays, magpies, brown owls, kestrels, merlins and sparrow hawks, for the benefit of natural history and my own instruction and amusement'.[4] But his teachers in no way appreciated their new pupil's need to climb trees and struggle into bushes, and so a battle was set in motion, with Waterton endlessly inventing new ways to escape from his captivity, and in return being punished, severely and repeatedly, for his defiance.

The master of the school was a 'profound Latin scholar' called Mr Storey. All that was remembered of him was the beatings he administered, the Pasche eggs which he dyed purple at Eastertime, and the fact that he had two curled wigs, in one of which the school cat gave birth to a litter of kittens. The other figure of authority was the Reverend Joseph Shepherd, a 'very correct disciplinarian', and on one occasion when he was being especially savagely beaten by this priest, Waterton managed to bite into the calf of his leg, and was proud to recollect how his sharp teeth pierced right through the worsted woollen stockings.

Waterton did have two good friends at Tudhoe. There was a fellow pupil called Jones, who later visited Rome with him when together they climbed the dome of St Peter's and fixed white gloves to the lightning conductor, much to the indignation of the church officials. It was this same Jones, or Captain Jones as he became, although what he was a captain of is never made clear, who in 1826 painted the portrait of Waterton riding sedately on the back of a crocodile, watched over by a cornucopia of jungle creatures. Then there was Old Joe Bowren who performed the duties of butcher, pig-server, scrub and brewer, and with whom Waterton was, as he described it, 'hand in glove'. Presumably it was from this man of 'vast bodily bulk' that he learnt some of the things he considered important in life: the whereabouts of otters and weasels; the habits of certain birds and animals; ways of trapping brown rats; ways of escaping or hiding in times of trouble.

Old Joe later migrated to Waterton's second school, Stonyhurst College in Lancashire, and there the two of them were able to renew their 'valuable acquaintance'. Once, when Waterton needed to escape detection, Old Joe enthusiastically hid him under a heap of straw in the pigsty, from which he emerged, grateful and stinking. But Stonyhurst was very different from Tudhoe, for Waterton soon found that here he was given the freedom to pursue his studies of natural history and was no longer beaten on account of what he called his 'ruling passion'.

For nearly four centuries Stonyhurst had been the seat of the powerful Shireburn family, with estates stretching for over 1,000 acres across the moorlands, woods and pastures of the Pendle region in Lancashire. The coast lay some twenty miles to the west, and in Waterton's time puffins, gannets and other sea birds would sometimes be buffeted this far inland when the weather was especially rough. There is a record of a final sighting of a sea eagle, which was shot in 1840 as it flew near the cricket pitch.

In 1717 the Shireburn line had come to an abrupt end. Sir Nicholas was dead and his son had predeceased him: according to legend the boy died from eating laurel berries while he was trapped in the heart of a thick labyrinth of laurels planted by his father. The house and the vast estates over which it presided then passed into the Weld family, who were based in Wiltshire, and since they had no wish to uproot themselves, Stonyhurst was left unoccupied, and for almost forty years the building stood empty, with an old servant called Mr Sparrow acting as caretaker, and witnessing its gradual dereliction. Then in 1794 Thomas Weld offered the house and its gardens to the English Jesuit Academy which had been based at St Omer in Belgium, but was about to be driven into exile because of the occupation of the French revolutionary armies. And so it was in October of that year, that a somewhat bedraggled group of Jesuit priests, along with twelve teenage boys, arrived to take over their new school. By the following year their numbers had risen to fifty-two pupils and seven masters.

The main building must have appeared huge and desolate: the cupola towers surmounted by perching stone eagles; the crested iron gateways; the wide stone steps; the enclosed stone courtyard. All the grandeur of the classical seventeenth-century style was offset by the fact of crumbling masonry, leaking roofs and the harsh Lancashire weather with winter drawing in quickly. Only the gardens, which Sir Nicholas had laid out in the Dutch manner, were said to be beautiful in their wildness: the laurels had grown huge, the avenues of holly and yew were a dark sanctuary for quantities of small birds and the forests of elm and oak had pulled in more closely around the stately carriage-ways and ornamental lakes.

For the first years this little community of priests and their pupils were almost cut off from the surrounding area. The local people, 'rude Protestants in the wilds of Lancashire', were withdrawn and suspicious—the last of the famous trials of the Pendle Witches had been conducted here as recently as 1720—and these Catholic strangers were carefully avoided. The pattern of the days was simple and austere. In the library, a little battered French grammar, compiled not long after Waterton had left the school, gives an unexpected insight into their way of life. It was printed exclusively for the use of the college 'comprising such words as we are in the constant habit of repeating at recreation'. There is talk of food and sickness, of work, games and the weather: 'What a nasty country this Lancashire is! We hardly have a day without rain. There has been no spring this year. Last year we had no summer . . . How did you get the cold? By lying in damp sheets. The chimney smokes. It wants sweeping. We shall be stifled. The playroom is full of dust. It is never swept. Nor the galleries either. The windows are all broken. Never mind.'[5]

One boy wrote a solemn letter home on 25 October 1795, the year before Waterton arrived. He provided his parents with the exact measurement of the firegrate in the schoolroom: 'length: 1 foot 1½ inches; depth: 8 inches; breadth at bottom: 3 ⅝th inches.' He then asked dismally how such a little device could be expected to warm thirty persons in a large room with a stone floor, and the wind coming in from all sides through chinks in the doors and windows.

The boys and the teachers worked together at restoring the buildings and taming the gardens. They slept together in a lopsided medieval building known as Sparrow's Hall, which stood within the main courtyard. They woke at 5 a.m. summer and winter alike. The college was still very poor and often the day's food consisted of nothing more than bread and beer. They studied French and the scriptures, but their main occupation was to learn and translate the classics. The house rules were strict, but not excessively so: Waterton was not flogged when he climbed to the top of one of the stone eagles, or when he wandered far from the college boundaries in search of birds' eggs.

Waterton's father had been educated at the English Academy in Belgium, and so it was logical that Charles should be sent to their new establishment at Stonyhurst. He arrived in 1796, and he stayed there, almost without interruption, for the next five years. The place rooted him and centred him and was a home to him in a way that Walton Hall had never been. Because of Stonyhurst he was able to become willingly fixated on his own youth. It was not a question of nostalgia, it was that throughout his life in some ways he never ceased to be a schoolboy. The college uniform of a dark blue tail coat with yellow buttons was what he persisted in wearing on formal occasions, and the fact that latterly the trousers were too short, the waistcoat too skimpy, and the cloth looked exhausted only heightened the impression that he was a schoolboy who happened to have become an old man. Once his wanderings were over and he had settled at Walton Hall, he would make regular visits to Stonyhurst, and tried to be there every Christmas. There are descriptions of him choosing to eat his meals with the boys instead of with the teachers, and of the sight of his thin and wizened figure being wildly applauded as he walked slowly across the stage balancing on his hands, or gave his impression of 'The Mountain in Labour', by heaving and sighing under a large red damask curtain.[6]

There was one curious and accidental phenomenon which made Waterton's love of Stonyhurst grow more intense as the years went by. It was situated in the heart of the cotton manufacturing district, and at the edge of what came to be known as the Black Country. It was near Preston and Blackburn and the many other sad cities which erupted during the machine age; places where, as Charles Dickens described them in the 1840s, 'struggling vegetation sickened and sank under the hot breath of kiln and furnace . . . where nothing green could live but on the surface of stagnant pools . . . where tall chimneys crowding on each other poured out their plague of smoke, obscured the light and made foul the melancholy air.'[7] And yet, thanks to a few odd factors in the history of industrial archaeology, there was a little pocket of some thirty square miles west of the Pendle Hills, which was left untouched by the industrial world, and Stonyhurst was situated in the centre of that pocket. There had been plans to build a railway line along the length of the Calder and Ribble Valley, which would have brought coal and steam power, factories and factory workers close to the gardens and gates of the college. But the railway was never built and the cottage industries of local spinners and weavers, who worked at their bobbin mills driven by water power, were never replaced by the huge machines that came to Preston and Lancaster. When the cotton industry collapsed in the 1840s, they died quietly, and left few traces of their passing.

The landscape around the Pendle Hills was bleak. Daniel Defoe, writing about his tour of the area in the 1740s said that there was an 'inhospitable terror' to be found there, and he complained, with the naivety of an earlier age, that there were no rich and pleasant valleys between the hills, 'no lead mines and veins of rich ore, as in the Peak; no coal pits as in the hills above Halifax; much less gold as in the Andes, but all barren and wild, of no use to either man or beast.'[8]

When Waterton made the journey from Walton Hall to his old school (twenty-four hours with coach and horses when he first went there; two hours by train to Preston via Leeds, and then an eight-mile journey with a pony and trap for his last visits), he would pass through the gates of his private sanctuary, and out into a landscape which every year became more crowded with the barbaric images of tall chimneys, dead water, slag heaps and slum dwellings. Then, as he drew closer to Stonyhurst, he entered an unmarked area, another sanctuary which had escaped from too much hurt. By the 1840s the River Calder, coming as it did on a long journey through the southern manufacturing districts, had become a 'stinking drain of effluents', but up to the turn of this century, the Ribble and the Hodder ran clear.

In the 1880s the *Stonyhurst Centenary Magazine* included a brief account of the flora and fauna to be found in the surrounding area. It makes for a simple and yet evocative description of the countryside as it once was. The pretty pink bird's eye primrose grew in abundance in the fields along the Hodder. Lily of the valley could be found by those who knew where to look. On the moors, sulphur-coloured pansies flowered in the early summer, and there also cloudberry, andromeda and deep blue columbines were to be found in profusion. There were frog orchids in the Forty Acre Field, and the heart-leaved twayblade orchid on Bowland's Slack. Peregrine falcons were abundant in the hills, and merlins inhabited the upland moors. Ravens had but recently disappeared—they lasted much longer here than in Waterton's district where he mourned the death of the last raven shot by a gamekeeper in 1820, since when 'I have never seen or heard a wild raven in this part of the country, and times are now so changed to the worse that I despair of ever seeing again this fine British bird in any of our woods.'[9]

Kingfishers were still a common sight along the Ribble, and the Hodder in the 1880s, although by the 1830s they were already becoming scarcer every year in the West Riding of Yorkshire.

On the canals too, it undergoes a continual persecution: not a waterman steers his boat along them, but has his gun ready to procure the kingfisher. If I may judge by the disappearance of the kite, the raven, and the buzzard from this part of the country, I should say that the day is no great distance when the kingfisher will be seen no more in this neighbourhood.[10]

The Stonyhurst list describes 162 species of birds, including goat-suckers, woodcocks, 'plagues' of hawfinches, and pied fly-catchers, as well as many of the big birds of prey whose numbers were being so decimated during this period.

When Waterton arrived at Stonyhurst as a fourteen-year-old boy, he was fully prepared to be again denied his right to freedom, and severely beaten if ever he was found 'bent on a ramble amongst the birds and beasts of the neighbourhood'. But the Jesuits did not punish him, instead they had the foresight to turn his obsession into an occupation. Having no hunting dogs kept for the purpose, they appointed him as the school rat-catcher and fox-catcher, with extra obligations to trap weasels and shoot at the swarms of fledgling rooks with a crossbow. It meant that he was free to go wherever he wanted, and he was, as he said, at the height of his ambition, 'I followed up my calling with great success. The vermin disappeared by the dozen. The books were moderately well-thumbed; and, according to my notion of things, all went on perfectly right.' Rat-catching was a serious business, and must have cost him many hours every week. An account book, dating from shortly after Waterton's departure, shows that £5. 11s. 4d. was paid for exterminating 666 rats, at 1½d. each.

As far as Waterton was concerned, his work as rat-catcher marked the beginning of his career as a naturalist and explorer, for although he had hunted rats and watched birds for as long as he could remember, it was only thanks to his Jesuit teachers that he felt himself to be 'armed with authority', and that gave him the inner strength to do as he pleased with dedication. One of his masters, Father Clifford, already anticipated the kind of life that he would be drawn to, after he had been at the college for two years: 'I have long been studying your disposition, and I clearly foresee that nothing will keep you at home. You will journey into far distant countries, where you will be exposed to many dangers.'[11]

At Tudhoe School Waterton's only close contacts had been with his friend Jones and Old Jim Bowren, his early mentor in the art of rat-catching. At Stonyhurst he was able to establish close friendships with several generations of teachers. The Jesuit temperament obviously suited him, and the 'paternal kindness' that was shown to him made him seem like a glad child, even when he was an old man in the company of teachers who were much younger than he. A long letter he received in 1804 from Father Clifford gives an idea of the closeness of the bond that had been established, and that would never be broken:

My dear Charles,
I received this morning your kind letter of the 17th and hasten to answer in the same day. Lay aside your fears about me, in all probability it is the will of God that I should live some years longer . . .
It gives me great pleasure to find you retain so great a sense of the little that I did for you, when I had the happiness of having you for my scholar . . .[12]

There were a couple of incidents dating from Waterton's time at Stonyhurst, which remained vivid in his mind, perhaps because of the sudden violence of the images. Once he was walking across the cricket field at night with a bundle of metal rat-traps under his arm. There was thunder in the air and suddenly, without knowing why, he dropped the traps and ran as fast as he could: he just escaped being struck by a bolt of lightning. On another occasion, the 'celebrated chemist' Dr John Dalton—the man who was later responsible for discovering the principle of radioactivity[13]—came to demonstrate the power of electricity by electrocuting an ox. Waterton was chosen as the assistant for this bizarre educational performance, and had to stand close by while the huge beast was scientifically executed.

In 1801 Waterton's education was completed. As a Catholic it was impossible for him to attend a university in England, and the natural decision was for him to travel, although where, and for what purpose, was as yet undecided. In the autobiographical essay which he wrote in 1838 he made only a brief mention of this time, saying that he spent a year at Walton Hall, and, following his father's example, he took up foxhunting and rode with Lord Darlington's famous pack of hounds. However there is an essay which he wrote in 1858 on the subject of the fox, which is a very damning description of that 'delightful, peaceful and national exercise, well known under the useful denomination of foxhunting'. In the essay Waterton says a good deal about the habits of the fox, and also about the foxhunting gentry who would hurtle through the countryside after its blood:

> See there! Sir Anthony is down in the mire, and his horse has rolled over him. Never mind. The horse has merely broken its neck and the baronet has lost his right ear by a kick from his dying steed. Sir Anthony will soon be sound again, if his surgeon bleeds him well—and as for the horse, there are many more in the stable, ready to take to the field. Dash on, my boys, grand and lovely is the sylvan scenery![14]

He tells of one hunt in particular which he would never be able to forget. He had apparently given up the chase and was resting his horse quietly, when the exhausted fox appeared before him

> panting and bewildered, his tongue lolling out of his mouth . . . on seeing me he stopped short and stared me full in the face. 'Poor little fellow!' I said to him, 'thy fate is sealed—thy strength has left thee, and in a few minutes more thou wilt be torn to pieces.' He then shrunk back again into the wood, as if to try another chance for life.[15]

It was here for the first time that Waterton suddenly found himself face to face with a member of the animal kingdom, the two of them staring at each other in a curious meeting of understanding. It was a meeting that was to be repeated many times over, and with many different creatures; but always it was as impressive and as unexpected as on this first occasion.

Then, inevitably, the moment was lost, the fox was killed, and the hounds began to 'snarl and quarrel over its bleeding carcass, which they devoured before the huntsman had made his appearance. Thus ended this day's sport.' It must also have helped to bring an end to Waterton's wish to pursue this way of life any further. In 1802 he set sail for Malaga in southern Spain, and it would be twenty-seven years before he felt able to come back for more than short visits and make Walton Hall into his true home.

CHAPTER III

Malaga and the Black Vomit

In November 1802 Waterton went to southern Spain to stay with two of his uncles who had chosen to live in a Catholic country rather than feel exiled in their native land. These uncles were businessmen, although the nature of their business is never mentioned in Waterton's brief account of them in his *Autobiography*. They had a house in the walled city of Malaga, and a country house not many miles away, situated near the foot of the Montes de Malaga, overlooking the farming lands of the coastal plain: red and yellow earth, white houses, olive and almond trees, and the intricate network of irrigation canals that had been laid out by the Moors in the ninth century.

For a year Waterton was a family guest, busy with 'rural amusements', and passing the days 'without misfortune, without care, and without annoyance of any kind'. He went by boat round the Straits of Gibraltar and stayed for some weeks at the port of Cadiz. He had plans to go to Malta, but this never materialized. He travelled, presumably by donkey, some hundred miles along the Mediterranean coast, to the little town of Algeciras. He had a chance to see the famous apes of Gibraltar—fifty or sixty of them moving across the rocky landscape in order to find shelter from a sharp easterly wind. In the hills above Malaga he watched 'remarkably large' vultures, red-legged partridges, goldfinches 'more common here than sparrows in England', and quantities of bee-eaters and quails, which migrated from North Africa in the early spring. On one occasion he had a brief vision of a flock of red flamingoes.

He learnt Spanish, and read the adventures of Don Quixote for the first time, so beginning his habit of reading a chapter from the book almost every day for the rest of his life, until he considered that erratic idealist and traveller an old friend as they shared many of the same opinions about human nature and the way of the world. It was from

21

Don Quixote that he learnt the proverb, 'Sometimes a man goes in quest of one thing and finds another,' and it was during his time in Spain that he first understood what the proverb could mean. He was wide-eyed and curious to see a country so different from his own, and was happy to enjoy the pleasures of 'this peaceful province, famous for its wine, its pomegranates, its oranges and its melons'. But then, after the year had come full circle and it was again the month of November, he was confronted by something altogether unexpected, which not only changed the character of the place that he was in, but changed him as a person as well. He found himself trapped in a landscape riddled with panic and disease, and he was one of many people for whom there seemed no hope of escape or survival.

In 1803 a severe epidemic of yellow fever erupted in Malaga and 50,000 people fled from the city as soon as they realized what was happening. Of those remaining, 14,000 were dead within a few weeks. The weather changed, and the progress of the disease was temporarily halted; then the weather changed again, and a further 38,000 people lost their lives.

Yellow fever was one of the most feared of all the dreadful epidemics of the time, and many stories and legends were told about its power and tenacity. The 'death ship', the *Flying Dutchman*, which was supposed to drift somewhere near the Bay of Biscay, was infected with yellow fever, and its curse was said to cling to any vessel that passed by too closely. The disease had been given more than a hundred names: to sailors it was Yellow Jack; to the people of Malaga it was '*il vomito negro*', the black vomit. The bacillus is carried by the domestic mosquito, *aedes aegypti*, an insect which lays its eggs in water casks, or open water containers, thus making it especially well-suited to travelling on board ship. It then establishes its hold at a sea-port where the atmosphere is warm and humid and there is a plentiful supply of uncovered, still water. A sea voyage lasting for months could be haunted by a chain of fatal attacks, and even if all the members of the crew were killed, the ship itself remained lethally infected for three months or more. The epidemic which reached Malaga in 1803 had probably come across the Atlantic from Cuba. It was one of the last of such outbreaks in southern Europe, although in the tropics the disease remained endemic until the turn of the century.

In Waterton's time there were many theories about the cause of such sickness, including vague references to miasmas rising up out of the ground, or pestilential vapours carried in the wind. It would be a long time before anyone suspected the part played by the mosquito, and there was still the lingering belief that all such wild and cruel afflictions were sent from Heaven to punish a sinful people. The standard treatment applied to all outbreaks of fever or plague had hardly changed since the time of the Black Death in the Middle Ages. What had been called devils were now called impurities, but in both cases the sick person's body was 'emptied' of the evil it contained by means of drastic purging and the letting of blood. Since the sixteenth century the importance of quarantine had been realized, and an afflicted area would be cut off from all contact with the outside world.

Waterton had just returned from Cadiz when the first signs appeared.

There began to be reports spread up and down the city that the black vomit had made its appearance; and every succeeding day brought testimony that things were not as they ought to be. I myself in an alley near my uncles' house, saw a mattress of most suspicious appearance hung out to dry. A Maltese captain, who had dined with us in good health at one o'clock, lay dead in his cabin before sunrise the next morning . . .[1]

A few days later Waterton was seized with a fever during the night; it was so violent that he was not expected to last for many hours. But after being racked by some 'dreadful spasms', he began to recover —and that in itself was a rare thing, since the disease tended to be fatal for an adult. For the next three weeks, and presumably while he was recovering some of his strength, he watched the crowds of people pouring out of the city, and then a 'state of pestilence' was declared, and it became a punishable offence to try to leave the area.

Waterton and his uncles returned to the house in the country, but the eldest uncle made regular business trips to the city. While away on one of these visits he fell sick, and Waterton at once set off on foot to be with him and to nurse him. After struggling for five days, 'much longer than we thought it possible', the man was dead.

We got him a kind of coffin made, in which he was conveyed at midnight to the outskirts of the town, there to be put into one of the pits which the galley slaves had dug during the day for the reception of the dead. But they could not spare room for the coffin; so the body was taken out of it, and thrown upon the heap which already occupied the pit. A Spanish marquis lay just below him . . .

The dogs howled fearfully during the night. All was gloom and horror in every street; and you might see the vultures on the strand tugging away at bodies which were washed ashore by the eastern wind.[2]

As if all this really was some form of divine retribution, the first wave of the epidemic was followed by an earthquake, which Waterton said he found even more terrifying than the yellow fever:

> The pestilence killed you by degrees; and its approaches were sufficiently slow, in general, to enable you to submit to it with firmness and resignation. But the idea of being swallowed up alive by the yawning earth at a moment's notice, made you sick at heart, and rendered you almost fearful of your own shadow. The first shock took place at six in the evening with a noise as though a thousand carriages had dashed against each other . . . I went to bed a little after midnight, but was roused by another shock about five o'clock in the morning. It gave the bed a motion which made me fancy it moved under me from side to side. I sprang up, and having put on my unmentionables (we wore no trousers in those days), I ran out in all haste to the Alameda. There the scene was most distressing: multitudes of both sexes, some nearly in a state of nudity, and others sick at stomach, were huddled together, not knowing which way to turn, or what to do.
>
> However, it pleased Heaven, in its mercy, to spare us. The succeeding shocks became weaker and weaker, till at last we felt no more of them . . .[3]

Waterton was by now desperate to escape from this nightmare, but there was no legal way to do so, and anyone defying the quarantine order was liable to be shot or imprisoned. Luckily, he was on friendly terms with the Swedish captain of a merchant ship, who was also anxious to get to England. Waterton managed to obtain a rather vague certificate from the British Consul, which declared that the city was now in a healthy state, and the Swedish captain already had a supply of false papers with him, in case he needed to leave from somewhere in a hurry. They slept on board ship for several nights, waiting for an east wind that would blow them round the Straits. Providentially the wind came, and at one o'clock in the afternoon, when the governor of the city had just set off for an airing in his carriage, and the officers from two Spanish warships had gone onshore for some amusement, the Swedish captain edged his boat away from the others in the harbour, and put out all sails in a cloud of canvas. 'The vessel drove through the surge with such a press of sail that I expected every moment to see her

top-masts carried away. Long before the brigs of war had got their
officers on board, and had weighed in chase of us, we were far out to
sea; and when night set in, we lost sight of them for ever, our vessel
passing Gibraltar at the rate of nearly eleven knots an hour!'[4]

They had more than a month of cold and stormy weather, and then,
because the English Channel was too rough to negotiate, they had to
weigh anchor by the Dorset coast for many more days. Their insub-
stantial legal papers were sent ahead of them to London, and although
Waterton fully expected to be ordered back to Malaga, they were
given a clearance to travel up the Thames to London. During the last
stage of the journey, while they were in the Channel, Waterton
suffered an 'attack of the lungs' which brought him near death for a
second time. He went directly back to Walton Hall to convalesce, and
there 'The late celebrated surgeon Mr Hay of Leeds, set me on my
feet again,' presumably by means of a great deal of purging and
bleeding.

Everything so far described of Waterton's experiences in Malaga is
taken from an autobiographical essay, which he wrote in his early
fifties. There is also the possibility of catching a glimpse of him at that
time from a letter he received shortly after he returned to Walton Hall.
Following his attack of yellow fever, and again when his uncle had
been unceremoniously flung into a plague pit, Waterton had written to
his old Stonyhurst master, Father Clifford. He wrote to him again as
soon as he was back in England. Those letters are lost, but Father
Clifford's reply has survived, and in it there are several references to
the experiences which Waterton had just lived through. One of his
letters had apparently been treated as if the envelope and the paper it
contained were themselves dangerous vessels of contagion, 'for it
arrived perforated in three different places, as if it had been cut with a
chisel, I suppose with a view of letting out the infection'.[5]

Father Clifford declared himself confident that the horrors Waterton had witnessed and suffered would make him unwilling to quit
England again in a hurry, and he went on to say:

I hope God will bless you and make you happy both in this world
and the next. What a terrible curse was that with which He visited
Malaga. What a picturesque and shocking description you gave me
of your illness. Are you sure it was the yellow fever? What were the
powders that cured you? Were they Calomel? The story of the death
of the rich merchant was very pathetic. I have kept that memorable
letter. You traced me a deplorable picture of the depravity that
reigns in Spain . . .[6]

In Malaga Waterton had been in a strange position. He contracted the disease very early on, and once that was past, he was immune, a charmed being who could not be harmed even though people were dying all around him. Like Dante being conducted through Purgatory and Hell, he could walk through the city, surrounded on all sides by the extremes of conflict, passion and spirituality which had been released by the epidemic. If he wanted to he could attend the sick without fear, as he did his uncle, and probably the rich merchant referred to in the letter. He could walk wherever he wished, whether to the awful places of burial, or through the streets where nobody knew him, or along the beaches where the vultures were always busy.

It has been said that people who have gone to the very edge of their own mortality and have then come back into the world see all the life that follows as an unexpected bonus, a gift which they hardly deserve. Waterton was just twenty-two when he experienced and witnessed so much human suffering, and yet survived it. Afterwards he was to spend many many years wandering from place to place, observing what he saw with a quiet and unjudging eye; many times he was on the brink of death, but perhaps it did not disturb him as it might otherwise have done.

No sooner was he a little stronger than Waterton felt restless, 'The bleak and wintry wind of England ill-suited a frame naturally chilly, and injured by what had already happened. I longed to bask in a warmer sun.' As the war in Europe against Napoleon was gathering momentum from all sides, there was no chance of a tour through more of the southern regions, and so he decided to go to British Guiana, or Demerara as it was then called. An uncle managed a sugar plantation out there, and Waterton's father had recently purchased a neighbouring estate which needed someone to act as an overseer. Slowly a pattern of life was evolving: 'Patience, and shuffle the cards,' as Don Quixote would say.

CHAPTER IV

British Guiana

In the early nineteenth century the colony comprised three provinces: Demerara, Essequibo and Berbice. Saying that a man had 'gone to Berbice' was a way of saying that he had gone to the dogs, with little chance of ever saving himself. Waterton told of the 'shoals' of poor Scotsmen who arrived in the colony, hoping for sudden wealth, and how once forty of them lay on the beach and drank rum until they were all dead.[1] He also said that out of every eleven men he had known there, ten had been killed by drink or by disease.

Before setting out he was introduced to Sir Joseph Banks, famous in his youth for his voyage across the Pacific with Captain Cook, and in later years as the President of the Royal Society, and an enthusiastic patron of explorers of lands that were still unknown. The old man and the young man liked each other at once, and kept in contact until 1820, the year of Banks's death. On the occasion of their first meeting Waterton was given a 'most pressing invitation to dinner'.

'I am a Catholic, Sir Joseph,' said I, 'and I am not allowed to eat meat on Fridays.'

'I am a Catholic too,' said he, 'as far as abstinence from meat is concerned; for the doctors have lately put me on a pudding diet; so you shall sit by my side and we shall have our eggs and pudding together.'[2]

It was Banks who gave Waterton a sense of scientific purpose in Guiana by encouraging him to try to obtain samples of the deadly blowpipe poison curare, and to find out if it had any important medical properties. It was Banks also who warned him of the 'very insalubrious nature' of low and swampy tropical countries, and advised him:

27

You may stay in them, for three years or more, and not suffer much. After that period, fever and ague, and probably a liver disease, will attack you, and you will die at last, worn out, unless you remove yourself in time to a more favoured climate. Wherefore, as you have not your bread to seek, you must come home once in three years, at farthest, and then all will go right.[3]

Waterton maintained this rule with strict obedience, but although during the twenty years that he was connected with the colony he persisted in not dying, he was often 'worn out', buffeted by dysentery, the wild fevers of malaria, and the ravages of countless parasites which fed on the blood and burrowed into the human body as if it were nothing more than the trunk of an old tree.

He set out from Portsmouth in November 1804 and arrived at his destination six weeks later. The colony had by then been a British possession for eight years; before that it had been occupied by the Dutch, the French, and briefly in the early seventeenth century by the English; it was only now that it was gaining status as an important commercial producer. The source of its wealth lay in the bleak expanses of black mud which stretched along much of the coastline and up the wide mouths of the river estuaries. This was alluvial silt, brought down by the rivers and caught and anchored by the roots of the mangrove and corrida trees, forming an area ten to twenty miles wide and mostly below sea-level: an area which if it was treated correctly was abundantly fertile. It needed a sea-wall, drainage canals and sluices to turn the brackish water sweeter, and for the mud to become a soil that was at first suitable for growing the bananas (plantains) used as a staple food for the slaves, and later the commercial crops of cotton, rubber, coffee and indigo, as well as the sugar-cane which eventually came to dominate all the cultivated regions.

A detailed map of the period shows the plantations lying in their hundreds in geometric regularity along the line of the Atlantic Ocean. They look like the carefully ordered strips in an allotment garden, although each strip covers some fifty acres. Above Georgetown lay Windsor Forest, and then followed Paradise, Non Pareil, Haarlem and Den Amstel, Bush Lot and Waterloo. Waterton's father called his plantation Walton Hall; his uncle Christopher was the owner of the incongruous combination of La Jalousie and Fellowship.

The plantation managers lived on their estates, along with their slaves and servants: about 300 slaves would be needed to run an average plantation.[4] The capital of Georgetown, or Starbroek as it was then called, kept them supplied with all their needs: new slaves from

West Africa; fresh soldiers to man the garrisons; fine wines, Irish butter, chandeliers, race horses and whatever other luxuries helped to maintain the idea of civilization. In Georgetown there were huge warehouses, 'casks and bales lie about as if every road were a wharf', municipal offices, whorehouses, a market, good and bad hotels, and a curiously shifting population who were all connected in some way or another with the booming agricultural business.

Dr George Pinckard, Inspector General to His Majesty's Forces, described his first impressions of Georgetown when he arrived there during the rainy season in 1796—it could hardly have changed very drastically in the few intervening years before Waterton's arrival:

> From the landing place we had nearly a mile to walk to town. From the nature of the road it was impossible to maintain ourselves upon our feet for a single step . . . we had to drag along in the rain, either ankle-deep in mud, or slipping and sliding upon the wet surface of the causeway, paved with bricks put edgeways into the ground. The land appeared one wide flat, intersected with dykes and canals; the road were mere banks of mud and clay, thrown from the ditches at their sides, and the houses were bedaubed with taudry colours like dutch toys . . . Canals and ditches have been dug at the back of the houses, being receptacles for mud and all the filthy drainage of the town. The causeway of bricks is carried through the whole length of the street, but the carriage road is mere mud and clay.[5]

All that warm mud and still water, and the tropical temperatures which hovered around 80 to 90 degrees fahrenheit throughout the year, made the area perfectly suited not only for growing plants and trees, but also as a breeding ground for disease. As one contemporary observer remarked, 'The financial interests of the planters overcame their love of life.' Yellow fever killed thousands of Europeans, especially those of a 'robust and plethoric constitution'; dysentery was endemic, so too was malaria, and rheumatic fever was suffered universally. The black slaves were especially susceptible to outbreaks of elephantiasis, yaws and leprosy, which turned them into grotesque living corpses; while everyone, no matter where they stood in the strict hierarchy of skin colour, could be attacked by mosquitoes, itch insects, jiggers, guinea worms, whip worms, *bêtes rouges*, and a number of other small and evocatively named creatures.

With the Atlantic Ocean before them, the vast rain forests behind them and all the roads petering out and leading nowhere beyond the outskirts of the town, there must have been a sense of being marooned, trapped in this artificially created landscape of drained silt. With a few exceptions, nearly all of the imported population of about 70,000 black slaves and 9,000 'free people of colour' and white Europeans lived along the coast. They lived in an area which occupied about 500 square miles, while behind them lay 83,000 square miles of a country that was unmapped, almost entirely unknown and considered to be teeming with dangers.

Georgetown was famous for social gaiety, immorality and steady, heavy drinking. Gin was taken at breakfast by the Dutch, while Madeira and water was favoured by the English. Since there were so few white women it was usual to buy oneself a mistress:

> The choice is various, a black, a tawny, a mulatto, or a nestee (forest Indian) can be purchased for 100 or 150 pounds sterling, fully competent to fulfil all the duties of her station: some are so much educated as to be able to read and to write. They are tasty and extravagant in their dress. They embrace all the duties of a wife, except presiding at table.[6]

The first club in Georgetown was opened in 1796, the Union Coffee House it was called, and it grew in size and splendour until it held regular concerts, theatricals and exhibitions. There was also a ball-room lit by 'four superb chandeliers, giving a wonderful effect to the dazzling splendour of the whole'. Within a few years that club had gone bankrupt, and it was sold off as lottery tickets with one item listed as 'a negro, George; a billiard table, boat, horse, cow, and etc'. But by then there were many other clubs and societies to take its place. In 1816 the Association for Promoting Manly Amusements in the United Colony was organized, and that brought in horse racing, boat racing, and any other colonial games that might prove helpful in 'promoting health, dissipating the spleen and abating scandal'.

Every tropical day, for the whites at least, began with the dawn, was broken by a long midday siesta, and approached a climax around 5 p.m. when the heat abated and all the gentlemen and ladies of fashion could parade in carriages or on horseback along the wide avenue flanked by cabbage palms, and known as the Ring. Waterton wrote a satirical piece in the local newspaper describing this human display where, 'Some were clodding in boots, some skipping in pumps; some had hats as big as umbrellas and others had snippets that scarce covered their noses; some had short jackets they could hardly move in, while the huge coats of the "dashers" would envelop a cabbage tree.'[7] The parading was followed by eating, after which there might be an entertainment or a ball to chase the night into the dawn of a new day. At night also 'there could be heard from every quarter the monotonous notes of drum and tambourine'[8] as the slaves gave expression to their need for gaiety in the face of all things, and danced their dances until the morning.

And always behind them lay the forests where there were no paths to be followed, only the wriggling tracks of the great rivers, and their countless tributaries. In these forests there were wandering tribes of Indians who mostly stayed clear of the coastal population, and whose numbers were estimated at about 20,000.[9] There were also bands of escaped slaves, or bush negroes as they were called, who formed small guerrilla communities deep in the forests or the swamps, who were hunted and rooted out of their hiding-places like wild animals, and had to struggle like wild animals if they were to outwit both their captors and the environment. There were also the occasional houses of Europeans: 'Protectors and Postholders of the Indians' whose job it was to maintain contact with the Indian tribes; plantation owners who preferred to live at a safe distance from the swamps and mosquitoes, and timber merchants who supervised the cutting and transporting of the monumental hardwood trees, whose commercial value was only just being recognized.

Where was Waterton to be found between the disparate worlds of the coast and the forest, and the white 'rollicking boys' who were now in power, and the people of other colours who worked for them in all manner of ways? If all of his life's work was a process of watching, watching with patience and trying to watch with impartiality, then here in South America for seven years he served his apprenticeship. He was a teetotaller in a land where 'custom never excused a man from having a drink', and a devout Catholic in a land where he often had to wait while the priest finished his game of backgammon before celebrating mass. He had an intense dislike for all the manly games on offer in Georgetown, and for the way of life which had made such an abundance of manly games possible. To make matters worse he was always outspoken in his opinions, he showed little regard for the formalities of his time, and in the eyes of most of his contemporaries he was becoming increasingly odd in his behaviour.

Between 1805 and 1812 he worked 'at intervals' as the manager of the plantations of Walton Hall, La Jalousie and Fellowship. Of the practice of slavery he wrote: '. . . it can never be defended; he whose heart is not of iron can never wish to defend it . . . it is a traffic that should have been stifled at birth.'[10]

To him it was not a separate issue of injustice, but just another example of the hypocrisy of governments which agreed to condone and encourage the trade for as long as it was useful to them. As a slave manager Waterton needed to ensure that the crops, the machines and the slaves were all kept in good order. He tended many of the slaves when they were sick, and learnt a lot from them about how they dealt with parasites and bouts of fever; it was probably from them too that he first learnt how to explore the swamps along the coast and behind the plantations.

In his later writings he says very briefly: 'Whilst I was on the estates I had the finest opportunity in the world of examining the water-fowl of Guiana; they were in vast abundance all along the sea-shore, and in the fresh-water swamps behind the plantations.'[11] But what he omits to explain, with his usual reticence about allowing any of his writings to 'savour too strongly of self', is quite how difficult it was to explore those swamps. From a distance they appeared like great meadows with hardly a shrub or flower to break the expanse of green sedges. During the dry season it was possible to weave between these, being careful not to be spiked by their sharp leaves; in the wet season even an Indian canoe could hardly make headway over the hummocks and tangle of vegetation, and if the water was less than three feet deep, then it was necessary to wade forward on foot. Waterton spent enough time among the fresh-water swamps and the salt-water mangrove swamps to be able to say later that he had studied 'minutely, the haunts, economies and character of all the birds of the Sea Coast', and he was sure that there was scarcely one whose detailed history had eluded him.[12]

Many times these expeditions left him shaking with malarial fever, and then he would ask for a slave or a servant to drench him with cold water and rub him with towels. He would take his own violent mixture of purgatives, and if there seemed no sign of improvement then he would apply a tourniquet to his arm and bleed himself of anything up to twenty ounces of blood. Later on when he was in the forests he would often have recourse to the bleedings and the purges, and it is painful to the imagination to think of a man who is hungry and exhausted draining his body of its blood and emptying his stomach and bowels. But still, he lived, and lived a long time.

Twice at least, and more often if he was true to the promise he made to Sir Joseph Banks, he returned to England. The first occasion was towards the end of 1805, when he received news of the death of his father. As the eldest son he was now the twenty-seventh Lord of Walton Hall and of all the lands and buildings that belonged to the estate; he had an income of about £700 per annum, and a number of duties that he was expected to fulfil. But his return home was only brief; he settled a few family matters and was soon back in South America. His brothers had inherited the estates in Demerara, and so he was now presumably working for their interests. His mother, whose outbursts of anger and panic he briefly described in his *Autobiography*, inherited from her husband the sum of one guinea, and a very meagre yearly income. She seems to have left Walton Hall, and disappears without trace and without any further mention until her death certificate was signed at Park Place near Liverpool in 1819.

Waterton was back in Guiana in the early part of 1806, and for the next two years he travelled a great deal, touring the islands of Tortola, Grenada, St Christopher, St John's and Barbados, and apparently staying at each place for several weeks. In 1808 he was appointed to deliver dispatches from Admiral Collingwood to the Spanish Government at Angustura (Ciudad Bolivar), a town which lay some 300 miles up the Orinoco River in Venezuela. It was 'the first commission that anyone of the name of Waterton had received from Queen Mary's days', and that pleased him immensely. The expedition gave him his first real sight of the life that was hidden within the forests: 'In the swampy parts of the wooded islands which abound on this mighty river, we saw waterfowl innumerable; and when we had reached the higher grounds it was quite charming to observe the immense quantities of parrots and scarlet aras [macaw] which passed over our heads. The loud harsh screams of the bird called the horned screamer were heard far and near . . .'[13] It was during the expedition that Waterton had the first of many confrontations with large snakes. On this occasion he was to be seen suspended above the river, clinging to a flimsy branch, on which an eight-foot-long, half-dead labarri snake was draped beside him.

Wherever he went he was watching, as if he was trying to unravel a mystery that haunted him, and sometimes he was as interested in the people who crossed his path as he was in the birds and animals. Waterton had set himself the private task of writing a report on the 'state of religion' among the Indians, the blacks, and, since they were there too, the white Europeans, and from the short summation of his study which has survived[14] there emerges his impression of the two worlds: the areas which had been affected by civilization and the areas which had not yet been touched. In all the towns and cultivated districts, the 'vice, ignorance and corruption' was the same, although to varying degrees, and it had infected almost everyone no matter what their race. In contrast, the people of the forest had a dignity and a spirituality which echoed the quality of the landscape they moved in.

33

Slowly Waterton himself was moving towards the need to cut himself off from the life of the coast, and to get closer to the life of the forest.

Partly the change came from within, but he also learnt a great deal from his friendship with a Scottish wood merchant called Charles Edmonstone. Edmonstone had come to Guiana in 1781 and had stayed there, living for the most part in an isolated house far from the coast for the next thirty-five years. During that time he never visited England, and he avoided having to visit Georgetown. Dr Pinckard, the same government official who described the mud in the streets of Georgetown in 1796, made a visit to Edmonstone's home, Warrow's Point on the Mibiri Creek, as part of an eleven-day journey up the Demerara River: an expedition which made him feel both proud and intrepid: '. . . no party, equally numerous, had been known to travel so great a distance from the coast, although individuals had occasionally journeyed as far as, or even beyond the falls of the river.'[15] He described how he and his party struggled to reach Mibiri Creek, travelling up

a confined channel, of deep black water, leading into the sombre gloom of the forest, and overhung with trees whose dark foliage meeting from the opposite banks formed a canopy which even at midday enveloped us, as it were, in the still shades of night. We were led into another creek, which was still narrower and darker than the former, and another called Mabeira [Mibiri] which was so narrow as totally to prevent the negroes from rowing, they were therefore obliged to stand up in the boat and push it on by resting the ends of their oars against the banks of the sides. Soon after we were conducted into a wide and open savannah at the remotest end of which we could just discern the lonely house of Mr Edmonstone . . . but before we came to the house, the windings of the creek took us back into the dark bosom of the forest . . .[16]

It was in this utter remoteness that Charles Edmonstone lived with his wife and children, a brother, a nephew and a curious mixture of friends and servants. Generals and colonels came to be entertained here, and so too did Indian chieftains and black slaves. Two families of freed slaves occupied the garden, and one of them accompanied the Edmonstones when they finally returned to Scotland and adopted their surname as his own,[17] while the others were still in the area in the early twentieth century, reminiscing about Edmonstone and his naturalist friend, Charles Waterton. On the edge of the garden, hidden among the trees, there was a little hut inhabited, at least at the time when

Pinckard was there, by an emaciated Scotsman called Old Glen, who had been a sailor, a soldier, a plantation owner and a preacher of his own visionary brand of Christianity. When he had grown too old and too seemingly mad to look after himself, Edmonstone had adopted him, and he concocted herbal remedies, read from his Hebrew Bible, and taught the young Edmonstone children how to read and write.

Mrs Edmonstone was a woman of two races. Her father was a Scottish wood cutter called William Reid, while her mother was an Arawak Indian, known as Princess Minda. The same book which gave advice about buying a coloured mistress said that it was sometimes possible to obtain an 'indigenous American, a more beautiful race than the mullattoes', and added that such unions might help to 'attract their kinsfolk into the habits of intercourse and civilization'.[18] But it was rare for a white man to take an Indian mistress, and very rare indeed to have the union solemnized by a church ceremony. Edmonstone's marriage with Helen Reid lasted almost forty years, and until the final years it seems to have been harmonious. She bore him a number of children, among them Waterton's future wife, and she provided him with an important link with the Indian tribes, a link which placed him in a unique position in the colony.

Because only the Indians knew how to travel safely through the forests, they were employed by the British Government to help track down the bush-negroes whose presence was considered a dangerous threat to the security of the whole province. In his role as Burgher-captain and later as Protector of the Indians, Edmonstone acted as an organizer of many such expeditions. He helped to root out several camps, and he was rewarded for his successes with an inscribed clock, a sword, a commemorative plate, tax exemptions, and even a piece of good black mud near Georgetown. He was also riddled with gunshot wounds, and finally afflicted with a headache which shadowed all the last years of his life. The idea of hunting for fugitives is abhorrent today, but to his credit Edmonstone managed to infuriate some of his superiors by his insistence that the slaves must not be maimed, and must be granted a pardon and dealt with fairly. 'The conditions on which they surrendered were, beside a full pardon of life or corporal punishment, that they never be returned to their former owners, but be sent from the colony and disposed of in some of the adjacent islands . . .'[19]

Edmonstone also tried to help the Indians in any way that he could. His role as an intermediary on their behalf was acknowledged when he was given the official title of Protector in 1810, a post which he held until he returned to England in 1817. He was especially aware of the dangers the Indians from the more remote areas faced on the occasions when they came to the coastal regions to sell tamed animals or little artefacts, but although he could help to provide them with food and shelter, no one could protect them from disease, from rum, or from the humiliations which they received from both the blacks and the whites. On one occasion he wrote an impassioned letter to the governor, saying that if the Indians were not fairly paid for their services to the colony, then he would cover the debt from his own pocket.[20] Yet when those gifts that were due to be paid by the Western world are set down in a list, they look naked and meagre, and somehow redolent of tragedy:

> For each man: 1 piece blue cotton cloth (Salempore); 3 hatchets; 3 cutlasses; 1 looking glass; 3 knives; 1 comb; 1 razor; 2 flints; 4 fishhooks; 1 pr. scissors; 1 tinder box; 1 lb coral.
> For each woman: 4 ells blue cotton cloth; 1 cutlass; 1 pr. scissors; 1 lb coral; 1 knife; 1 looking glass.[21]

It is not clear at what point Waterton came to know Edmonstone, but certainly by the year 1808 they were firm friends. From Edmonstone and from his family and connections with both the Indians and the blacks, Waterton came to learn the naming of trees, birds, animals, reptiles and insects. He learnt where he might find them and what to expect of them. He was taught how to communicate with the Indians and was accepted by them. And once he was ready to set out on his first expedition then Edmonstone's trusted guides and servants came with him. Much later, in 1820, the house at Mibiri Creek, which was by then deserted and derelict, became his home, and throughout his life something of Edmonstone's way of thinking, a philosophy born of spending long years in the hugeness and density of the rain forests, stayed with him.

In 1804, at the meeting with Sir Joseph Banks, Waterton had worn a powdered wig for the last time. By 1812 he had given up wearing shoes and was able to run and climb barefoot like an Indian. In 1820 he spent eleven months in the forests, and rarely saw another white man, living on whatever meat, plants or fruit were offered to him or he could find for himself. Perhaps even the barrage of heat and pain and sickness which he often suffered taught him a different kind of acquiescence; a stillness and a passivity which helped him to immerse himself in what he saw; a form of submission.

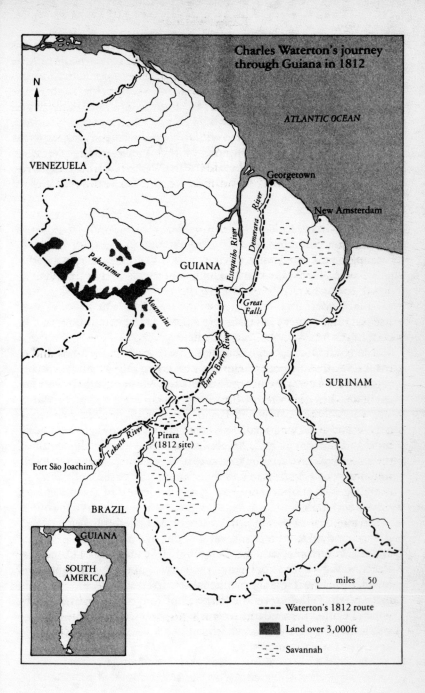

Charles Waterton's journey
through Guiana in 1812

N

ATLANTIC OCEAN

VENEZUELA

Georgetown

New Amsterdam

Essequibo River

Demerara River

Pakaraima

GUIANA

Mountains

Great
Falls

Burro Burro River

SURINAM

Takutu River

Pirara
(1812 site)

Fort São Joachim

BRAZIL

GUIANA

SOUTH
AMERICA

0   miles   50

- - - - Waterton's 1812 route

Land over 3,000ft

Savannah

CHAPTER V

A Search for El Dorado

In 1812, when Waterton set out on his first journey to explore the 'far extending, unexplored wilds of Guiana', he was one of the first white men to enter a landscape that had long kept itself secret and hidden; a landscape that seemed to be as powerful and as indestructible as the sea; a place where, in the words of a later traveller, 'a man would lose his senses, and forget the world. Nothing was important besides the silence of the forest, the solitude, the light.'[1]

Recently all that has been changing: the secrets are uncovered; the great forests are being opened up and cut down; the savannahs can be explored with the help of cars and aeroplanes. Where once there were no clear maps, and no means of travelling any distance except by water or on foot, there is now the steady growth of roads, towns and airstrips, and wide wounded areas stripped of trees. Where before, in Waterton's time, there were no books that could accurately describe, or even perhaps give a name to some of the creatures that were to be found here, now the toucan and the scarlet macaw, the sloth and the anteater, the giant otter which could reach a length of seven feet and was so highly prized for its dense sleek fur, the armadillo, and the other ancient inhabitants of those intense worlds have been studied and classified, and many of them are on the edge of extinction.

It took Waterton several days, travelling by canoe up the Demerara River from the outskirts of Georgetown, to reach the sugar plantation known as the Loo. Here the cultivated regions were interspersed with tangled trees, and wherever the cleared land had been neglected it was quickly reclaimed by undergrowth and new trees. Beyond the Loo lay the sugar works of Amelia's Waard, and after passing these:

There is not a ruin to inform the traveller that either coffee or sugar have ever been cultivated . . . an unbroken range of forest covers each bank of the river, saving here and there where a hut discovers itself, inhabited by free people of colour, with a rood or two of bared ground about it; or where a wood cutter has erected himself a dwelling, and cleared a few acres for pasturage. Sometimes you see level ground on each side of you for two or three hours at a stretch; at other times a gently sloping hill presents itself, and often on a turning point the eye is pleased with the contrast of an almost perpendicular height jutting into the water. The trees put you in mind of an eternal spring, with summer and autumn kindly blended into it.[2]

Today that first stage of the journey can be accomplished in an hour, driving along a wide tarmac road. The deserted remains of Amelia's Waard were cleared away long ago, and the estate has become part of the mining town of Linden. Huge furnaces for extracting bauxite stand by the riverside, and the smoke and the dust from their chimneys fill the air for miles around. Further up-river another road cuts right across the area where Waterton followed a rugged path which took him overland from the Demerara to the Essequibo; a short distance even then that could be managed 'with ease' in a day and a half. 'So matted and interwoven are the tops of the trees above you, that the sun is not felt once all that way, saving where the space which a newly-fallen tree occupied lets in his rays upon you . . . In this retired and solitary tract, nature's garb, to all appearances, has not been injured by fire, nor her productions broken in upon by the exterminating hand of man.'[3] It is this same stretch of land which has been chosen as the site for a new town. It can be seen growing up amongst the wreckage of cleared bush and the stumps of trees; a huge saw-mill is busy, cutting and slicing its way through countless tall straight trunks: 'The Green-heart, famous for its hardness and durability; the Hackea, for its toughness; the Ducalabali, surpassing mahogany; the Ebony and Letter-wood, vying with the choicest woods of the old world; the Locust-tree, yielding copal; and the Hayawa and Olou-trees, furnishing a sweet-smelling resin, are all to be met with in the forest, betwixt the plantations and the Rock of Saba.'[4]

Waterton was able to resign from his job as plantation manager in the early part of 1812, and at once he was impatient to set out. The fact that the rainy season was on its way, making such an expedition more difficult than ever, did not seem to deter him. Perhaps it was stubbornness, perhaps he saw it as an added challenge, but because of this choice of timing, the expedition proved almost suicidal. Waterton was away in the wilds for something over four months, and for most of that time it rained; at first spasmodically, and then almost without ceasing, with the noise of cascading water drowning all other sounds. When finally he got back, he was, in his own words, 'so wayworn, sick and changed',[5] that it was three months before he could stand without shaking, and three years before the ferocity of his bouts of malarial fever subsided and he felt strong again.

Before his second journey, in a letter addressed to Pope Pius VII and dated 1817, Waterton states his intention of undertaking his journeys, to 'penetrate into the interior, in order to examine its productions'—presumably this means his study of the animal and vegetable kingdoms—'see the state of the different tribes of Indians ... to find out the vegetable composition with which the Indians poison their arrows, to search for Lake Parima, and ultimately to reach the frontier fort of Portuguese Guiana.'[6] After his first trip he felt himself to be sufficiently 'seasoned' to be able to withstand sickness and physical hardship. He knew he was able to travel with his Indian guides as if he were one of them; and so at last he was ready to be submerged in the wet heat and sometimes the daytime darkness of the forests, and the bleak expanses of the high savannahs. In that way his second expedition was a private pilgrimage, and had little to do with poisoned arrows, or a lake that was said to be hidden in the mythical land of El Dorado, or a garrisoned fortress that lay some 400 miles inland on the borders of what is now Brazil. He wished to be cut off from all the familiar landmarks of his civilization, and to know what it was like to be lost in what could be a merciless land. In terms of his inner development he must have learnt a great deal, but in the eyes of the world the expedition would only look brave, foolhardy, and lacking in any noteworthy achievements.

No one had asked Waterton to explore Guiana; only Sir Joseph Banks, now confined by gout to a wheel-chair, was interested in curare, and would be glad of another meeting in London. No eager public was waiting to learn more about the lost lake of El Dorado, and Waterton seemed almost relieved when he could come to no conclusive evidence about its existence: 'So much for Lake Parima, or El Dorado, or the White Sea. Its existence at best seems doubtful; some affirm that there is such a place, and others deny it.'[7] At this stage also, Waterton had not even decided to write a book about his adventures, in fact the idea seems to have come several years later, when he had failed to persuade a friend and fellow naturalist to take on the task.[8] But on this his first expedition, and on the subsequent ones, so long as he had the strength in him, he did keep a detailed journal, writing, 'every night by the light of the fire, or whatever light there was; I have done so once or twice by the light of the firefly'.[9]

All these journals have been lost, and there is no reference to anyone having seen them during Waterton's lifetime, but there are two notebooks which he made in the 1840s,[10] when he was travelling across Europe with his two sisters-in-law, which have survived. From these it is possible to see how he was in the habit of quoting long sections from his own softly pencilled scrawl, and using them un-altered in his published writing. Only the few more personal refer-ences, anything that placed the man too clearly in the landscape, were carefully removed. *Wanderings in South America* must have been compiled in the same way. It is an anthology of notes made while travelling. The people, the creatures, even the trees that are met along the way, crowd into the text in almost chaotic profusion, and the words follow the traveller's eye as he gazes at one thing and then another, always ready to be distracted, always ready to move on.

A few small Cayman, from two to twelve feet long, may be observed now and then in passing up and down the river; they just keep their heads above water, and a stranger would not know them from a rotten stump.

Lizards of the finest green, brown and copper colour, from two inches to two and a half feet long, are ever and anon rustling among the fallen leaves and crossing the path before you; whilst the Chameleon is busily employed in chasing insects around the trunks of the neighbouring trees.

The fish are of many different sorts, and well-tasted, but not, generally speaking, very plentiful. It is probable that their numbers are considerably thinned by the Otters which are much larger than those of Europe. In going through the overflowed savannahs, which have all a communication with the river, you may often see a dozen or two of them sporting among the sedges before you.[11]

The *Wanderings* could not be used as a text-book for naturalists or anthropologists; there are some accurate and evocative descriptions of both human and animal life, but they are brief and fleeting, and it was not Waterton's intention to be more thorough: 'I merely penned down a few words concerning them [birds], in order to inspire Naturalists with a desire of going to look for them in their native woods.'[12] Nor could the book serve as a guide for geographers; it proved helpful to the Schomburgk brothers, and others who explored this territory shortly after Waterton, and it is still possible to follow his route from

Georgetown to the Fort of São Joachim, but he provided no maps, and once he had left the rivers and was crossing the flooded savannahs, he was unable to give any proper names for the landmarks he passed by:

> Half of this day's march is in water, nearly up to the knees. There are four creeks to pass: one of them has a fallen tree across it. You must make your own bridge across the other three. Probably, were the truth known, these apparently four creeks are only the meanders of one.
>
> The Jabiru (a member of the stork family), the largest bird in Guiana, feeds in the marshy savannahs through which you have just passed. He is wary and shy and will not let you get within gun-shot of him.
>
> You sleep this night in the forest, and reach an Indian settlement about three o'clock the next evening, after walking one-third of the way through wet and miry ground.
>
> But, bad as the walking is through it, it is easier than when you cross over bare hills, where you have to tread on sharp stones, most of them lying edgeways.
>
> The Indian place you are now at is not the proper place to have come to in order to reach the Portuguese frontier. You have advanced too much to the westward, but there was no alternative.[13]

The strength of the writing lies in its immediacy; the way it reads like the notes made for a documentary film. And like a documentary film-maker, Waterton's main aim was to draw his audience into the landscape, and then to show them how to look and what to look for, while he himself remained hidden and out of sight. He calls himself the 'accidental traveller', ill-equipped in the task he has set himself, someone who can 'merely mark the outlines of the path he has trodden, or tell the sounds he has heard, or faintly describe what he has seen in the environs of his resting places'.[14] And if, as a guide, he can help people to see the world of nature as he sees it, either in reality or in their imagination, then perhaps some of them might learn what it means to be merciful, and might not be driven by the wish to uproot and to slaughter whatever wild life they come across. Over and over again Waterton is saying 'Look close with a quiet mind'; learn from all that you see, and do not try to assert your power by accumulating a heap of useless corpses. 'Having killed a pair of Doves in order to enable thee to give mankind a true and proper description of them, thou must not destroy a third through wantonness, or to show what a good marksman thou art; that would only blot the picture thou art finishing, not colour it.'[15]

> This too is the native country of the Sloth. His looks, his gestures and his cries all conspire to entreat you to take pity on him. They are the only weapons of defence which nature has given him. While other animals assemble in herds, or in pairs range through the boundless wilds, the sloth is solitary, and almost stationary; he cannot escape from you. It is said his piteous moans make the tiger relent, and turn out of the way. Do not level your gun at him, or pierce him with a poisoned arrow—he has never hurt one living creature. A few leaves, and those of the commonest and coarsest kind, are all he asks for his support.[16]

The reader of the *Wanderings* must bear one important fact in mind. They were written with the intention of encouraging others to see and marvel at such a land as Guiana. Because of this, and because of Waterton's aversion to letting anything he wrote 'savour too strongly of self', the text ignores or minimizes all the difficulties he encountered during the journey. He tells of flooded swamps and torrential rains, but not of what it was like to lie in wet clothes in a wet hammock with a fever, and the rain clattering through the trees. He tells of the solitude and emptiness of the savannahs, but not of the desperate hunger they suffered while crossing them, because there was no food to be found anywhere, and for days they had nothing to eat but cassava bread sprinkled with cayenne pepper. He tells of insects, but omits to say that by the time he was back at the Edmonstones' house his body was pitted with ulcerated sores brought on by their bites. It is only from letters, and one letter in particular, that a clearer picture can be made, allowing the more personal details to be added into the framework of the story of an adventure.

On his first journey Waterton left Georgetown on 5 April 1812. His friend Charles Edmonstone went with him past the deserted sugar estate of Amelia's Waard, and as far as a high rock formation overlooking the Demerara River and known by the Indian name of the Saba. It was here that the government postholder had his house, and here also that the boundary between the known and the unknown world was defined. With six Indians and a negro slave belonging to his uncle Christopher, Waterton set off up-river. He was barefoot and bareheaded, dressed in wide canvas trousers, a shirt, and a thin flannel waistcoat worn next to the skin, 'flannel is a great preserver of health in the hot countries'.[17] He had with him a gun, a pocket telescope, a lancet for letting blood in case of emergencies, a hammock, and a canvas 'painting' for protecting the hammock during rainstorms. Whatever other equipment he took, it fitted into a single canoe, along with eight men.

Having left the Saba Rock, 'beyond which there are no more habitations of white men, or free people of colour', Waterton begins to describe the forest vegetation that towers and tumbles around him on all sides. There are wild fig-trees, as big as a common apple tree, rooted among the crowning branches of the great moras, 100 feet above the ground. The trailing bush-rope vine is everywhere: 'Sometimes you see it nearly as thick as a man's body, twisted like a corkscrew round the tallest trees, and rearing its head high above their tops. At other times three or four of them, like strands in a cable, join tree and tree, and branch and branch together.'[18] An uprooted tree can be stopped in its fall by these great cables, and then, hanging suspended at some impossible angle, it sends out new roots into the rich soil and begins to grow again. Waterton examines the earth that produces such a profusion of growth, and sees that it is made chiefly of fallen leaves and decayed wood, and, as many a modern ecologist has since emphasized, he warns that if the land is left exposed, then this rich blanket is easily swept away by the rains, leaving behind something 'little better than sand'.

He tells of the four-footed animals that are to be seen in the forest: tapirs and tiger cats (one of which he took back to Walton Hall where it became an excellent ratter); monkeys and opossums; ant-bears 'sometimes seen on the tops of the wood-ants' nests'; armadillos in holes in the sand hills 'like rabbits in a warren', and porcupines, 'now and then discovered in the trees above your head'. He tells of the birds whose colours are more vivid than those of the finest jewels; of the vampire bats which so intrigued him on his later expeditions, and the many snakes: the camoudi or bull-killer, the speckled and dirty-brown coloured labarri, and, 'unrivalled in his display of every lovely colour of the rainbow and unmatched in the effects of his deadly poison', the couanacouchi, popularly known as the bush-master.

Not far up-river from the Saba Rock, they come to a settlement of Acoway Indians:

Though living in the midst of the woods, they bore evident marks of attention to their persons. The hair was neatly collected and tied up in a knot; their bodies fancifully painted red and the paint scented with hayawa. This gave them a gay and animated appearance. Some of them had on necklaces . . . many wore rings, and others had an

ornament on the left arm, midway betwixt the shoulder and the
elbow. At the close of day they regularly bathed in the river below,
and the next morning seemed to be busy in renewing the faded
colours of their faces . . .

They are a poor, harmless, inoffensive set of people, and their
wandering and ill-provided way of living seems more to ask for pity
from us, than to fill our heads with thoughts that they would be
hostile to us.[19]

As they go on they pass five more settlements, two of them right on the
edge of the water, the others set back amongst the trees. From one of
these Waterton obtains his first sample of curare, and at once he tests
its strength on a middle-sized dog. Having inflicted the fatal wound
with the point of an arrow, he describes the animal's death in a
curiously lingering and gentle manner. Later he stopped all killing,
even for scientific purposes, but often in Guiana he watched this act of
dying, mesmerized by the sight of life slipping out of a body:

In three or four minutes he began to be affected, smelt at every
little thing on the ground around him, and looked wistfully at the
wounded part. Soon after this he staggered, laid himself down, and
never rose more. He barked once, though not as if in pain . . .[20]

They approach the great fall of the Demerara, the water white with
foam, 'fretting and boiling amongst the huge rocks', and much too fast
to navigate. The Indians try to hack out a path alongside the bank
where huge crabwood trees grow, but the task proves too difficult and
they are forced back. It is decided that they should take the canoe up a
little estuary which will lead them to the Essequibo River in four days,
while Waterton sets out alone—or perhaps the negro slave stays with
him—on a shorter route which need only take him a day and a half.
This is the same path that is now intersected by a wide road, and the
same land that is now stripped of its trees and dominated by a
saw-mill. The path is like a tunnel, and in the half-light Waterton sees
wild pigs moving about in droves; curious rodent-like creatures called
acouris whose front teeth are used by the Indians as the sights for
blowpipes; the large wild guinea-pigs known here as labbas; a bird
called the powise, as big and as awkward as a turkey; the beautiful
macaba or trumpeter-bird, black with flashes of red and gold. Slowly
he moves amongst this twilight world, amongst the scuttling creatures
of the forest floor, and the great carcasses of dead trees, which rot and
return to the earth with extraordinary speed: 'Put your foot on that

large trunk, that seems entire amid the surrounding fragments. Tread on it, and like the fuss-ball, it will break into dust.'[21]

It seems that he stays close to this path for four days. Maybe occasionally he sees clear sunlight when he uses the trailing bushropes to hoist himself up into the high trees, but for most of the time he is on ground level. When finally he reaches the banks of the Essequibo River there is the sudden transition from darkness to brightness, from the suffocating containment of the vegetation to the dazzling brightness of water reflecting the sky, with hills on one side and, far away to the south-east, a high mountain like a bluish cloud on the horizon. A recent traveller has tried to put words to the qualities of light and colour that are to be found on the Essequibo River in the early morning when, 'Not a ripple disturbed it: air and liquid seemed spun of the same opalescent substance, lilac green and palest blue, shot through with straw-yellow, sunshine fingers.'[22] And beyond the light and the colours the imagination must see the soft outlines of hills and valleys and lowlands; all linked together by a chain of forest, luxuriant and unbroken.

So, they travel on and on, following the course of the river past wooded islands; past estuaries that disappear into tunnels of branches and leaves. It is now three weeks or more since they left the Saba Rock. There is no mention of the rain falling, but the river is so full of water that the journey becomes increasingly difficult. Sometimes to avoid the force of the rapids, they have to cut a passage through the branches and vines that hang over the banks along the edge of the water. On one occasion they make a path along the bank itself, carrying the canoe with them. The forest here is too dense even for Indian settlements, and so at night they sleep in the open, their hammocks hung amongst the trees, and they hunt for whatever food they can find.

Another two weeks go by and they come to a settlement of Macusi Indians. Here Waterton manages to obtain some very potent curare, although the Indians are reluctant to part with it. In the distance the Crystal Mountains can be seen. Once it was thought that they were made of diamonds, or some other bright jewel, but their brightness is an illusion, the coincidence of clear light and smooth rock.

Their route now takes them along the Burro Burro River, which has its source in the high savannahs. The Indians point out an unmarked site on the river bank where they say a white man once lived. It seems that he was an unsuccessful businessman, and 'because his creditors had treated him with as little mercy as the strong generally show to the weak' he escaped from them by retreating further and further into the forest. On the banks of the Burro Burro River, about 300 miles inland from Georgetown, he ended his days; his hut, his body, and all signs of how he spent his time soon overwhelmed by greenness.

They are on the edge of the forest. Here they leave the river and the canoe, and taking their meagre baggage with them they follow a path that leads them into the sudden openness of the savannah. It is a very different landscape that confronts them.

The finest park that England boasts, falls far short of this delightful scene . . . quite surrounded by lofty hills, all arrayed in the superbest garb of trees: some the form of pyramids, others like sugar-loaves towering one above the other, some rounded off . . . the ridges of others resemble the waves of an agitated sea. Beyond these appear others, and others still farther on, till they can scarcely be distinguished from the clouds.

There are no sand-flies here, nor *bêtes rouges*, nor mosquitoes in this pretty spot. The fire flies during the night vie in numbers and brightness with the stars in the firmament above; the air is pure, and the north-east breeze blows a refreshing gale throughout the day.[23]

There is solitude and silence, but there are also no four-footed animals to be seen, and not even any tracks to be found; no birds anywhere, except a few vultures flying high up above the hills, and the stork-like jabiru is out on the marshes and out of reach of gunshot. Every day they are dependent on whatever food they can catch or gather, and if they get nothing, then they must live off their supply of cassava bread, and hide its taste of mould and age with sprinklings of cayenne pepper. For three days at a stretch they eat this cassava, and it punishes them all with a severe attack of dysentery. The familiar insects are indeed absent, but there is a little fly, a quarter the size of a house-fly, and with a bite more tormenting than that of the mosquitoes from the coastal regions.

They travel in a south-westerly direction, following a winding path that has been walked by the Indians for countless generations. But this is not the season for travelling. The way is rocky and steep, and every so often they come to swampy areas where they have to wade knee-deep in water. The rain falls spasmodically but heavily, and the path becomes so badly flooded that they are forced to abandon it. They come to a wide creek, with steep banks and fast-flowing water, and this they must swim across. It takes them a day to construct a simple raft that can carry the clothes and the baggage, and the best part of another day to beat the banks with long sticks to chase out the

47

crocodiles that would otherwise attack them as they struggle through the water. They sleep that night by the side of the creek, and the next morning they walk for nine hours until they reach an Indian settlement, the first they have seen for many days. Here they can rest and gather some strength.

Before them lies a wide, flooded plain that looks like a huge lake. Waterton wonders if the legendary Lake Parima is in reality nothing more than this stretch of submerged scrub and grassland; an optical illusion that would retreat and vanish every year when the rains stopped falling. In the far distance he sees deer, spur-winged plover, curlews, the huge jabiru birds, ducks and egrets. Flocks of scarlet macaws fly through the air. Yellow termite nests, spiralling upwards eight to ten feet high and impervious to the weather, stand in clusters on the raised patches of ground, like the remains of some forgotten civilization.

South-west of this plain lies the Pirara River, and that joins up with the Takutu River which flows close by the Fort of São Joachim. In less than a week they can reach their destination. They have been travelling for two months, or maybe it is longer; they have covered a distance of 400 miles, or maybe more. The last stages of the journey have worn them out. They have suffered from dysentery, and 'a severe inflammatory complaint', and all of them have fevers of mounting intensity. Their destination is near, but what of it? The Portuguese soldiers who man the fort have orders to forbid strangers from approaching , and even if they are allowed entry, it would only provide a brief respite before turning round and going back the way they have come.

They reach the banks of the Pirara River, and there by chance they meet up with some Portuguese soldiers. Waterton masters his fever sufficiently to be able to compose a letter in impeccable Spanish, addressed to their commanding officer at the fort. Sitting in a little hut by the river, skeleton-thin and trembling, his body pitted with sores, he writes:

Respected Sir,
Since I do not have the honour of your acquaintance, I thought it more proper and fitting to wait here until I have received word from you. Having travelled as far as this little hut, I do not wish to return without having seen the Portuguese Fort, and I beg your permission that I might be allowed to visit it. My motives are honourable. I am not a man of business, nor am I a soldier or a government official. I am a Catholic nobleman, with a country estate in England, and many years of my life have been spent in wandering . . .[24]

It seems that at this stage the Indians have no more energy or resistance left in their bodies, 'they lie disabled in their hammocks, unable to move',[25] and so Waterton must go on alone. The Portuguese soldiers lend him a canoe, and three Carib Indians who can take him slowly up the river. The rain falls, the nights are cold, the sun is never to be seen. Waterton's fever grows more fierce, but still he notices the flocks of macaws and parakeets, and the tapirs plunging heavily into the water, showing no signs of fear as the little canoe approaches them.

When they are close to the fort, Waterton waits to hear whether his request has been granted. The officer in charge comes to talk to him, and takes pity on such an unexpected stranger, saying that his orders were never meant to be 'put in force against a sick English gentleman'. For six days Waterton is carefully nursed and fed until his fever has subsided and he can stand up again and is ready to leave.

The Indians are still lying in their hammocks where he left them, but they also are ready to stand and to walk again. They retrace their steps across a flooded land. Several times they are near death.

> Perceiving that life was ebbing fast, I asked the negro if he thought I would struggle through till daylight. 'Ah massa. You go dead in four hours more.'
> 'Then,' said I, 'when you see me quite dead, throw my body out of the hammock and try to get back to the settlements.'
> At this time our hammocks were suspended from stunted trees of miserable foliage, a foot deep in water. The rain was falling in torrents, while the painted sheet, which I usually carried with me, afforded little or no shelter; it had been rent and torn in a hurricane about a week before, on the top of a hill.[26]

Because there is no time to be lost if they are to come out of this alive, they decide to risk going down the falls of the Essequibo River, rather than trying to get across country to join up with the Demerara. In the *Wanderings*, Waterton ignores all the difficulties they went through and describes just one incident. The river gathers strength and ferocity as it approaches the falls. They lash the canoe to the branches of a dead tree that has been trapped amongst the rocks. Beyond the tree is a narrow channel of rushing water, barely twelve feet wide:

> Nothing could surpass the skill of the Indian who steered the canoe. He looked steadfastly at it, then at the rocks, then cast an eye on the channel, and then looked at the canoe again. It was in vain to speak. The sound was lost in the roar of the waters; but his eye showed that

he had already passed it in imagination. He held up his paddle in a position, as much as to say, that he would keep exactly amid channel; and then made a sign to cut the bush rope that held the canoe to the fallen tree. The canoe drove through the torrent with inconceivable rapidity. It did not touch the rocks once all the way.[27]

Maybe hurtling down this stretch of the Essequibo River was all that Waterton could clearly remember of his return journey, and everything else was confused by the delirium of fever, the ceaseless battery of the sound of rushing water, falling rain and the reverberations of thunder. He arrived back at Mibiri Creek in the month of August, towards the end of the rainy season. When his friends first saw him they could hardly recognize him, and for three months Mrs Edmonstone nursed him through the worst of his sickness. She was at the same time nursing a new baby, her daughter Anne, who seventeen years later was to become Waterton's wife and the mother of his child. He stayed long enough in Guiana to attend the little girl's christening, and then he made preparations for his voyage back to England.

CHAPTER VI

The Park

Towards the end of 1812, Waterton was strong enough to leave the Edmonstones' home and come to Georgetown. He had with him the spoils of his travels: an odd collection which included a ball made from the juice of the Indian rubber tree, painfully collected while he was suffering from a 'double fever'; many balls of 'delightful, odiferous gum, which I think equals frankincense for burning in church . . . about 150 of the most rare and beautiful birds, and fine, fine blowpipes'.[1] He also had 'considerable quantities of the famous vegetable poison', curare, and a fair idea that its potency was far greater than had previously been thought by Sir Joseph Banks and others, for he had already tried some of the stuff on a large and well-fed ox weighing 960 pounds. As he recorded with a characteristic combination of anecdote and scientific observation, 'The poison seemed to take effect in four minutes . . . In five and twenty minutes from the time of his being wounded he was quite dead. His flesh was very sweet and savoury at dinner.'[2]

Although others before him had obtained small samples of curare, it was still not known that the bark of the liana vine contained the poison, *strychnos toxifera*, for it was only one of the many ingredients which the Indians used in recipes which included the fangs of poisonous snakes, the crushed bodies of ants, and cayenne pepper. Waterton was the first white man who had been allowed to watch the ceremonial preparation of curare, and he even managed to obtain all the separate ingredients used, each one 'carefully folded up in leaves as is the Indian custom'.[3] But all of these little packages were swallowed up by the Essequibo River, on one of the occasions when the canoe capsized while making its perilous way back home.

Because of his expedition to the Fort of São Joachim, Waterton had become briefly famous. While he was away the governor of the province of Demerara, General Carmichael, had written to Lord Bathurst, recently appointed as the British Secretary for War and the Colonies, 'to say that I was in the forest; and that, if he wanted a person to conduct an exploring enterprise, he thought I might be safely recommended to his lordship's notice'.[4]

During the weeks that he stayed on the coast, waiting for the departure of the next boat bound for England, Waterton was swept into the social life of the colony. General Carmichael asked him if he would deliver some official dispatches to Lord Bathurst in London, and these were accompanied by a warm letter of introduction, which added still more weight to his status as a candidate for future explorations in other forests or plains which had been coloured red by the growing British empire.

The night before he set sail he was invited to a 'splendid' ball. It was held at the Union Coffee House, now in its glittering prime, and in advance of its bankruptcy. There was dancing under the lights of the four chandeliers which had just been installed, and rousing English music played by a band called the Royals. It must all have seemed very strange, in contrast to the life he had grown accustomed to during the last long months. And he must have looked very strange too, amongst the people of the coast, with his skeleton-thin body, skin 'the colour of mahogany' and his face still showing the shock of sickness and hunger. By some odd coincidence, the vessel that was to take him to England on the following morning was called the *Fame*.

Slowly he made his way back, stopping off at the islands of St Thomas and Grenada on the way. The 'tertian ague' which gave him regular bouts of fever every forty-eight hours, starting punctually at midday, and racking his body without respite for six to twelve hours, accompanied him throughout the voyage. When he finally arrived in Liverpool in March 1813, he was too weak to consider travelling on to London immediately, and so sent the precious dispatches and the letter of introduction ahead by post. Before long he received an enthusiastic reply from Lord Bathurst, asking him to come for a meeting as soon as he could, in order to discuss the possibility of going out to Madagascar.

In May, Waterton went to meet his lordship in London. He was at once offered a government commission to explore 'the interior of Madagascar, with permission to visit Monomotapa and the Sechelles Islands, &c; and that a man-of-war would take me out early in October following.'[5] He did not give an immediate answer, but returned to Walton Hall, where he might consider the matter carefully, and having done so he wrote to Lord Bathurst, saying that because of

1 Waterton at the age of forty-two. The tropical bird and the wild cat's head are both hollow specimens prepared by his own method of taxidermy.

2 Walton Hall in 1831. The house on its wooded island could only be reached by means of the iron bridge. The old watergate provided shelter for numerous birds and one spring Waterton counted forty-nine pairs nesting there.

3 For many years Waterton was an 'accidental traveller' in the wilds of British Guiana. When rivers could not be navigated it was necessary to carry the canoe through the shadowy world of the forest floor.

ill-health he must refuse. Later, with hindsight and a sad bitterness he wrote,

> I never acted so much against my own interest as when I declined to go to Madagascar. I ought to have proceeded thither by all means and let the tertian ague take its chance. My commission was a star of the first magnitude . . . and the star went down below the horizon to appear no more.[6]

It was quite true. This was the first, and really the only occasion when in spite of his Catholicism and his naturally defiant spirit, the door was opened for Waterton to join the establishment. If he had gone to Madagascar, and presuming that he came back alive, he would have ceased to be a wanderer and an accidental traveller, instead he would have become an explorer, backed by the blessing and finance of the British Government: an important person in the eyes of important people. His private hobbies and obsessions would have been given unquestioned authority, and no one would have doubted his word when he described the intricate preparation of curare, or the upside-down habits of the sloth, or told how he rode on the back of a crocodile. Nevertheless, if he had gone to Madagascar, there would have been many restrictions to his freedom and his way of going about things, and perhaps his stubbornness and his need for privacy were as important as the waves of fever when he refused the commission. For the rest of his life all his work as a traveller, a naturalist, a conservationist, a taxidermist and an occasional scientist was financed out of his own pocket and performed in the manner of an inspired amateur. With the wisdom of a far wider hindsight, perhaps it was better that way.

For the next three years, instead of watching the sunbirds, the horned chameleons and the thirty-nine species of round-eyed lemur that were to be found on the island of Madagascar, Waterton turned his attention to the lands which surrounded his family home. In Guiana he had seen a profusion of wild life that can now hardly be imagined even with the help of contemporary drawings or the solemn lists of estimated numbers; back at Walton Hall he began to be painfully aware of the systematic destruction of wild birds and animals which was taking place all around him. Some species were becoming increasingly scarce, others had been entirely banished from this part of England:

> Kites were frequent here in the days of my father; but I myself have never seen one near the place. In 1813, I had my last sight of the

buzzard. It used to repair to the storm-blasted top of an ancient oak which grows near the water's edge; and many and many a time have I gone that way, on purpose of getting a view of it. In the spring of that year it went away to return no more, and, about the same period, our last raven was shot on its nest by a neighbouring gentleman.[7]

The fault lay with the English game laws which protected the grouse, the pheasant, the blackcock, the partridge and the bustard, but allowed every other bird, from the sea eagle to the clouds of little finches, to be shot or trapped indiscriminately. The fault lay in the steady improvement in the efficiency of firearms which led to such refinements as the punt-gun with which one hunter claimed to have killed 617 sandpipers with just two shots.[8] The fault lay with the parliamentary Acts of Enclosure which systematically removed so many of the commons, heaths, moorlands and 'wastes' which had been the natural habitat for many birds, especially the birds of prey.[9] There were also the inevitable changes brought about by the growth of industry and the human population, the tangled network of canals and roads and soon the railways that were spreading out across the countryside. But beyond all this there is the image of the need for slaughter: people killing like a fox kills chickens trapped in a hen-house, stripping the countryside of its life. The American naturalist John James Audubon, famous for his vivid and often savage paintings of birds and animals, a man with whom Waterton had terrible and subjective quarrels in later years, once said, 'I call birds few when I shoot less than a hundred a day.'[10] Everywhere there are echoes of this attitude, and the image of heap upon heap of useless corpses.

When Waterton came back from Guiana, something had changed in him. He had, in his own words, 'suffered and learnt mercy'. It was not only that he did not want to kill, unless he considered it really necessary, he more especially wanted to foster and protect the living creatures whose existence was so important to him. Here he had a park which since the death of his father, and more recently the death of his mother, was entirely his own. The park was filled with the trees which he had known since he was a child: thousands of trees holding in their history thousands of long quiet years. There were the spreading oaks in whose branches he used to lie when he watched the foxes playing at night, and by whose roots he eventually chose to be buried. On the island, near the gatehouse, there was a huge sycamore tree, which had been the home of a tawny owl for as long as he could remember. Before he left for southern Spain he had scooped twenty-four gallons of dark water the colour of strong coffee from a deep hole in its side, then he had carefully prepared the hole with a metal perch and a floor of stone chippings and wood shavings in the hope that the tawny owl would return with the following spring. There were other oaks, and other sycamores, elms and beeches, willow and ash: they could all play a part in protecting and feeding the birds and animals that belonged to the area. And yet, thanks to the assiduous work of the gamekeeper who concentrated on owls, hawks, herons and anything else which could be accused of disrupting the well-being of the pheasants; of the gardener who spared the robin because of old superstitions, but shot blackbirds, finches, thrushes, ring-doves and other birds that might threaten the orchard or the vegetable plots; and thanks also to the local farmers and poachers, and maybe because of other factors as well, there was no longer that loud clamour of joyful noise to celebrate the arrival of spring, such as Waterton remembered from his childhood. When he walked out among the trees at night he often listened in vain for the cry of an owl or a nightjar, and the sudden scream of a heron.

In the spring of 1813 he began the long slow process of enticing birds and animals back to the park. He started with the barn owl.

Up to the year 1813, the barn owl had a sad time of it at Walton Hall. However, on my return from the wilds of Guiana, having suffered myself and learned mercy, I broke in pieces the codes of penal laws which the knavery of the gamekeeper and the lamentable ignorance of the other servants had hitherto put in force, far too successfully, to thin the numbers of this poor, harmless, unsuspecting tribe.

On the ruins of the old gateway, against which, so tradition says, the waves of the lake have dashed for the better part of a thousand years, I made a place with stone and mortar about four feet square, and fixed a thick oaken stick firmly into it. Huge masses of ivy now quite cover it. In about a month or so after it was finished, a pair of barn owls came and took up their abode in it. I threatened to strangle the keeper if ever, after this, he molested either the old birds, or their young ones.[11]

With the success of the 'settlement on the gateway', Waterton 'set about forming other establishments'. In the broken trunk of a hollow sycamore tree he built stonework with sixteen compartments in it, and these were soon occupied by sixteen pairs of jackdaws. If he found an old ash tree with a honey fungus erupting from its side, then he would take a hammer and chisel to cut away the soft affected wood until he had excavated an ideal compartment for the tawny owl. He was busy, immensely busy, planting new trees and ground cover, making boxes and chambers, roofing in hollow trunks, constructing holes, erecting perches and resting places; and finding new places for himself too, where he could sit quietly amongst the branches of his trees watching and waiting.

> I often go into the topmost branches of a wide-spreading oak, and there, taking the *Metamorphoses* out of my pocket, I read the sorrows of poor Halcyone. A brook runs close by the tree, and on its bank I have fixed a stump for a resting place for the kingfisher. On it this pretty bird will tarry for a while in passing up and down, and then plunge into the stream and bring out a fish.[12]

Many years later he noted with great satisfaction that spring at Walton Hall was once again celebrated with a barrage of bird song; the old gatehouse was occupied by no less than forty-nine pairs of nesting birds; and when he was walking through the woods at night he heard

> the heron screaming, the wigeon whistling, the barn owl screeching, and the tawny owl hooting in rapid succession. The moon was playing on the water at the time, and the air was nearly as warm as summer. I thought of times long past and gone, when I was enjoying nature's richest scenery in the interminable forests of Guiana.[13]

But the spring of 1813 was just the beginning. The birds needed time to grow accustomed to safety, and the local people needed time to adjust to the habits and demands of their new squire. If in Guiana Waterton had seemed strange and wild to the white colonials of the coast, here in Yorkshire he must have appeared like a being from another world, and only his broad north-country accent would have made him familiar. Admittedly he had been back home quite regularly over the years. On at least a couple of occasions he had brought back live tropical birds, and in 1811 he arrived with a 'Blackamore' who appears briefly in the household account books and then disappears without trace; but this was the first occasion since his adulthood that he had come to live at Walton Hall.

He arrived with his extraordinary luggage of skins, weapons and poisons. When a fever was on him his thin body took on a shrunken look and dark rings appeared around his eyes. In warm weather he went barefoot and spent a great deal of time working with his trees, but if it was cold he became fretful and impatient. Unless he was going to some formal appointment he would be so shabbily dressed that he could easily be mistaken for a beggar or a farm labourer. But no matter how he looked he was still the Squire of Walton Hall, and the fourteenth male inheritor to occupy the family mansion. When the local people saw him, even if he was sitting high up in the branches of a tree, the women would bob a curtsey, and the men would touch their forelocks in the formal greeting owing to their master. Already there must have been that innocent gentleness which was noticed by everyone who met him; a quality which infuriated some people and charmed others. Added to that there was his impatience, which would break out in sudden anger or rudeness, if he felt himself to be stretched too far.

The gentleness and the anger were both busy. Slowly, inexorably, Waterton declared war on the attitudes of almost everybody who lived in his area. Within his own household he forbade the gamekeeper and the gardener to use either traps or guns, and if they disobeyed him they would forfeit their jobs: 'My keeper both hates and fears a magpie, but self-interest forces upon the fellow the unpleasant task of encouraging the breed in order to keep well with me.'[14] He argued with his ancient housekeeper and anyone else who cared to listen about the superstitious fears which the country people had about many creatures: '. . . ravens, owls and magpies have long since dropped all dealings with people in the other world; and hedgehogs are clearly proved never to have sucked a cow . . .'[15]

When his neighbour Sir William Pilkington showed him the freshly killed body of the last raven in Yorkshire, he called the man a scoundrel, adding that his father before him had been no better for he had boasted of shooting the last kite. He defended every living creature from the polecat to the carrion crow, but with the exception of the Hanoverian rat, and nearly all his careful studies of birds and animals were concerned with finding valid reasons why this one or that one should be spared.

The windhover [kestrel] is perpetually confounded with the sparrowhawk, and too often doomed to suffer from the predatory attacks of that bird on the property of man. But when your gun has brought the poor windhover to the ground, look, I pray you, into the contents of his stomach; you will find nothing there to show you that his life ought to be forfeited. On the contrary, the remnants of the beetle, and the field mouse, which will attract your notice, prove indisputably that his visits to your farm have been a real service to you.[16]

I attribute the bad character which the heron has with us for destroying fish more to erroneous ideas than to any well-authenticated proofs that it commits extensive depredations on our store-ponds. Under this impression I encourage the poor persecuted wanderer to come and take shelter here; and I am glad to see it builds its nests in the trees which overhang the water, although carp and tench and many other sorts of fish are here in abundance. Close attention to its habits has convinced me that I have not done wrongly.[17]

The carrion crow does very little injury to man during nine or ten months of the year; and if in this period he is to be called over the coals for occasionally throttling an unprotected leveret or a stray partridge, he may fairly meet the accusation by a set-off against it in his account of millions of noxious insects destroyed by him.[18]

I am a great friend of the weasel and the polecat, although I know they will commit depredations on game whenever the opportunity shall occur. Still I consider that the havoc which they make amongst mice and rats far overbalances their transgressions against the game laws.[19]

I protect the magpie, with greater care, perhaps, than any other bird, on account of its having nobody to stand up for it. Both rich and poor seem to entertain so great an antipathy for this gay and lively bird in its wild state, that I often wonder how the breed has managed to escape utter extirpation in this populous district.[20]

The fox require no particular attention at our hands by way of keeping up the breed. Only let us prevent poisoned food and traps being placed in its runs, and nothing more will be asked of us.[21]

Were I just now requested to find a hollow tree in the woods of the neighbourhood, I should say that it were useless to go in quest of one, so eager have the proprietors been to put into their pockets the value of every tree which was not 'making money', according to the cant phrase of modern wood valuers. No bird has felt this felling ancient timber more than the tawny owl . . . Were it not for my park, I believe that the tawny owl would be extinct in this part of Yorkshire.[22]

The *Essays on Natural History* from which these accounts have all been taken, first began to appear as articles in Loudon's *Magazine of Natural History* after the year 1831, and later they were published, along with additional essays in three bound volumes. Many of the incidents referred to, and the studies of bird and animal life, however, stem from those three early years.

CHAPTER VII

Curare

In the early nineteenth century, no one knew anything about curare except that it killed quickly and gently and had no cure. Then, quite unexpectedly, it was discovered that the drug did not poison the body, it simply stopped all the bodily functions, and if the lungs could be kept working the victim would eventually wake up, unharmed, as if from a deep sleep. This opened up all kinds of speculations about how curare worked, and how its powers could be used to alleviate pain or to resist the progress of a disease. Still, it proved a difficult substance to work with, and after innumerable trials and experiments it was not until 1945 that it came into general medical use.[1]

When he was in Guiana for the first of his wanderings, Waterton used curare to kill animals of various sizes, watching their manner of dying and trying to understand more: 'Neither attribute to cruelty, nor to want of feeling for the sufferings of the inferior animals, the ensuing experiments. The larger animals were destroyed in order to have proof positive of the strength of a poison which had hitherto been doubted: and the smaller ones were killed with the hope of substantiating that which has commonly been supposed to be an antidote.'[2]

For the rest of his life he remained fascinated by the drug. It has been said that his own experiments were probably of 'limited importance',[3] and it seems likely that for the most famous of these in which an ass was successfully revived after having been given a lethal dose, he simply acted as a spectator to the whole proceeding. Nevertheless the observations he made in Guiana provided a clear and accurate description of how the drug was prepared, how it was used, and how it affected a living organism; and the curare he brought back with him was very strong, and so well-packaged that it was still potent when it was tested more than 150 years later.[4] Also, and this was perhaps the most important factor, he was always willing to give samples of his

60

supply to anyone who showed a genuine scientific interest in it. Doctors, veterinary surgeons, and those who were simply curious, were presented with a little package, often sent in the post, and accompanied by an explanation of the nature and the strength of the contents.

My good friend Mr Menteath . . . will start today on his way to London. I have requested him to be the bearer of a few poisoned spikes to your Grace; and as he has no connection with the Pope, I flatter myself that they will be safe in his hands . . .

A professional gentleman by the name of Davis wrote to me from Cardiff the other day, for some Wourali [curare]; and I sent him a poisoned spike in a letter.[5]

I had intended to have sent you a poisoned spike,—but on reading your favour of the 2nd I perceive that you are occupied in making a very scientific experiment which will require great care, and the use of the very best wourali . . .[6]

He had several boxes in which he kept a collection of small wooden spikes which each impaled about one gramme of solid curare paste coated in wax, poisoned arrows tightly wrapped in the long leaves of the coucourite palm, and a number of carefully sealed pots and bottles.

Numbers 1, 2, 3 contain Macushi poison which I have not tried; but I have every reason to believe that it is very strong, and its effects are very fatal. Number 5 & 6 contain Macushi poison which I have tried. It killed the ox mentioned in the *Wanderings*. It killed an ass in London in 1813; and one in Rome in 1818, and I have killed several dogs with it . . .

All the poison in the lumps of wax is in a moist state, and will remain so as long as air is excluded. It is quite ready for use.

In Numbers 7 & 8 the poison is in a glass bottle, with bladder inserted instead of a cork. You have only to cut off the top, at the circle which I have made in the wax, and you will get at the poison immediately.[7]

He took his role very seriously. He was the custodian, the keeper of a mysterious substance which could kill without causing pain, and which took away life with such an extraordinary gentleness that it made death a thing not to be feared: '. . . life sank in death without the least apparent contention, without a cry, without a struggle and without a groan . . . it sank to the ground, but sank so gently, that you could not distinguish the movement from an ordinary motion; and had you been ignorant that it was wounded with a poisoned arrow, you would have never suspected that it was dying.'[8]

Until Waterton's strange and lingering descriptions of the working of curare, the only other information had been provided by Edward Bancroft, an English physician who was in the colony in the 1760s,[9] and the dramatic and totally inaccurate account of the 'winged death' which is to be found in the *Discoveries of the Large, Rich and Bewtiful Empire of Guiana*, written by Sir Walter Raleigh in 1595.

There was nothing whereof I was more curious than to find out the true remedies of these poisoned arrows, for besides the mortalitie of the wound they make, the partie shot endureth the most insufferable torment in the world, and abideth a most ugly and lamentable death, sometimes dying stark mad, sometimes their bowels breaking out of their bellies . . . as black as pitch and so unsavoury as no man can endure to cure, or to attend them; And it is strange to know that in all this time there was never a Spaniard, either by gift or torment, that could attain to the true knowledge of the cure, although they martyred and put to invented torture I know not how many of them.[10]

By the early nineteenth century the myth and the confusion had hardly shifted. No one knew what was the active constituent among the many unlikely items that were boiled together to make a black and sticky mixture, and no one knew how it affected a living organism with such a quiet speed when it entered the bloodstream, although it could be tasted and even swallowed without lethal effect. It was called by many names: Waterton chose 'wourali', others 'woorara', 'urali' and 'urari', although now the generic name 'curare' has come into general use. To make matters more complex, there are several types of liana vine which yield the crucial substance, and the tribes of the South American forests all had their secret recipes which produced a poison of widely differing potencies.

If Waterton had not had the misfortune to lose 'all the collected materials of which the poison is composed' in the rushing waters of the Essequibo, he would have had no difficulty in identifying the toxic ingredient. Then he could have made a name for himself by describing it and giving it a Latin classification; this would have won him the quiet though perhaps ambivalent congratulations of the men of science. As it was he did say that he thought the vine was the 'principal ingredient', and that the poison 'affects the nervous system and thus destroys the vital functions', but the problem was that he included this information as part of the narrative of the *Wanderings*. He published no separate scientific paper on the subject, to give credibility and dignity to his assertions, and he delivered no lecture, something which surely Sir Joseph Banks would have been pleased to arrange for him at the Royal Society. Instead he simply sandwiched all of his careful observations amongst the curious and haphazard adventures of a barefooted traveller, and the book did not get published until 1825, twelve years after he had returned from the first of his wanderings. Notoriety was something he achieved easily, even though he was made to carry it all his life like a tin can tied to a dog's tail, but the kind of recognition he deserved both as a scientist and as a naturalist always eluded him, and he himself tended to dismiss all of his achievements as 'feeble efforts'.

In 1836, more than ten years after the *Wanderings in South America* was published, two German explorers, Robert and Richard Schomburgk, set off to Guiana with the declared intention, among others, of finding out how curare was prepared, and of what it was composed. They followed a route which Sir Robert once admitted was 'entirely guided'[11] by Waterton's directions, and after much trouble and persistence, they were able to isolate the crucial liana vine and experiment with its powers. Sir Robert further complicated the history of curare by 'recognizing' the vine as a member of the *Strychnos* family, thus implying that it was a strychnine-type convulsive poison, whereas the opposite was true since it works as a muscle relaxant. Both brothers, for whatever reason, chose to mock at Waterton with an odd vindictiveness, and denigrated the importance of his earlier achievements. Richard Schomburgk, in his book *Travels in British Guiana*, declared that 'no earlier traveller' could have witnessed the preparation of curare,

> . . . their information is always supported only by the accounts of the Indians, who naturally take care to keep the manufacture of the poison as dark as they possibly can . . .
>
> It was to be expected that the mysterious details of the earlier travellers in British Guiana, of Waterton for example, were too inrooted amongst the Colonists for them to believe the simple method of preparation with which my brother furnished them on his return. The certainty that only the vegetable effect of a plant gave rise to the terrible effects was doubted, these being ascribed to the poison fangs of snakes, the ants, and to peppers.[12]

It was, to say the least, very unfair, and as Waterton's devoted friend and editor, Sir Norman Moore, wrote in the preface to his edition of the *Essays on Natural History*, published in 1871:

> Schomburgk was the first to publish a good map, and it is still the best, of Guiana, though it is impossible to avoid the expression of a wish that he had been as candid as he was laborious. He has copied whole passages from the *Wanderings*, with no other change than the transformation of an interesting into a heavy style, and notwithstanding all his obligations to Waterton, he never once mentioned him in his books with respect.[13]

However all that is a long jump in time, and it leads into areas of rivalries and quarrels which are not relevant here. The first scientific study of the effect of curare was made by a young English physician called Benjamin Collis Brodie (1783–1862). He was a prolific experimenter and a tireless contributor to learned magazines, and he later became, among other things, the sergeant surgeon to Queen Victoria. In 1810 Brodie set himself the task of trying to understand the 'Influence of the Brain on the Action of the Heart, and the Manufacture of Animal Heat'.[14] With the terrible simplicity that must perhaps so often accompany such pioneering research, he developed a method of administering artificial respiration to a number of decapitated cats and rabbits, while carefully noting the length of time that the heart could be kept beating without the help of the head, and the speed at which the body temperature fell. He then moved on to 'Experiments and Observations on the Different Modes in which Death is Produced by Certain Vegetable Poisons', which involved poisoning dogs, cats, guinea pigs and rabbits and seeing what happened. He used all sorts of poisons: essential oil of almonds, the juice of aconite leaves, oil of tobacco, proof spirits, and something called Upas Antiar which had been obtained in Java. He was also provided with some very stale and inactive curare which had been given to him by the son of that earlier traveller, Edward Bancroft.

The crucial experiment, which came to be seen as a landmark in the history of anaesthesia, involved a young cat which had been given a lethal dose of curare. For more than two and a half hours the limp body of the animal was given artificial respiration, and after that time the stillness of her apparent death was replaced by a state of 'profound sleep', and then she 'awoke and walked away'. On the following day she appeared 'slightly indisposed', but otherwise healthy, and she was subsequently given to a friend of Brodie and 'lived, I have been informed, for some years'.[15]

Brodie's experiments were published in detail in 1811 and 1812. It is not known whether Waterton had been introduced to him by that time, but it is certain that Sir Joseph Banks acted as an intermediary between the two men. Following the experiment with the cat Brodie was eager to obtain a fresh supply of curare, and Waterton had set himself the difficult task of reaching the Macushi Indians who made the most potent poison. Banks had intensified Waterton's determination by saying, 'I have been a great traveller, and all the investigations which I have been able to make concerning the nature of the poison, tends to convince me that it is not sufficiently strong to kill the larger animals, such as men and cattle; but it may answer very well in the ordinary pursuit of winged game, and in that of minor quadrupeds. When you yourself shall have witnessed its deadly effects on man or cattle, we will no longer doubt its deadly virulence.'[16]

Waterton does not mention Brodie by name in either the *Wanderings* or in his *Essays* and there is the impression that the two men felt a natural antipathy for each other, but he did refer to Brodie's work when talking about possible antidotes for curare poisoning. The only remedies mentioned by the Indians were drinking quantities of rum, or filling the mouth with salt or the juice of sugar cane, and then being immersed in water. He tried out these practices on some unfortunate chickens, but they showed no sign of improvement and died quickly. But he mentions,

> It is supposed by some, that wind, introduced into the lungs by means of a small pair of bellows, would revive the patient, provided the operation be continued for a sufficient length of time. It may be so; but this is a difficult and tedious mode of cure, and he who is wounded in the forest . . . stands but a poor chance of being saved by it.
>
> Had the Indians a sure antidote, it is likely they would carry it about with them . . .[17]

When Waterton came to London in the May of 1813 to see Lord Bathurst, he had with him samples of his Macushi poison Numbers 5 and 6, and he took the opportunity of killing an ass with it, presumably to demonstrate its potency to a small invited audience. In April of the following year he was again in London, and the poison was used in an important experiment which was performed at the Veterinary College. A she-ass, acquired for the purpose by the President of the College, the

Duke of Northumberland, was injected with a dose of curare. When she was insensible, Brodie performed a tracheotomy, and the noted veterinary surgeon Professor William Sewell worked at the bellows. Waterton must have supervised the administration of the poison, but apart from that he had no other function. According to Dr Brodie's rather terse report, the artificial respiration lasted 'more than an hour', after which the ass recovered and seemed to suffer no inconvenience. Waterton chose to describe the proceedings in more detail.

A she-ass received the wourali poison in the shoulder and died apparently in ten minutes. An incision was then made in its windpipe, and through it the lungs were regularly inflated for two hours with a pair of bellows. Suspended animation returned. The ass held up her head, and looked around; but the inflation being discontinued she sank once more into apparent death. The artificial breathing was immediately recommenced, and continued without intermission for two hours more. This saved the ass from final dissolution; she rose up and walked about; she seemed neither agitated nor in pain.[18]

The two men both added the information that the Duke of Northumberland subsequently presented the ass to Waterton, that she was given the name Wouralia, and lived on at Walton Hall for a further twenty-five years.

It was Professor Sewell, the man who was working the bellows at sixteen to eighteen breaths a minute, who suggested that curare might be used as a treatment for rabies and tetanus, diseases which terrified the imagination, and for which there was no known cure. The principle of this theory was quite sound: 'frightful spasm is the prominent symptom of those awful maladies; complete quiescence is the effect of the administration of wourali'.[19] Indeed curare did come to be regularly used on tetanus victims, with a certain measure of success, although in the case of rabies it never helped, even though Sewell and Waterton were both convinced of its potentiality:

So confident was he [Sewell] of a favourable result, that I heard him declare before Sir Joseph Banks and a large company of scientific gentlemen, that were he unfortunate enough to be bitten by a mad dog, and become infected with hydrophobia, he would not hesitate one moment in having the wourali poison applied.[20]

I am so certain that the Indian poison will cure hydrophobia, that were I labouring under the dreadful disease, I would undergo the operation in preference to any treatment that the faculty could suggest.[21]

At this point, although serious scientific progress was being made, things kept on verging on a macabre absurdity. In 1838 Sewell put his theories into practice and inoculated a horse suffering from tetanus with a dose of curare. For two hours the horse was given artificial respiration, and when it revived all the symptoms of tetanus had disappeared. Unfortunately it celebrated its recovery by gorging itself on too much warm bran during the night which proved fatal. Still, the experiment was counted as having been a success.

Inspired by Sewell's achievement, Dr Francis Sibson, the Resident Surgeon and Apothecary at Nottingham General Infirmary, contacted Waterton about the possibility of using curare on human victims of rabies. Sibson had been working with ether and chloroform, and he was experienced in administering artificial respiration to both animal and human patients, so it was natural that he should want to include curare in his researches. Now there were six men under his care who had recently been bitten by a mad dog, and he was waiting to see if they would soon show the signs of madness and hysteria which presaged the onset of the disease.

The house surgeon [Sibson] has written to me, and ardently begged some wourali poison, requesting at the same time that I will send him instructions how it ought to be used in case of need. I have answered him saying that if any of the patients show symptoms of hydrophobia, and if the attending scientific men declare the case to be hopeless, he must send me an express, and I will be with him without loss of time . . . He says my letter is most satisfactory.[22]

The six men were not affected, but in the spring of the following year a Nottingham policeman contracted rabies and an 'express' was duly sent off to Waterton. However, although he set off without delay, armed with his poisoned spikes, the policeman died a few hours before he arrived. He and Sibson then decided that in order to be able to act quickly and without hesitation should another case arise, it was necessary to win over public confidence by giving a demonstration of how a victim of curare poisoning could be safely restored to life.

The first of these demonstrations seems to have been welcomed by the people of Nottingham as a public entertainment. Early on a

Monday morning, the hospital schoolroom where the experiment was to take place was so overcrowded with 'professional gentlemen from the town and the county' and whoever else could get in that one reporter from the *Nottingham Journal* complained that it was impossible to keep an accurate account of the proceedings. The first day was not very propitious. To demonstrate the strength of the poison a brindled dog was injected and allowed to slip into death. To demonstrate the effectiveness of artificial respiration, a second dog was injected and attempts were made to revive it; but something went wrong and it died without a return to consciousness. On the same day, an 'aged ass' was also injected, and once the curare had taken effect it was heaved on to a large table, and seven men, headed by Waterton and Sibson, began the work of bringing the animal back to life. For seven and a half hours they kept the bellows going, sixteen to eighteen breaths a minute, and, for fear of losing the momentum, Sibson did all of this part of the work himself. Finally the ass revived, but he was very weak, and developed an infection which killed him shortly afterwards.

On the following day they were better organized. A stronger ass was procured, the room was less crowded, the table was not used, and the experiment was mercifully much briefer. After two hours the ass resumed its natural breathing, and by the end of the day it 'showed every symptom of liveliness, strength and even playfulness, betraying no signs of having been operated on'.[23] A person mounted on its back and was carried around the room with no difficulty.

The experiments 'gave universal satisfaction'[24] and everyone present declared themselves confident that if another case of rabies occurred, then curare should at once be resorted to. Dr Sibson was provided with a 'fair store' of Macushi poison Numbers 5 and 6, and he and Waterton parted on the understanding that they would both be at the ready if and when the need arose.

For the next twenty years and more, the two men maintained their friendship with a regular correspondence and occasional meetings, but not once did they have a chance to test their shared belief. In 1855 they were informed of a rabid child in London, but she had been ill for four days, and they despaired of being able to help. 'I conceive that the child will be dead, or at least beyond the power of receiving advantage from the application of Wourali, before I can reach the hospital. Let us have a good case, as everything will depend on a good trial.'[25]

But they never got their 'good case'. In June 1856 Waterton wrote to Dr Harley, who was also busy with curare, lamenting the fact that, 'we have never been able to operate on a patient, as the patients have always died before we could get to them.'[26] He even resorted to advertising his willingnesss to offer his services and those of his friend, in an essay entitled *The Dog Tribe*, but there is no evidence that he received any replies:

Both in the *Wanderings*, and in the *Essays*, I have spoken of the Indian Wourali poison as a supposed cure (I say supposed because it has never yet had a trial) for hydrophobia; but as the subject is one of vast importance, perhaps I shall not do amiss if I add here a few plain instructions.

Supposing a person has been bitten by a mad dog. That person may, or may not, go mad; but should symptoms of the disease break out, and a competent practitioner in medicine pronounce it to be undeniably hydrophobia, and the family wish to have the wourali tried, I beg attention to the following remarks: Do not, I pray you, let any medicines be administered. The paroxysms will generally occur at intervals, during two or even three days before the final catastrophe takes place. Lose no time in telegraphing for Dr Sibson, No 40 Lower Brook Street, London; and for Charles Waterton, Walton Hall, near Wakefield, Yorkshire. We will promptly attend.[27]

CHAPTER VIII

The Second Wandering

There is perhaps the danger of looking at a person in the distant landscape of a time long since past and giving them more clarity, more of a sense of ambition and purpose than they ever felt themselves to have as the years of their life followed each other. It is presumed that the traveller knew where he was going; that the explorer knew what he was looking for.

Waterton's second wandering in South America was in many ways very confused and uncertain, and for the first six months at least it would seem that restlessness and disappointment drove him on to each new place. He did have several plans, but they were all either forgotten, or proved impossible for one reason or another.

Just before he left England, in the March of 1816, he received a letter from Sir Joseph Banks. The letter was friendly, complimentary and paternal. Waterton is warned to avoid the 'Noxious Miasmata of the Swampy Regions which lie near the Roots of the Hills',[1] and he is requested to make a collection of the seeds from any of the curious or beautiful plants that he might find in places not before explored by Europeans. If these seeds could be put in packets and presented to the Royal Gardens at Kew, then his name would be 'as much Respected in the Botanical World as it now is in the Zoological'. However, Waterton did not avoid those 'Noxious Miasmatas' for the sake of his health, nor is there any indication that he collected seeds.

On one occasion, after several months of seemingly aimless travel, he unexpectedly declares that his real motive for coming to South America again was so that he could return to the Crystal Mountains of El Dorado, approaching them by travelling up from the mouth of the Amazon. But if that was indeed so, then he made remarkably few preparations for such an ambitious undertaking, and he gave up the whole idea at the first sign of difficulty.

It could be said that he had privately set himself the task of completing his study of the 'state of religion among the Indians', and other peoples in the regions he visited. But he was no historian, and the political, social and religious situation at that time was in such a state of upheaval that he could only take a rather blinkered look at a few of the issues involved. In the report which he completed on his return to England in December 1817, and which he sent to Pope Pius VII, he wrote about the troubles caused by the expulsion of the Jesuits from Portuguese territory in 1759, ignoring all the other troubles caused by revolution and rebellion, the growth of the sugar industry, epidemics, the defeat of Napoleon at Waterloo, the collapse of money markets, the gradual abolition of slavery, and the many other shock waves caused by the collision of the Old World with the New.

In a way, Waterton's dissatisfactions could be seen simply as a reflection of the prevailing mood in the countries he passed through. Everywhere he went there was a sense of impending chaos. The old order was under threat from all sides, and colonies could change hands from one day to the next, according to the shifting balance of power in Europe or the success of an internal revolution. The energy which had brought commercial centres suddenly into existence among the mud flats and the ransacked forests could turn in the opposite direction if a new wind blew. There was already a state of 'domestic war' among many of the slaves, and furtive guerrilla wars were being fought by fugitive slaves living in the forests and swamps. The idea of revolution and nationalism was spreading across the whole continent amongst those who felt that the colonial powers had no right to bleed their land of its riches, and there was yet another state, although it had not the energy to be warlike, among the forest Indians who were being pushed further and further inland, and who were witnessing the death of the world as they had known it. It comes as a shock to realize that those scattered and hidden communities had once been numerous all along the coast of southern Brazil and the Guianas. It comes as a shock to hear an early Portuguese settler giving an impression of their numbers by saying, 'They are so many, that were they to be cut up in a butcher's shop, there would never be a shortage.'[2]

In April 1816 Waterton arrived in the town of Pernambuco on the southern coast of Brazil. England had recently established strong commercial links with that country: barrels of porter and whisky and crates of fine china for the luxurious houses of the planters were regularly unloaded at the ports, along with an extraordinary assortment of less helpful items such as ice-skates, warming pans and corset

71

stays sent over from the manufacturing towns of the north, and wooden coffins from goodness knows where.

The climate, the commercial life, the imported population of slaves, whites and free people of colour, all that was by now familiar, but Pernambuco was much harsher than Georgetown. The strangeness of the place was heightened by the fact that in the month of April everyone was in deep mourning following the recent death of the very old and very mad queen of Portugal, Maria I. Or, as one commentator caustically explained, it was a time when 'the price of all black articles felt a sudden and enormous increase.'[3]

In spite of the sea breezes, the streets stank of human and animal refuse. Sick slaves were often left to die in the streets, and dead bodies were dumped on the sea-shore to be eaten as carrion by the vultures.[4] The maintenance of public services was performed by convicts chained together in pairs and watched over by an armed guard, and the clanking of their chains could be heard throughout the centre of the town. The shops were without windows, the houses were built haphazardly and with no apparent coercion of style: 'As you walk down the streets, the appearance of the houses is not much in their favour. Some are very high, and some very low; some newly whitewashed, and others stained and mouldy, and neglected as though they had no owner.'[5] Several travellers from this period remarked on the balconies which were latticed with narrow strips of wood, giving a blind and closed look to the buildings and a sense of claustrophobia to the person walking between them. During the daytime there were

No females to be seen, excepting the Negro slaves, which gives a sombre look to the streets. The Portuguese, the Brazilian, and even the mulatto women in the middle ranks of life, do not move out of doors in the daytime. They hear Mass in the churches before daylight, and do not again stir out, except in sedan chairs, or in the evening on foot, when occasionally a whole family will sally forth to take a walk.[6]

At first Waterton was shocked by Pernambuco where 'vice and ignorance reign triumphant', but then in a week or two he began 'to feel less the things which annoyed him so much on his first arrival'. It is not clear how many weeks or even months he stayed there, or quite how he occupied himself. He visited pretty villages in the area, he enjoyed 'hospitality, elegance and splendour'; he collected fifty-four specimens of birds and narrowly escaped the consequences of grabbing the rattle of a rattlesnake's tail which he mistook for a grasshopper. He wrote about the immorality of the priesthood, and about the beauties of the countryside, but always his concentration seems to have been distracted, and his descriptions never penetrate beyond the superficial. A French cotton buyer who was in Pernambuco during that same year provided in a few sentences a much more evocative sense of the precarious mood of the place when he told of the wealthy plantation owners who

> . . . living in the midst of the forests seem to fear shadows, or more precisely stated, up to the edge of the forest, around the mill, everything is denuded and scorched to a distance of a quarter of a league . . .
>
> Luxury consists of a great variety of silverware. When a foreigner is entertained, in order to wash himself he is given splendid vessels made of this metal, of which also the coffee trays used at table, the bridles and stirrups of the horses, the knife hilts are made . . .[7]

According to Waterton the people of Pernambuco were content and satisfied with their way of life. But maybe he was simply too distracted by his own thoughts to see them clearly, for while he was there an important rebellion against Portuguese rule was fomenting which broke out shortly after he departed, leaving many hundreds dead, and spreading unrest throughout the colony.

For the next several weeks he zigzagged from place to place, always being thwarted in his apparent purpose by one inconvenience or another. The heavy rains came just when he was considering going from Pernambuco to 'the interior' on horseback, although where he wished to go is never mentioned. A journey to the state of Maranhao, about 500 miles to the south, would take at least forty days by land, and he complained peevishly, 'The route was not wild enough to engage the attention of an explorer, or civilised enough to afford common comforts to a traveller.'[8] If he had chosen to reach the same destination by sea, then the only means of transport available were the terrible slave ships which carried their cargo from port to port along the coast. Not surprisingly Waterton avoided the experience of being enclosed in such a human cage of misery.

Some months later, he planned to travel from Cayenne in French Guiana, to the port of Para on the mouth of the Amazon, and, '. . . to have ascended the Amazon from Para, and got into the Rio Negro and from there to have returned towards the source of the Essequibo, in order to examine the Crystal Mountains and look once more for Lake Parima, the White Sea.'[9] But although suitable ships were available, this huge enterprise was cancelled because the current along the coast was running at such a speed that it would make the first stage of the journey 'long, tedious, and even uncertain'. A Portuguese vessel had already taken four weeks to battle with the first half of the sea voyage, but still Waterton's excuse for not going has a hollow sound to it.

The irritations and the problems followed each other thick and fast, and there were so many abortive schemes that to follow Waterton's peregrinations through Brazil, Cayenne, Surinam, and into British Guiana is like playing a game of snakes and ladders. Finally defeated in all his plans for exploration, he eventually retired to the forests above Georgetown where he could once more potter about barefoot, with his hammock and his canvas sheet, watching birds, noting down their habits and appearance, and making a collection of some of the finest specimens, which he shot down Indian-fashion with a blowpipe and a little arrow tipped with curare.

The narrative of the second wandering closes with a long catalogue of quiet and clear descriptions of many of the different birds he saw, along with enthusiastic but not always convincing reassurances about how safe and easy it is to live in the wilds.

> Custom will soon teach you to tread lightly and barefoot on the little inequalities of the ground, and show you how to pass on, unwounded, amid the mantling briars.
>
> Snakes in these wilds are certainly an annoyance, though perhaps more in imagination than reality; for you must recollect that the serpent is never the first to offend . . .
>
> Tigers are too few, and too apt to fly before the noble face of man, to require a moment of your attention.
>
> The bite of the most noxious of the insects, at the very worst, only causes a transient fever, with a degree of pain more or less.[10]

But in spite of the enthusiasm and the lyricism of his evocation of life in the forest, it is the early stages of the expedition which seem to stay in the mind, leaving the impression of a man hurrying with an almost desperate haste through towns and villages, making a quick note of the smell of the air, the filth in the streets, the appearance of a prison or a government building, a distant silhouette of hills. Even when he stays for several weeks in one place, the sense of restlessness is not lost, even when he is effusive in his praise for the prettiness of a particular area, or the hospitality of those who entertained him, the places and the people seem to merge into a sameness which is disquieting. Events which took place long ago, and people long since dead, are bundled together with fragments of modern politics and encounters with the living. It is only the brief vision of a bird or a flock of birds, a shoal of flying fish, the fading rainbow skin of a dolphin left to die on a ship's deck, which have any reality to him, and make sense out of the lands through which he was passing and the time that was passing with him.

Leaving Pernambuco still in the black clothes of mourning, with social gaiety spinning through the houses of the rich, and a bloody and defeated revolution only a few months away, Waterton took a passage on a Portuguese brig bound for Cayenne in French Guiana. For the fourteen days of the journey he slept on a hen-coop on deck, where he was much bitten by some unnamed blood-sucking insect, but at least he was spared the noise and the stench of a slave ship.

From a distance, as the ship approached the harbour, the view of Pernambuco had been charming. Frigate pelicans flew above the bay, and hurtled down into the water when they saw the gleam of a fish. The town nestled in a landscape of gentle hills, forests and plantations. The entrance to the port of Cayenne was also charming: wooded islands near the shore, and behind them the stately hills of the mainland, showing the 'sublimest scenery on the sea coast from the Amazons to the Oronoque'. About twelve leagues out to sea was a great tower of rock called the Constable, barren of vegetation and thick with nesting birds. Here were the breeding grounds of pelicans, rosy flamingoes, snow-white egrets, scarlet curlews and spoonbills.

But in Cayenne also, as in Pernambuco, this was not a propitious time for visiting. Since the turn of the century the colony had been shifting precariously between English, Portuguese and French control. When Waterton arrived the Portuguese were the unwelcome rulers, and the people were in compulsory mourning for the mad Queen Maria, as well as in secret mourning for the recent defeat of Napoleon, who was now banished to the island of St Helena. Waterton realized that 'this was not the time for a traveller to enjoy Cayenne'. The sadness of the people blunted their hospitality. He stayed in the town for a few days and saw the deposed French governor, Victor Hugues, 'broken down and ruined and under arrest in his own house', gloomily pacing along the balcony of his prison every evening in the company of his four daughters. One day he went to the plantation of La Gabrielle where he saw 22,000 clove trees in full bearing. One evening as he sat under a cinnamon tree, a knife-grinder insect cut through the branch above him, so that it fell on his head, and he took the branch home to Walton Hall as a memento. One day he went to a huge cavern in the side of a mountain not far from Cayenne where he watched the birds known as cock of the rock, with their pale orange feathers, and a tufted fan of feathers on their heads. The days passed in such snippets of experience.

From Cayenne he had planned to go to Para and from there up the Amazon, but the plan was easily abandoned, and instead he took an American ship along the coast to Surinam. Here too the delicate equilibrium of colonial society was teetering dangerously. The crops were plagued by disease, and the planters lived in a virtual state of siege from the fugitive slaves. Waterton described the capital of Paramaribo as 'handsome rich and populous', and did not mention the oppressive humidity which was said to make the place like a Turkish bath within the orchid house at Kew, nor did he mention the unease of the people. He went on to New Amsterdam, found it 'languid' and wondered vaguely what had held back its commercial progress. Two years after he left, the colony was virtually bankrupt, the sugar harvest collapsed, and 15,000 slaves died in a single smallpox epidemic. But for Waterton New Amsterdam was only important because it was near to British Guiana and Georgetown. Now at last he knew exactly where he was going and what he was doing: 'If, gentle reader, thy patience be not already worn out, and thy eyes half closed by the dull adventures of this second sally, then we will return to the forests of Demerara . . .'[11]

Once again he was back in the familiar vast solitudes of a landscape where he could move freely, and there he remained for a further six months, cut off from the clamours and confusions of the outside world that was for him far more frightening or dangerous than any snake bite or fever. He says nothing of where he stayed, nor how far he wandered. He went to the mountains, to the creeks, to the swamps, the savannahs and the plantations. He watched birds before the dawn and after dusk and through the night. He travelled far into Macushi country to catch sight of the rich orange and shiny black colours of the troupiale, the nightingale of Guiana. He clambered among the mangrove swamps where he could find a large member of the toucan family which the Indians called bouradi, the nose. He studied the six species of kingfisher, and by the light of the moon he watched the goatsucker jumping up to catch flies from under the bellies of goats and cattle. He collected more than 200 specimens and devised a way of preserving the vivid colours of the toucan's beak. He apologized for the fact that so much more could have been written, and each bird could have been more particularly described. The words tumble out in a stream of strange names; the bright colours of feathers and beaks; the hushed air echoing with the tolling bell sound of the campenero bird, the 'dura-quaura' of the partridge just before the dawn, the yelping 'piam-po-o-co' of the toucan, and the 'ha, ha, ha, ha, ha, ha, ha, who-are-you, who-who-who-are-you?' of the goatsucker. Waterton was far from human society and in the company of creatures he could understand.

CHAPTER IX

The House on Mibiri Creek

Having written his report on the state of religion among the Indians in South America, Waterton decided to arrange to have an audience with Pope Pius VII, so that he could discuss the matter further. With the help of his powerful Jesuit connections, a date for a meeting was fixed and he duly arrived in Rome in the winter of 1817. However events did not follow according to plan, for while in the celestial city he happened to meet up with his old Stonyhurst school friend, Captain Jones, and the two of them, 'with nerves in excellent trim . . . mounted to the top of St Peter's, ascended the cross, and then climbed thirteen feet higher, where we reached the point of the conductor, and left our gloves on it. After this we visited the castle of St Angelo, and contrived to get on the head of the guardian angel where we stood on one leg.'[1]

The Pope was neither pleased nor impressed by this demonstration of skill. He ordered the immediate removal of the offending gloves, which had to be done either by Captain Jones or by Waterton himself, since no one else was prepared to try and reach them. He also decided that he had no wish to discuss the state of the Catholic faith in South America with an acrobatic Englishman who showed so little respect for Vatican property and Vatican dignity.

Sometimes, as Don Quixote so often discovered while on his rambling travels, 'a man goes in quest of one thing and finds another'. While in Italy, Waterton happened to visit the Cascini gardens in Florence. It was noisy with carriages and people, and yet it was teeming with pheasants and innumerable other birds. The secret of this unusually harmonious combination lay in the ivy which trailed everywhere over the ground, and hung in thick cascades in the trees, providing endless sheltering and hiding places.

We live to learn. I was not sufficiently aware of the value of ivy for the protection of the feathered race . . . At the grove of the Cascini, you see the ivy growing in all its lofty pride and beauty. As I gazed at its astonishing luxuriance, I could not help entertaining a high opinion of the person, be he alive or dead, through whose care and foresight such an effectual protection had been afforded to the wild birds of heaven, in the very midst of the 'busy haunts of men' . . .

I have profited by what I saw in Tuscany for, on my return to my native place, I began the cultivation of ivy with an unsparing hand.[2]

Waterton's particular ability to tumble into near-fatal accidents ensured that when he got home to Walton Hall he had plenty of time to work on the cultivation of the ivy plant. He was making his way back to England in the early spring of 1818, and his carriage was crossing the Mont Cenis Pass, when he had the idea that the baggage on the roof had broken loose. He climbed on to the wheel to inspect it and, as bad luck and the darkness of the night would have it, smashed a side window, and two pieces of glass broke off into his leg, just above the knee-cap. He examined the wound as best he could, and bound it up tightly with his cravat, but by the following morning he had a high fever, and when the carriage finally arrived in Paris, both he and the wound were in a 'deplorable state'. After several weeks of careful nursing, he was declared strong enough to return to Yorkshire, but it was two years before the stiffness in the knee had worn off, and he could once again walk with ease. During that time of enforced inactivity, he hobbled around the park, planting ivy wherever it might be willing to spread its dark and sheltering leaves.

But still he was restless, and by the end of 1819 the plans for a third wandering in South America had evolved. This time, instead of exploring unknown lands or struggling towards distant boundaries, he chose to return to the area in British Guiana which he knew the most intimately, and even to stay in the house where he had been welcomed as a guest on so many occasions before. The fact that the Edmonstones' home on Mibiri Creek had been standing empty and uncared for during the last three years, and the possibility that the climate and the vegetation had already eaten through much of the roof, the walls and the floors, did not deter him. To be more precise, the idea filled him with added enthusiasm.

In planning this expedition Waterton had two declared aims. He wanted to learn the 'habits and economies' of the creatures of the forest, and by this he meant not only what a certain animal or bird looked like and where it was most likely to be found, but also the details of its behaviour which could only be learnt by regular and patient observation. He went, and when he came back he knew how a three-toed sloth placed its feet when preparing for daytime sleep in a high tree; he knew the range of food eaten by vampire bats at night; he had explored the possibilities of approaching a poisonous snake in such a way that it did not feel threatened. He had learnt to understand something of the pattern of the days and the seasons in a forest where human beings were rarely to be seen, and his own presence was scarcely noticed.

His other determination was to master the technical difficulties involved in preparing birds and animals as museum exhibits, so that he could bring back with him to England a small but perfectly preserved collection of some of the wild life to be seen in Demerara. It must be remembered that at this date many of the inhabitants of the tropical rain forest were known in Europe only from dried-out skins, or from the ungainly creatures prepared by taxidermists who had to guess at the appearance of the strange animal they were trying to represent. The first specimens of the bird of paradise, for example, were shipped to England without legs (for the convenience of packing, as it turned out), and their leglessness caused great excitement among the scientific ornithologists. Snakes in museums usually had wooden heads and tigers' teeth, because of an overriding fear of their deadly poison. Neither the giant anteater nor the sloth had been seen in lifelike representations, and were still regarded as close relatives to the mermaid and the unicorn. And so it was with a very serious and public-spirited purpose that Waterton arranged to have ten black hair trunks specially made for him in Wakefield. Each trunk was large and strong and fitted with a lock, and one of them was the right size and shape to hold a full-grown crocodile. Waterton also ordered a canvas bag to be made for him; something which could contain an angry adult boa constrictor, should that prove to be necessary.

Before leaving, Waterton paid a last visit to Sir Joseph Banks; talking incongruously with an old and dying man about the technical difficulties of stuffing dead quadrupeds.

I saw with sorrow that death was going to rob us of him. We talked much of the present mode adopted by museums, in stuffing quadrupeds, and condemned it as being very imperfect; still we could not find out a better way; and at last concluded that the lips and noses ought to be cut off, and replaced with wax; it being impossible to make these parts appear like life, as they shrink to nothing, and render the stuffed specimens horrible to look at. The defects in the legs and feet would not be quite so glaring, being covered with hair.[3]

Banks was indeed dead by the time that Waterton returned, and so he never had the satisfaction of learning that a solution had been found, and there was now no need to cut off noses and lips and hind legs and feet.

Before setting sail from the Clyde, Waterton visited the Edmonstones at Cardross Park. Charles Edmonstone had already sent word to his old negro slave at Mibiri Creek, Daddy Quashi, telling him to expect a guest, and there was nothing else that he could do to prepare a distant welcome. In February 1820 Waterton set out on a familiar journey across the ocean. He arrived in Georgetown to be confronted by an epidemic of yellow fever. Many people he had known in the colony were dead or dying, and he stayed only long enough to collect a few supplies, and then set off to Mibiri Creek, escaping from the image of the slow and silent processions of coffins being carried past the brightly painted houses and past the canals filled with waterlilies and mosquitoes.

He reached the site of Charles Edmonstone's wood-cutting establishment:

> All was changed; the house was in ruins, and gradually sinking under the influence of the sun and rain; the roof had nearly fallen in; and the room where once governors and generals had caroused, was now dismantled, and tenanted by the vampire . . .
> On the outside of the house, nature had nearly reassumed her ancient right: a few straggling fruit-trees were still discernible amid the varied hue of the near-approaching forest; they seemed like strangers, lost and bewildered, and unpitied in a foreign land . . .[4]

So there he was, this solitary Yorkshireman, with his empty black trunks, his cotton and needles and bottles of bichloride of mercury, his canvas awning and hammock, his copies of Horace and Cervantes, his little medicine chest and a few items of essential clothing, and he was coming home to a very derelict house which he intended to use as a 'head-quarters for natural history' for a number of months. As a concession to physical comfort he had the roof repaired, and then as far as he was concerned he was ready to begin.

> . . . neither the frogs nor serpents were ill-treated, they sallied forth without buffet or rebuff, to choose their place of residence; the

world was all before them. The owls went away of their own accord, preferring to retire to a hollow tree rather than to associate with their new landlord. The bats and vampires stayed with me, and went in and out as usual.[5]

Daddy Quashi was there as arranged, and a coloured family called Backer was living in a hut in the garden which had once been used to store provisions. At some point they were joined by a young mulatto boy called James, who was taught to help with the long and often tedious process whereby an empty skin was transformed into a creature that seemed to be vivid with life and energy.

This little group became Waterton's family for the next eleven months. He never clearly describes quite how they all lived, but certainly they all lived more or less together under several leaking roofs. Apart from an expedition to go and catch a large crocodile, they stayed in the vicinity of Mibiri Creek. In the evening they would all meet up and tell stories and inspect each other's bodies for the daily infestation of ticks, lice and leeches and the 'beautiful scarlet coloured' *bêtes rouges*, insects which were almost too tiny to be seen with the naked eye and yet could produce the most intolerable itching. There was also the prolific and determined chegoe or jigger, which could raise a large family under a toe-nail within twenty-four hours.

> As soon as you perceive that you have got the chegoe under your flesh, you must take a needle, or a sharp-pointed knife, and take it out. If the nest be formed, great care must be taken not to break it, otherwise some of the eggs remain in the flesh, and then you will soon be annoyed with more chegoes. After removing the nest, it is well to drop spirit or turpentine into the hole . . . Sometimes I have taken four nests out of my feet in the course of the day.[6]

They ate whatever they happened to catch or find, or whatever was offered to them by the Indian tribes. They ate turtle eggs and baby alligator, howler monkey, ant-bear and toucan. Waterton tried wasp grubs 'as a dessert after dinner' but found them somehow unpalatable, nor did he share Daddy Quashi's fondness for partially rotten meat. If an interesting specimen was caught it was first carefully skinned before being cooked, and in that way a meal and a museum exhibit could both be had. Large but inedible corpses, such as the boa constrictor, were left out in a good position where the habits of vultures could be studied.

Waterton acted as the doctor for the group. He bled himself when he was ill, and no doubt offered to bleed his companions. He regularly treated the Backer children with his mixture of jalap and calomel. He made use of quinine or Jesuit's bark as it was still called, and concocted his own castor oil from castor oil seeds. Once when he lacerated his foot on a hardwood stump, he decided that the wound needed a poultice so he instructed Mrs Backer to prepare one for him from freshly boiled cow dung: 'Since heat and moisture are the two principals, nothing could produce these two qualities better than fresh cow dung boiled . . . Had there been no cow dung, I could have made do with boiled grass and leaves.'[7]

The narrative of the eleven months that Waterton spent in the forest on this trip is perhaps the most personal writing that he ever produced. Not that he tried to explain his private thoughts, or the particular energies which he felt guided him, but in his haphazard and enthusiastic style he conveyed an image of himself meandering through the days and through the heat and the damp of the seasons. His attention would be distracted now by a red-headed woodpecker, now by the sudden magnificence of the trees, now by the gaze of a snake and the gleam of its skin. Somehow he managed to climb up into the canopy level of the vast trees, so that he could watch the activities of the howler monkeys, the sloths and the birds. He would also potter about in the semi-darkness of the forest floor, knowing where he might encounter a tortoise or a bustling armadillo. He would light a little fire at the base of hollow tree trunks, for the sake of the extraordinary opportunity of seeing a billow of smoke erupt some hundred feet or more above him, and the scuttling of strange creatures who were suddenly frightened out of their hiding places. When he encountered pain or fear or sickness in his own body he observed it with the same detached fascination as he watched everything else. Sometimes with a kind of idle curiosity he would court danger, and then sit back to observe his own response to it. Throughout the writing there is a sense of deep contentment which never seems to leave him, even when he was extremely frightened or uncomfortable.

He wanted to allow his senses to experience everything: the taste of honey in a hummingbird's stomach; the unexpected musk-like smell from the empty craw of a vulture; the sight of a chegoe urgently digging its way into the flesh of his hand:

> Wishful to see how he worked, I allowed him to take possession. He immediately set to work, head foremost, and in about half an hour he had completely buried himself in the skin. I then let him feel the point of my knife and exterminated him.[8]

Charles Waterton

In his hammock suspended in the attic he would wait hopefully for one of the vampires to come and drink his blood.

> I have often wished to have been once sucked by the vampire. There can be no pain in the operation, for the patient is always asleep when the vampire is sucking him, and as for the loss of blood, that would be a trifle in the long run. Many a night I slept with my foot out of the hammock to tempt him, but it was all in vain . . .
>
> As there was a free entrance and exit to the vampire in the loft where I slept I had a fine opportunity of paying attention to this nocturnal surgeon. He does not always live on blood. When the moon shone bright, and the fruit of the banana tree was ripe, I could see him approach and eat it. He would also bring into the loft from the forest a green round fruit, something like a wild guava, and about the size of a nutmeg.[9]

In June the rainy season was at its height. 'Nothing could exceed the dampness of the atmosphere' was all that Waterton had to say in trying to evoke the steaming and sodden world that surrounded him and the quiet unease that would settle on the forest before each deluge of rain, when everything was silent and waiting. For several days he had been on the edge of sickness: 'I had been in a kind of twilight state of health, neither ill nor what you may call well. I yawned and felt weary without exercise, and my sleep was merely slumber.' Then a fever broke out in all its force:

> I awoke at midnight, a cruel headache, thirst, and pain in the small of the back informed me what the cause was . . . I dozed and woke and startled, and then dozed again, and suddenly awoke, thinking I was falling down a precipice . . .
>
> The return of the bats to their diurnal retreat, which was in the thatch above my hammock, informed me that the sun was fast approaching to the eastern horizon . . . I was saved the trouble of keeping the room cool, as the wind beat in at every quarter.[10]

He doctored himself with violent bleeding, by setting his feet in warm water, drinking quantities of weak tea and purging himself relentlessly. This was followed by a fourteen-day course of quinine which 'put all to rights'. It would seem that this was the only sickness he suffered during the eleven months, apart from the lacerated foot and two cases of severe sunburn.

Waterton's account of his third wandering contains some beautiful

4 A visitor to the Edmonstone home on the Mibiri Creek needed to travel up the Demerara River and along narrow channels that were in perpetual darkness.

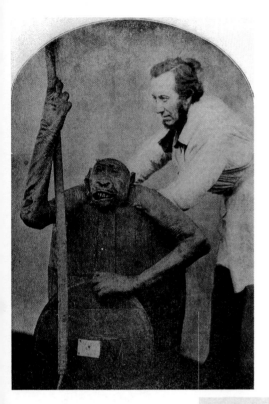

5 In 1865 Waterton was delighted to receive a large male gorilla which was delivered to him immersed in a barrel of rum. This photograph, taken in 1858, shows a similar pickled specimen.

6 Waterton moulded the 'noble countenance' of the Nondescript from the hindquarters of a monkey and offered it to a suspicious public as a Wild Man of the Woods.

descriptions of animals. Whereas before he had described the appearance of the sloth, and the way he had watched one dying from the
effects of curare poisoning, now he spent much time observing them in
their natural habitats high in the trees. He described a sloth preparing
itself for sleep or travelling 'at a good round pace' from tree to tree, and
there is a curiously touching story of finding a large two-toed sloth
stranded on the ground by the banks of the Essequibo River. Waterton
took a long stick and offered it to the helpless creature so that it could
hook its arms around it, he then carried it over to a high tree, and
watched it race up the trunk and set off towards the heart of the forest
with a 'wonderful rapidity'.

He noticed the peculiar hair of the sloth, 'thick at the extremity and
tapered at the root where it becomes as fine as a spider's web',
although it would be many more years before it was realized that algae
grew within the hollow shafts of the hair, giving the animal's body a
faint greenish tinge. He watched the three species of ant-bear in the
'inmost recesses' of the forest, and was the first person to report
accurately how the giant anteater walks, not on the soles of its feet, but
on the curled-over outer side of its forefeet. He described armadillos
burrowing in sandhills like rabbits, and swimming well in times of
need; tortoises pottering about on the forest floor looking for fallen
fruit and with no enemies except the boa constrictor 'who swallows
him shell and all', and man who 'takes him up and carries him away',
but 'man is scarce in these never ending wilds, and the little depredations he may commit upon the tortoise will be nothing, or a mere
trifle.' He also described himself, another creature in the forest.

Time and experience have convinced me that there is not much
danger in roving amongst snakes and wild beasts, provided only
that you have self-command. You must never approach them
abruptly; if so you are sure to pay for your rashness; because the
idea of self-defence is predominant in every animal, and thus the
snake, to defend himself from what he considers an attack on him,
makes the intruder feel the deadly effect of his poisonous fangs. The
jaguar flies at you, and knocks you senseless with a stroke of his
paw; whereas, if you had not come upon him too suddenly, it is ten
to one but that he had retired in lieu of disputing the path with
you.

The labarri snake is very poisonous, and I have often approached
within two yards of him without fear. I took care to move very
softly, and gently without moving my arms, and he always allowed
me to have fine view of him, without showing the least inclination to

make a spring at me. He would appear to keep his eye fixed on me, as though suspicious, but that was all. Sometimes I have taken a stick ten feet long, and placed it on the labarri's back. He would then glide away without offering resistance. But when I put the end of the stick abruptly to his head, he immediately opened his mouth, flew at it and bit it.[11]

Snakes held a lifelong fascination for him. Not far from Mibiri Creek some negroes were working for a woodcutter, and he offered a reward to any of them who could lead him to a good-sized one, for snakes were not easy to find since they slept hidden during the day and came out to hunt at night.

One afternoon, sitting on the mouldering steps of his house, reading from his pocket edition of the *Odes* of Horace, a negro came running to tell him that a snake had been found. So off he went, barefoot and dressed in an old hat, an old shirt and his trousers held up with braces. Daddy Quashi went with him, armed with a cutlass, while he took his eight-foot wooden lance. They were led to a fallen tree, and there, hidden among the branches and a mantle of woodbine, lay the coiled form of a boa constrictor, 'not poisonous, but large enough to have crushed any of us to death'.

Since the day was on the decline and since a dead snake would be a stinking carcass if left in the tropical air until the morning, Waterton thought it would be wise to capture this specimen alive. As slowly and as gently as possible, he cut away a hole in the woodbine and bent back the twigs until he had a good view of his victim's head. Then, having talked over his battle plans with Daddy Quashi and the other negro, he advanced at the head of his battalion, keeping his head and arms still and with the lance held stiffly in front of him. Through a process of grappling and pinioning the snake was overpowered, and as a final indignity Waterton tied its mouth shut with his braces. It was carried back to the house and inserted into the canvas bag, to await its execution in the morning. That night Waterton slept in his hammock in the loft. Through the holes in the floor he could see the bag in the room below him and hear the boa constrictor thrashing and hissing all through the night. By six o'clock the next evening the snake was dissected, and by the following year it was in a glass cabinet at Walton Hall.

There was another battle with a boa constrictor, a younger one, ten feet long, and 'not thick enough to break my arm in case he got twisted around it'. Waterton met this one unexpectedly and since there was 'not a moment to lose' he grabbed it by the tail, punched it on the nose and 'allowed him to coil himself around my body, and marched off with him as my lawful prize. He pressed me hard, but not alarmingly so'.[12] Since he had no wish to eat snake meat, he set the skinned corpse out in the forest, at a place where it would attract the vultures. 'In a few days it sent forth that odour which a carcass should send forth, and about twenty of the common vultures came and perched on the neighbouring trees; the king of the vultures came too; and I observed that none of the common ones seemed inclined to begin breakfast till his majesty had finished.'[13]

Although most of Waterton's time was spent in the vicinity of Mibiri Creek, he was determined to take a large cayman back with him to England, and large specimens could only be found on the Essequibo River. With Daddy Quashi, James the mulatto and an Indian guide called Jan, he went to Georgetown by canoe to collect the necessary supplies and then they set off up the Essequibo. On the first night that they were camping by the great river he had the pleasure of seeing a jaguar. 'The Indian would have fired, but I would not allow him to do so, as I wanted to see a little more of our new visitor; for it is not every day or night that the traveller is favoured with an undisturbed sight of the jaguar in its own forests.'[14] When the Indian could not stand the prowling presence any longer he let out a tremendous yell which was an efficient as gunshot in removing the danger.

In four days they had reached the first falls of the Essequibo and there Waterton hired a negro and a coloured man who 'pretended to know everything about the haunts of caymans, and how to catch them'. By the next evening they had reached what appeared to be a good place, and there they made camp and prepared themselves for the hunt. They had tortoise for supper, and the sound of the jaguars roaring through the night was 'awfully fine', like distant thunder.

They baited a shark hook with fish and anchored it deep in the river, with a length of strong cord fixed to the hook and bound to a tree on the sand-bank. That night the caymans were indeed 'upon the stir', they answered each other in the dark water, letting out loud menacing sighs which could be heard a mile off. For four nights in succession the bait was skilfully removed from the hook and nothing was caught. Waterton watched sting rays gliding over the bottom of the river. He saw giant iguanas, scarlet macaws, sun birds, innumerable parrots, and two to three hundred fresh-water turtles all gathered together on a sandbank. And so the days passed in 'exercise and knowledge', but still there was no cayman. Waterton realized that the coloured man who was supposed to be the authority on cayman catching was going about it in the wrong way, and he determined to seek the more expert help of the forest Indians, 'the coloured man fancied I could not do without him, so I convinced him to his sorrow that indeed I could, and paid him what I had agreed to give him, . . . and ordered him back.'[15]

They set off towards an Indian settlement, turning up a creek which was 'dark, winding and intricate' beyond any that Waterton had seen before. They met up with three Indians who were willing to help, and that night they stayed in the settlement. They were given boiled howler monkey which Waterton found 'very good indeed' and boiled ant-bear which he found less good since it had been kept beyond its time, and stank 'like our venison does in England'.

The next day the Indians led them to a still and deep part of the Essequibo, flanked by an immense sandbank. They laughed at the shark hook and the cord, and promised to come up with something much more efficient: '. . . probably this poor wild man of the woods would succeed by means of a very simple process; and thus prove to his more civilised brother that, notwithstanding books and schools, there is a vast deal of knowledge to be picked up at every step, whichever way we turn ourselves.'[16]

One of the Indians, who had long ago seen his father catch a cayman, made a bunch of barbed wooden hooks which he bound together with a cord and baited with a little rodent called an acouri. One end of the rope was tied to a tree and the hooks were suspended just above the water, propped up by a stick stuck in the sand. With the simple trap completed, the Indian took the shell of a land tortoise and banged it with his axe to inform any cayman in the area that something interesting was going on in this section of the river: 'In fact the Indian meant it as the cayman's dinner bell.'

They slept fitfully through the night, the darkness filled with the sound of jaguars roaring and caymans sighing, and at half past five the Indian went to inspect his trap and at once let out a shout of triumph. 'The Indians got there before me, for they had no clothes to put on, and I lost two minutes in looking for my trousers and in slipping into them.'

Waterton's ambition was finally realized, for there was a cayman, ten and a half feet in length, thrashing angrily at the end of the cord. Now, 'nothing remained to do, but to get him out of the water, without injuring his scales'. However, when he explained to the Indians that he wished to draw his prize quietly out of the water, and then secure him, without the use of any weapons, they simply sat down and refused to move, and he knew that they would walk off into the forest if he tried to force them to obey him. They were prepared to help if they could use their arrows, and Daddy Quashi was filled with thoughts of guns, 'considering them our best and safest friend. This would have ruined all. I had come above three hundred miles on purpose to get a cayman uninjured, and not to carry back a mutilated specimen.'[17]

It is difficult at this point to disentangle Waterton's scientific purpose and perfectionism from his stubbornness and his love of excitement. In any case he was determined that his specimen must be unblemished, and paced up and down the sandbank, 'revolving a dozen projects' that might achieve this aim. His solution was simple. He would take the canoe's mast as a defensive weapon, and would personally heave and steer the creature out of the water, and then it would only be a question of tying it up. Since he was placing himself directly between the Indians and the danger, they were willing to help pull on the rope.

> I then mustered all hands for the last time before the battle. We were, four South American savages, two negroes from Africa, a creole from Trinidad, and myself a white man from Yorkshire. In fact a little tower of Babel group, in dress, no dress, address, and language.[18]

Waterton wound the sail around the end of the eight-foot-long mast and, holding it before him like a fixed bayonet, he crouched on one knee about four yards from the water's edge, and faced his prey. He had decided that if the cayman charged open-mouthed at him, then he would force the mast down its throat; an attack which would still leave its skin undamaged. His assistants were ordered to pull until the cayman appeared on the surface of the water, and to slacken their grip if he plunged. He surfaced, plunged, surfaced again:

> This was an interesting moment. I kept my position firmly, with my eye fixed steadfast on him.
> By this time the cayman was within two yards of me. I saw that he was in a state of fear and perturbation; I instantly dropped the mast, sprang up, and jumped on his back, turning half round as I vaulted, so that I gained my seat with my face in the right position. I immediately seized his fore legs, and, by main force, twisted them on his back; thus they served me for a bridle.
> He now seemed to have recovered from his surprise, and, probably fancying himself in hostile company, he began to plunge furiously, and lashed the sand with his long tail. I was out of reach of the strokes of it, by being near his head. He continued to plunge and

strike, and made my seat very uncomfortable. It must have been a fine sight for an unoccupied spectator.

The people roared out in triumph, and were so vociferous that it was some time before they heard me tell them to pull me and my beast of burden further inland. I was apprehensive the rope might break, and then there would have been every chance of going down to the regions under water with the cayman . . .

The people now dragged us above forty yards on the sand: it was the first and last time I was ever on a cayman's back. Should it be asked how I managed to keep my seat, I would answer, I hunted some years with Lord Darlington's fox-hounds.[19]

After a good deal of struggling the cayman was finally secured, and then tied into the canoe and carried back to the site where they had their hammocks. 'There I cut his throat; and, after breakfast was over, commenced the dissection.'

So Waterton had conquered his cayman, and made a beautiful job of preserving it as well. It is still possible to stare into its gaping mouth and see a pinpoint of light at the far end of its unblemished tail.[20]

The journey back down the Essequibo was not a pleasant one. At the falls they were almost swamped by the roaring waters and sucked into a whirlpool. On reaching the coast they were twice grounded on mudflats and had to wade about in deep mud trying to get their little vessel back afloat.

Waterton stayed for only one day in Georgetown, and then returned to Mibiri Creek to complete his tasks. He finished off work on the cayman as well as the other birds and quadrupeds he had collected over the months, and had the satisfaction of seeing that he had now fully mastered the art of taxidermy. His creations were perfect, and extraordinarily lifelike. The rainy season returned, the lightning and the thunder were incessant, the days were cloudy and the nights cold and misty. It was time to return to England: 'I had now been eleven months in the forests, and collected some rare insects, two hundred and thirty birds, two land tortoises, five armadillos, two large serpents, a sloth, an ant-bear, and a cayman.'[21]

CHAPTER X

The Tax Inspector and the Nondescript

Waterton once said that he was 'for ever crying stinking fish in the streets'.[1] By this he meant that no matter what he was trying to relate, whether it was the story of one of his adventures, some information about animal behaviour, or indeed an aspect of his own personality, he had an extraordinary ability to make people mistrust him, disbelieve him, or think him a fool. There was an occasion when he met a grand lady in the house of a grand friend. He was standing by the fire in a dark and gloomy sitting room when this unknown person entered and, since he said nothing, she made the first approach, and spoke to him in what seemed to be an artificially slow and loud voice.

> Now here commenced the mischief. Whether a spirit of impudence, or of satire, or of rudeness seized me at that moment I cannot say—but turning my face to the speaker, and putting my hand to my ear thumb downwards, I said in a tone unusual to me, 'Speak louder, Madam, for I am hard of hearing,' and this tone I most unfortunately spoke throughout our conversation.[2]

It was an aspect of this same spirit which must have persuaded him to leave his gloves fluttering on the Vatican's lightning conductor, before a meeting with the man who was, as it were, the owner of this piece of apparatus so useful in keeping the wrath of God away from high buildings. And when Waterton came to write his book about his travels, *Wanderings in South America, the North West of the United States and the Antilles in the Years 1812, 1816, 1820 and 1824* a number of people were left with the disconcerting impression that he had constructed a strange hoax, a hybrid of truth and fantasy, and he seemed to have done it purely for the purpose of ridiculing his more serious or scientifically-minded readers.

91

Baron Munchausen himself would have been proud to tell of the ride on the back of the crocodile and the battles with boa constrictors, and it was difficult to know how to respond to Waterton's assertion that it was more dangerous to walk down a crowded London street of an evening than to spend a number of months in a steaming tropical forest. But all this was as nothing compared with the Nondescript, that bizarre taxidermal creation which looked like the head and shoulders of a very worried man, and which Waterton claimed to have shot down in the forests while on his final expedition to Guiana in 1824. The story of the Nondescript is a complex one, and its presence in the *Wanderings* did Waterton's reputation a great deal of damage. When asked why he had included it, and indeed even its portrait, in his book, he said it was all because of an unfortunate encounter with a tax inspector at the Liverpool docks in 1821.

Waterton's homeward journey from Guiana was a very pleasant one. Having finally 'hit upon a way of doing quadrupeds', and with such superb examples of how well his method worked, he was filled with a private sense of triumph at the knowledge of what was contained in the ten black hair trunks. He decided that when he arrived in England he would give a series of lectures, explaining in practical and scientific terms exactly how he prepared his insects, serpents, birds and animals. Then the museums of Europe would be able to discard the 'ragged, rotten and deformed' specimens which they now housed, and replace them with creatures whose symmetry and natural beauty was in itself a cause for wonder. Admittedly Waterton's method involved a great deal of time, patience and skill, but his techniques could no doubt be improved and simplified. While crossing the Atlantic he unlocked his trunks every day to check his specimens, and also to allow the ship's crew and his fellow passengers to examine and admire them.

They docked at Liverpool, and the officials at the customs house received him as an old friend.

> They considered that it would be difficult to fix a price on specimens which had never been bought or sold, and which never were to be, as they were intended to ornament my house. It was hard, they said, to have exposed myself, for years, to danger, and then be obliged to pay on returning to my native land. Under these considerations, they fixed a modest duty, which satisfied all parties.[3]

It was while the marvellous contents of the trunks were being examined that Mr Lushington appeared, a paradigm of bureaucratic principle, and a most Hanoverian rat: 'He was an entire stranger to me, and seemed wonderfully aware of his own consequence. Without preface or apology, he thrust his head over my shoulder, and said, we had no business to have opened a single box without his permission.'[4] Mr Lushington decided that the duty which had been fixed was far too low, and a second valuation of the specimens must be made. Until that had been done, the boxes were to be kept at His Majesty's pleasure, in His Majesty's Liverpool depot. He made matters worse by taking Waterton to one side and assuring him that he '. . . had a great regard for the arts and sciences, he lamented that conscience obliged him to do what he had done, and he wished that he had been fifty miles from Liverpool at the time when it fell to his lot to detain the collection. Had he looked in my face as he said this, he would have seen no marks of credulity there.'[5]

Waterton was allowed to take a pair of live Malay fowls with him, but everything else had to be left behind while their value was assessed. He was particularly distressed at being parted from a collection of the eggs of 'curious birds' which he had 'done-over' with gum arabic and packed in charcoal, in the hope of being able to hatch them out under some unsuspecting broody hen at Walton Hall.

The Treasury deliberated for six weeks, and no amount of appeals from Waterton or certain of his influential friends could speed up the process. Finally he received a very curt letter from Mr Lushington, in which he was informed that any specimens he wished to donate to public institutions could pass duty free, but there was to be a hefty charge on each item that he intended to keep for himself. Inevitably Waterton's ancestral black rattedness was aroused. Lushington and the Treasury confirmed all his worst suspicions about the whole race of Hanoverians who ruled his country and had the power to hem him in with such petty restrictions. Now he would not give his public lectures, nor would he invite an eager public to come and see the strange treasures he had brought back with him. And it was surely no coincidence that in this same year, 1821, he began the enormous task of building a high stone wall, an invincible barricade that was to encircle the entire estate; cutting him off from unwanted intruders and leaving him alone with the birds, animals, trees and those particular visitors who were granted access.

For three years he stayed at home, working on the park, overseeing the building of the wall, and nursing his resentments so that they grew and took strange shapes. Then in 1824 he set off on his fourth and last wandering. For several months he was in North America, but before returning to England he paid a hasty visit to Demerara. He had evolved a plan, a curiously thought-out practical joke which he felt would enable him to kill several birds with a single stone. As soon as he arrived, he set about obtaining the bodies of two howler monkeys. With one he took great pains in preparing it as a perfect specimen 'in order to show the immense difference that exists betwixt the features of this monkey and those of man'.[6] The hindquarters of the second monkey were used in the construction of the Nondescript.

> The features of this animal are quite of the Grecian cast, and he has a placidity of countenance which shows that things went well with him when in life. Some gentlemen of great skill and talent, on inspecting his head, were convinced that the whole series of its features had been changed. Others again have hesitated, and betrayed doubts, not being able to make up their minds whether it can be possible, that the brute features of a monkey can be changed into the noble countenance of a man.[7]

This ambivalent creature served several functions. On the simplest level it was a demonstration of Waterton's skill as a taxidermist. Where others could not even make a dead cat look like an approximation of a living cat, he could achieve this disconcerting metamorphosis. If he told a dramatic story of how he had captured this wild man of the woods, then the game entered a new dimension. What would the eminent naturalists say when confronted with such a solemn-faced link between man and the brute creation? What would Mr Lushington and the Treasury say when they had to decide on the import duty to be paid for the head and shoulders of something which appeared to be a human being?

It has been said that Waterton tried to give his Nondescript a marked resemblance to Mr Lushington, but of that there is no proof. As a first test of the power of his new creation, Waterton exhibited it in Georgetown in December 1824, and in the local paper he provided a dramatic and farcical account of how he had captured this Wild Man, this 'creature approaching to our form infinitely nearer than the famed orang-outan of Borneo'. He had heard of a 'cruel and malicious race' of men, who lived in the tops of trees deep in the forest. With an Indian guide he made a 'long and dreary march' into the interior, until they reached a place where the trees were of an immense height:

> We had not advanced more than half a mile, before he pointed out something very thick near the tops of the trees, resembling rooks' nests, but vastly more bulky. 'There,' said he in a mournful whisper,

'*there* is one of their settlements, and I can see smoke coming out of some of them.'

'If there be smoke,' said I, 'it must be about their dinner-time, and I wish I was up at them, for I am confoundedly hungry.' I could see this piece of false wit of mine vexed him, he said I had better be thinking of something else—and then staring wildly in my face, he lifted up his hands in despair and fled precipitately.

Just as he left me I heard a rustling in one of the high tufted trees near me. I instantly took aim with my air-gun, and down dropped the animal, lifeless at my feet. Here for the first time I saw the real wild man of the woods.

I looked at him again and again, and was sorry I had ever gone in quest of him. There was no time to be lost . . . The animal was too large to carry—so taking out my knife I cut off his head and shoulders, threw them on my back, and set off in the direction the Indian had gone—looking up every now and then in the trees behind me to see if I were not pursued by some of their police; for I strongly suspected I had unfortunately killed a man—nor have I yet made up my mind upon the subject.[8]

In Georgetown the exhibit was welcomed as a good practical joke, and a number of letters subsequently appeared in the paper with claims of meetings with 'men whose heads do grow beneath their shoulders', with angels, with a 'giant humbug', and other 'superior beings'. However, once back in England, Waterton kept very quiet about his 'discovery' and decided that he would use it to 'baffle the united talents and information of the first naturalists of the day'.[9] For several months he worked on preparing his journals for publication, and was very insistent on the way that the *Wanderings* should be produced, with no glossary of terms, and no illustrations.

I could have written ten volumes as easily as one. My sole object was to incite the reader to go and wander in that far distant region . . . I could have given the scientific name and the Indian name of every bird and beast, but I carefully refrained from doing so. I gave the world an original and scientific account, written down in pencil at the close of every day . . . not sullied by caricatures, or mystified by notes of closet naturalists.[10]

But no matter how honest and unadorned his account was, no matter how closely he adhered to the daily notes that he had made, 'sometimes writing by the light of a fire, I have even written by the light of the fireflies',[11] he could not resist the temptation to 'cry stinking fish in the streets'. As a frontispiece for the first edition of the *Wanderings* he included a well-executed lithograph of the Wild Man of the Woods, now renamed as the Nondescript, or, to give it its local Indian name, the Itouli (surely the 'I too lie'). At the end of the account of the fourth wandering, after 230 pages of idiosyncratic but scrupulously honest descriptions of what he had done and what he had seen while on his travels, he told how he had found and killed this strange creature. The circumstances are made slightly less ridiculous than they were in the Georgetown newspaper, but the joke is, if anything, more thinly disguised, and the damage was done.

> I also procured an animal which has caused not a little speculation and astonishment. In my opinion, his thick coat of hair, and great length of tail, put his species out of all question; but then his face and head cause the inspector to pause for a moment, before he ventures to pronounce his opinion of the classification. He was a large animal, and as I was pressed for daylight, and moreover, felt no inclination to have the whole weight of his body upon my back, I contented myself with his head and shoulders, which I cut off: and have brought them with me to Europe.[12]

The joke meanders along over several paragraphs, with Waterton often implying that his Nondescript is nothing but a clever fake, but never openly saying so.

The *Wanderings* were a great success, and were widely read up until the early part of this century. But although 'Captain Waterton' the crocodile rider entered very speedily into popular mythology, and although many readers were profoundly impressed by his descriptions of his life in the tropical rain forests, neither his prose style nor his exploits pleased his reviewers or his fellow naturalists. It cannot be presumed that they would all have been kinder if the Nondescript had not raised its Grecian head, but certainly for many this was simply the last straw. Even Sidney Smith, one of Waterton's most tolerant and friendly critics, added sadly that by including the portrait, and the story of the Nondescript, 'our author is abusing his stuffing talents, and laughing at the public . . . It is foolish to trifle with science and natural history.'[13] Others were much less generous, branding him as a man with 'the greatest possible love of the marvellous, and a constant propensity to dress up truth in the garb of fiction'.[14]

Waterton did his best to defend himself whenever he was so 'unmercifully pummelled'. 'Some people imagine that I have been guilty of deception by placing the Nondescript as a frontispiece to the book . . . I never had the slightest intention to act so dishonourable a part.'[15] The waves of critical animosity which the book received only served to strengthen his sense of being a different species of rat, and he never seemed to try to unravel his own motives in the whole complex business. No matter how much he struggled, he had now provided his enemies and his potential enemies with a wonderful weapon to use against him if ever they wished to throw scorn on his credibility, even his veracity, as a traveller and a naturalist.

CHAPTER XI

America, its Birds and its Bird Men

Waterton decided to go to North America because he was shown a book called *American Ornithology* written and illustrated by Alexander Wilson, a Scotsman who in 1794, at the age of twenty-eight, had emigrated to the United States and settled in Pennsylvania. In Scotland he had worked as a weaver, travelling from place to place trying to sell his goods, and he was also a moderately successful poet. In America he got a job as a teacher, and went on writing poetry. In 1803 he quietly decided to 'make a collection of all our finest birds', by which he meant that he intended to be the first person to attempt systematically to catalogue, describe and make accurate drawings of all the birds of the eastern states. For the next ten years he devoted himself to this task, and then he died of severe dysentery, having just completed the eighth of the proposed ten volumes.

Wilson had no training either as a naturalist or as a painter. He taught himself the basic principle of drawing by trying to make a likeness of a stuffed owl which he kept on his desk. He began his work as a naturalist by filling his room with a random assortment of live specimens.

While others are hoarding up their bags of money, without the power of enjoying it, I am collecting, without injuring my conscience, or wounding my peace of mind, those beautiful specimens of Nature's works that are forever pleasing. I have had live crows, hawks and owls—opossums, squirrels, snakes, lizards etc., so that my room has sometimes reminded me of Noah's ark, but Noah had a wife in one corner of it, and in this particular our parallel does not altogether tally.[1]

When preparing for one of his long expeditions, he was 'in the habit of taking a walk every morning, and when he could make twenty miles without much fatigue' he started. He would set off with his water-colour paints, his notebooks, his flute, and a green parakeet called Poll sitting in his pocket wrapped up in a piece of cloth. On one exhausting six-month journey, he and the parakeet travelled a distance of over 2,000 miles.

> Philadelphia to Pittsburgh, 320 miles; down the Ohio in small boat alone 720. By land to Lexington 75. Ditto to Nashville 200. Through the wilderness to Natchez 470. To New Orleans along the Mississippi 252. Total to New Orleans 2,037.[2]

Wilson was a solitary person, dedicated and efficient in his work, often stubborn and irritable in his dealings with others. But as a traveller, dependent on the hospitality of strangers, or in the company of wild nature, he was filled with gentleness, humility and a quiet pleasure, and was able to communicate this aspect of himself in his meticulous drawings, and in his descriptions of places and people and, above all, of birds.

In order to make his drawings, Wilson needed to have specimens. Whenever possible he captured a bird and kept it a prisoner for as long as he needed to study it, and if it died he grieved its loss as he grieved for his parakeet when it was swept into the sea, or as he grieved for an ivory-billed woodpecker which cried like a child and refused to take any food for three days. Once he told almost apologetically about how he had been on the point of killing a mouse, but had relented when it looked into his face with an eye of 'supplicating terror'.[3]

For Waterton, the reading of Wilson's *American Ornithology* seemed like a meeting with a rare friend, and he determined to go to America so that he could, as it were, walk beside him. He wanted to see the birds that Wilson had described with such careful intensity, and the landscape he had known. He wanted to go to Philadelphia so that he might meet the people who had been his friends during his life, and who were now working for him after his death: the Peale family whose museum housed many of his specimens; George Ord, a peppery zoologist who had completed the ninth volume and written a brief biography of the man; Charles Bonaparte, the young cousin of the dispossessed emperor, who was busy on a supplement of *Birds not Mentioned by Wilson*; the printer Alexander Lawson, who had made the plates for all the watercolours 'drawn from Nature by A. Wilson'. And so it was that Waterton landed in New York in the early summer of 1824, a tourist and also a pilgrim.

Throughout the eastern states of America in the 1820s, much of the landscape that Wilson had known was already lost or about to be lost, and many of the birds that he had thought of as common were becoming increasingly rare. But the landscape was still vast and extraordinary in its beauty.

First to New York, with the tall trees of an ancient hardwood forest lining the wide avenue of Broadway. Droves of scavenging pigs, 'their backs like the lids of old horsehair trunks',[4] roaming at their ease through the streets of that young city. Stately houses, and 'no steam engines filling the air with soot'. There were very few dogs to be seen, 'still fewer cats, and but a very small proportion of fat women'.[5] When Waterton walked along Broadway he felt that he was surrounded by a gentle people. He was not robbed, nor jostled, nor stared at, and when he stood for an hour on end to watch the passers-by—especially the women, he became obsessed with the 'immense number of highly polished females to be seen'—nobody seemed to resent his curiosity.

He went by steamboat from New York to Lake Eyrie; he saw the Niagara Falls, passed through Ontario, Montreal and Quebec, and returned to New York via Albany and the newly-opened Hudson Canal. When the weather became too cold for comfort he set off towards British Guiana. He spent some weeks in the neighbourhood of Philadelphia where he met Wilson's circle, and made an unexpectedly close friendship with George Ord. He mentioned only one bird-watching expedition which he made with the ornithologist Titian Ramsay Peale along the Delaware River, and was so scorched by the sun that one genteel lady remarked, 'He was the darkest white man I ever saw.'[6]

In his account of North America, Waterton said very little about the birds he saw, maybe because he felt that Wilson had said it all already. Mostly he was busy with people: the gentry who were not haughty; the academics who were not too self-opinionated; the working people who showed no subservience; the ladies who confused him with their openness, yet did not quite terrify him, and even awoke the vague stirrings of desire. There was one lady in particular whom he met when he had just sprained his foot. He commemorated his confusion by writing a thoroughly pre-Freudian poem in the guest book of the inn at the Niagara Falls:

> . . . he sees all that which can
> Delight and calm the soul of man,
> But feels it not—because his toe
> And foot together plague him so.[7]

He also, perhaps for the benefit of that same lady, held the sprained foot under the fall of Niagara: '. . . I hobbled on the scene of action. As I held my leg under the fall, I tried to meditate on the immense difference betwixt a house-pump and this tremendous cascade of nature, and what effect it might have upon the sprain; but the magnitude of the subject was too overwhelming, and I was obliged to drop it.'[8]

Once he complained of being bitten by a bug, once he slept on a straw mattress inhabited by a family of mice, and the approaching winter of New York brought on a severe cough, but in spite of such minor disturbances he was highly content, skittish even, and filled with enthusiasm.

> I was wonderfully pleased with my trip to the United States—that country seems to me to be what England must have been fifty years ago. Public crime is very seldom heard of, and the whole country seems to be at peace and good fellowship with itself. I prefer the United States much to England.[9]

Eighteen years later Charles Dickens could not have disagreed more thoroughly. He complained that he was not able to drink a glass of water 'without having a hundred people looking down my throat when I open my mouth to swallow'.[10] He was shunted from crowded lecture halls to crowded parties, from bleak prisons to bleak prairies to dirty steamboats, in a state of 'perpetual worry', and he concluded that it was 'impossible, utterly impossible for any Englishman to live here and be happy'.[11]

Of course the two men had different wishes and expectations. Dickens travelled as a celebrity, whereas Waterton travelled as an unknown tourist, without even any letters of introduction, 'for I am one of those who depend upon accidental acquaintance'. But there was also the fact of the extraordinary speed at which America was changing, and maybe Waterton would have liked New York and the surrounding countryside less in the 1840s than he did in the 1820s. Already in his time the stretches of wilderness were being lost, and would never be regained.

Those lofty and luxuriant trees, which served to relieve the 'perpetual sameness' of Broadway, were soon to be cut down. The immigrant population was multiplying and spreading in all directions. Throughout the eastern states the great hardwood forests of oak and chestnut, tulip trees and plane trees were being cleared for firewood, for building material, and to make way for agricultural developments. A letter written by an early settler in the state of Indiana gives a haunting description of the enormity of what was happening:

> Everywhere you hear, from the river, the ringing of axes. The sound of axes splitting firewood salutes the ear every morning instead of birdsong.
> The trees growing on the banks [of the Big Wabash River], from their immense size, astonish everyone. The Plane with its long white arms, and the Tulip tree attain to an enormous magnitude.
> Indian summer haze is caused by millions of acres being in a wide-spreading fire, the haze rising up through the woods and prairies, hill and dale, darkening the heaven and earth.[12]

Waterton was not oblivious to what was happening, but he wanted to believe that here there was more chance that people would understand the need to protect the wildness of nature, before that wildness had been eradicated.

> Nature is losing fast her ancient garb, and putting on a new dress in these extensive regions. Most of the stately timber has been carried away; thousands of trees are lying prostrate on the ground; while meadows, cornfields, villages, pastures, are ever and anon bursting upon the traveller's view as he journeys through the remaining tracts of wood. I wish I could say a word or two for the fine timber which is yet standing. Spare it, gentle inhabitants, for your country's sake; these noble sons of the forest beautify your landscape beyond all descriptions; when they are gone a century will not replace their loss, they cannot, they must not fall.[13]

But against these words could be placed another extract from that letter written by an early settler, 'The everlasting sound of falling trees . . . is a relief to the dreary silence of these wilds.' And then there are the numerous accounts of the havoc of hunting expeditions, with almost no restrictions on what was killed: '. . . you may walk out north, south, east, or west, and sport everywhere at your pleasure; no man will attempt to stay your course over any field, or through any woods.'[14] There was a vastness of landscape, a profusion of life that it was able to support, and the sense that these resources could never be exhausted, no matter how much they were used.

To take a single image. In the early nineteenth century a flock of passenger pigeons could number as many as 2,000 million birds, darkening the sky for miles around as they travelled south in the autumn, moving over the land in search of food. And yet, within the span of a single century, the whole species had been made extinct, and was remembered most clearly in the descriptions of its extermination. Wilson once told how he spent several hours watching a 'living torrent' fly over his head, and John James Audubon, Wilson's rival who was to become America's most celebrated wilderness man, told how he was present at one of the massacres, when the men from miles around came to take part, and once it was all over pigs and dogs were let loose to devour some of the many thousands of useless corpses.

The noise which they made, though yet distant, reminded me of a hard gale at sea, passing through the rigging of a close-reefed vessel. As the birds arrived, and passed over me, I felt a current of air that surprised me. Thousands were soon knocked down by the polemen. The birds continued to pour in. The fires were lighted, and a magnificent, as well as wonderful and almost terrifying scene presented itself . . . It was a scene of uproar and confusion, I found it quite useless to speak, or even to shout to those persons who were nearest to me. Even the reports of the guns were seldom heard, and I was made aware of the firing only by seeing the shooters reloading.[15]

Waterton in America missed all such scenes of devastation, although he could not help but be aware that in just the same way as the forests were being cut down many of the creatures he expected to see were becoming increasingly scarce.

Since [Wilson's] time I fear the white-headed eagles [bald eagle], have been much thinned. I was perpetually looking for them, but saw very few. One or two came now and then and soared in lofty flight over the falls of Niagara. The Americans are proud of this bird in effigy, and their hearts rejoice when its banner is unfurled. Could they not then be persuaded to protect the white-headed eagle, and allow it to glide in safety over its own native forests? Were I an American I should think I had committed a kind of sacrilege in killing the white-headed eagle.[16]

Ironically, although this bird had been chosen as the national emblem, it was still treated as vermin, and even as a creature which had such a peculiarly nasty character that it was every citizen's duty to destroy it. Benjamin Franklin writing in 1783 said, 'I wish the bald eagle had not been chosen as a representative of our country. He is a bird of bad moral character . . . he is generally poor, and often very lousy. Besides, he is a rank coward.'[17]

Some years after Waterton's visit to North America, Audubon wrote his description of this same eagle in his *Ornithological Biography*. Not only was it cruel and merciless, it 'delighted' in inflicting suffering on its victims.

> It is then that you may see the cruel spirit of this dreaded enemy of the feathered race . . . He presses down his powerful feet and drives his sharp claws deeper than ever into the heart of the swan. He shrieks with delight as he feels the last convulsions of his prey, which has now sunk under his increasing effort to render death as painfully felt as it can possibly be.[18]

Something must now be said about John James Audubon. He is known as the father of American conservation, and a string of national parks have been named after him. His books, *The Birds of America*, *Ornithological Biography*, and *The Viviparous Quadrupeds of North America*,[19] have made him the most famous of all illustrators of animal life, and some of his descriptions of his travels through the uninhabited regions of the United States together with his accounts of the creatures he saw have become classic evocations of a world as it once was.

Waterton and Audubon met only once in New York in July 1824, when they took tea together at the house of a mutual acquaintance, and Waterton was shown Audubon's portfolio of drawings of birds.[20] Very little has been said about that meeting, but it was almost inevitable that the two men would dislike each other at first sight. The easiest way to begin to understand why is to look at a portrait of each of them. Audubon is shown with his gun and his dog, and a sweep of magnificent landscape behind him. He wears a wolf-skin jacket, his hair is long, curled and shining with bear grease, and his expression is intense, romantic and undeniably theatrical. A portrait of Waterton made during his North American travels shows him with a little crested bird—one of his own hollow specimens—perched on his finger, and the head of a wild cat with round mad eyes perched on a book in front of him. His hair is cropped close to his head, he appears formal and diffident, and there is a disquieting look of self-mockery on his face.[21]

To pursue the simple contrasts further: whereas Waterton was the product of generations of careful marriages amongst the English Catholic aristocracy, Audubon was the illegitimate son of a French soldier turned plantation owner, and a Creole woman called Mademoiselle Rabin. He was born in San Domingo in 1785, shipped over to France when he was still young, and at the age of nine was legally adopted by his father and his father's childless wife. In 1803 he went to America and, apart from a few trips to Europe, there he stayed until his death in 1851. In telling his own life story he once hinted that he was the Dauphin, the son of Louis XVI and Marie Antoinette. He claimed to be ten years older than he really was and even his wife never knew his true age. He told people that he was the heir to vast estates in America, that his mother was a Spanish lady of noble blood—so many of the stories of the adventures of his life moved and changed and shifted according to the mood of the time, and the expectations of an audience.

Audubon was, above all, a showman. He was ambitious, handsome and charming. He was one of those people who was able to create a character for himself, as if he were an actor obeying his own stage directions. For many years his life was confused and restless, as he moved from one disastrous business venture to the next; trying to make himself rich, and using up other people's money in the process. It was not until 1820 that he formulated his Great Idea of producing a set of illustrations of the birds of America along with descriptions of their behaviour and habitat, and it was not until 1826 that it became possible for him to realize his ambition. The moment that the chance of success appeared, he exploited it relentlessly. As one biographer has written:

> He made use of the slightest connection with those of rank or royalty. He sought out and cultivated the rich and powerful, those who could aid him best. In his campaign to advance his scheme, Audubon combined many of the traits of the French courtier and the American salesman.[22]

He emerged not only famous for his drawings and his writing, but also for his flamboyant personality and appearance. In England he was recognized as the personification of the pioneering spirit, a 'natural man' formed in the Rousseau mould. And in his own adopted country he became the American Woodsman, noble, brave and untamed, a man who knew how to survive in regions where no human beings dared to wander, even though by the time he was writing about his adventures the frontier wilderness was receding fast in all directions.

This is not to say that Audubon was insincere as an artist or as a writer. His fascination with birds and wild nature had been with him since childhood, and it never left him. But whereas Waterton, and indeed Alexander Wilson, entered into their forests, swamps and empty plains in order to find quiet and an inner stillness, confident that even the fiercest creature had no wish to cause them harm, Audubon's wilderness was a place that challenged him with danger and excitement, fear and triumph. Hunting delighted him, and many conservationists must wince to read of his enthusiasm for the 'bloody havoc' of a buffalo hunt, the 'rare sport' of shooting pelicans on their nests, or the wonderful sight of dead spoonbills, flamingoes and other wading birds, piled up in a heap as high as a hayrick.

Such killings were not simply a random slaughter. Audubon had the desire, it could be called the metaphysical desire, to capture and to hold the fleeting and vivid splendour of a living creature. In his *Autobiography* he wrote about how he first discovered the magical power of drawing: 'The moment a bird was dead, however beautiful it had been in life, the pleasure arising from the possession of it was blunted . . . I wished to possess all the productions of nature, but I wished life with them.'[23] This act of possession came about with the creation of an image, and once Audubon had perfected his art he could reproduce a creature caught in a flash of movement more real than the fleeting glance of reality: a trumpeter swan, lifesize, its neck curved back to snap at a moth struggling in the water; a white-headed eagle crouching over the glistening dead body of a catfish; a cluster of parakeets in the branches of a hickory bush. In this respect Audubon was close to Waterton in his meticulous and strangely loving preservation of museum specimens which could look as if they were still alive, but he was very different from Wilson, who could draw his birds with intensity, but transfixed them in a death-like pose.

Wilson and Audubon had had one fateful meeting. It was in 1810 when Wilson was tramping the countryside in search of sponsors, with Poll the parakeet in his pocket and two completed volumes of *American Ornithology* as exemplars to show to prospective buyers. He walked into a general grocery store in Louisville, Kentucky, and there he met the store's joint owner, John James Audubon. The volumes were examined, and Audubon also produced his own work, which by that time comprised about 200 drawings.

I rose, took down a large portfolio, laid it on the table, and showed him, as I would show you, kind reader, or any other person fond of such subjects, the whole of the contents with the same patience with which he had shown me his own engravings . . . But reader, I did not subscribe to his work, for, even at that time, my collection was greater than his.[24]

According to Audubon, Wilson stayed at his house and met his family and friends; the two men went hunting together; obtained birds which Wilson had never seen; and Audubon offered his fellow naturalist the results of his researches and the drawings he had made, 'on condition that what I had drawn, or might afterwards draw and send to him, should be mentioned in his work as coming from my pencil'.[25] But here the plot thickens, for Wilson in his rather sombre diary from this period makes only a brief mention of meeting Audubon—'examined his drawings in crayon, very good . . . went out shooting this afternoon with Mr A.,'—he says nothing at all about the hospitality, the help and the offers of further help. It could have been that one of the two men chose to make later adaptations of the truth. It has also been suggested that Wilson's journal was expurgated and altered by George Ord and Waterton, as part of their angry battle with Audubon.[26] Be that as it may, ten years after this meeting Audubon set off on the first of his true wanderings, for which he kept a disorderly account of daily events, impressions and bird notes:

I left Cincinnati this afternoon at half past 4 o'clock, on Board of Mr Jacob Aumack's flat boat—bound to New Orleans—the feeling of a Husband and a Father were my Lot when I kissed My Beloved Wife and Children with an expectation of being absent for Seven Months . . . Without any Money My Talents are to be my Support and My enthusiasm my Guide in My difficulties.[27]

During the next three years he perfected his extraordinary style as a painter of birds, and in April 1824, dressed 'with extreme neatness', he went to Philadelphia, the centre of science and scholarship, to try to find a printer and subscribers so that he could realize his project. He met George Ord who was finishing a new edition of Wilson's work and had no interest in a rival publication; he met the engraver Alexander Lawson who refused to print his work and quarrelled with him; and he met the naturalist Titian Ramsay Peale who refused to lend him any of Wilson's specimens from the museum and also quarrelled with him. He travelled aimlessly to New York, and on to Buffalo and Niagara, and at some point he realized that his only chance of success lay in Europe. In May 1826 he sailed for Liverpool.

When he arrived he knew no one, although he did have some powerful letters of introduction from people who had appreciated the quality of his work. Within a few days he was invited to show a selection of his birds at the Royal Institution, and suddenly he was a celebrity. He was taken from one grand function to the next. He had a meeting with Sir Walter Scott who appeared 'wrapped in a quilted morning-gown of light purple silk',[28] and he dined with Lord Elgin, 'a small slender man, tottering on his feet, weaker than a newly-hatched partridge'. With his trapper's coat and his shoulder-length hair, he appeared as a creature from another world, to be stared at, and plied with questions. He told stories about his adventures; he gave impressions of the gobbling of a wild turkey, the hooting of a barred owl, the cooing of a dove; he wrote papers for scientific societies; he accumulated a list of learned letters after his name; he got drunk and sober and drunk again. He also got himself a good printer and a list of wealthy subscribers, and his career was under way. The story of his subsequent struggles and successes is not relevant here, what matters is the quarrel which erupted between him and Waterton.

Waterton was the aggressor and perpetuator of the quarrel and for several years he hated Audubon with a dangerous intensity. Although he succeeded in drawing attention to a number of mistakes or inconsistencies in Audubon's work, he did very little to undermine the American Woodsman's reputation, and in the process he did a great deal of damage to his own. His quarrel had several roots. There was his fondness for Alexander Wilson, and the sense, shared by the Philadelphia circle, that Audubon had stolen from Wilson's inspiration and taken for himself the glory. George Ord was especially bitter in this belief, and he wrote Waterton interminable letters filled with fresh evidence against their mutual enemy. The two fuelled each other's anger, and both seemed to suffer a curious identification with Wilson, which coloured everything they said in a highly subjective light.

Because of his own temperament, Waterton naturally disliked the type of person that Audubon was. His moral sense of truth and falsehood allowed for such elaborate jokes as the Nondescript, or such schoolboy pranks as riding bareback on a crocodile, but he was severely shaken by Audubon's habit of merging his imagination with his experience, to such an extent that he was himself convinced by his own stories, no matter how they contradicted each other. But most of the English aristocracy, along with many of the scientists and naturalists of the time, were happy to be convinced by Audubon's evocation of the American wilderness, teeming with fierce and blood-thirsty creatures and their innumerable victims. After the famous pigeon massacre, Audubon described how, as the dawn rose: 'The howling of the wolves now reached our ears, and the foxes, the lynxes, cougars, bears, racoons, opossums, and polecats were sneaking off. Eagles and hawks, accompanied by a crowd of vultures, took their place and enjoyed their share of the spoils.'[29] In response to this crowded gathering of scavengers, Waterton replied with typical scorn:

Mr Audubon may boast a sight never before seen by mortal eyes under similar circumstances. Great, indeed, must have been the yearning for pigeon flesh, to have caused such a wide variety of wild animals to assemble there, and irresistible the flavour which induced them to tarry so long beyond their wonted times of prowling. Their very nature seems to have changed. In general the flash of a gun, the crackling of a flame, or the shout of a huntsman will scare any of them, even when concealed in their lonely retreat, but, on this ever memorable occasion, the nerves of the animals, both large and small, were strung up to an astonishing degree of intensity.[30]

In a series of letters and essays, mostly first published in Loudon's *Magazine of Natural History* between 1830 and 1833, Waterton fought step by bitter step to prove that Audubon had lifted information from other sources, had been helped in his scientific writing by other hands, had invented things he had never seen, and had elaborated on the things which he had seen. Could a rattlesnake race up a tree and swallow a squirrel tail first? Did Audubon really witness a mid-air battle between an eagle and a vulture over a piece of offal? Was he sure of the inherent malice in a bald eagle?

Audubon never answered these attacks directly, although he made a number of scathing references to 'that Demerara gent' or 'Charli the alligator rider'. However he followed the accusations carefully, and friends and relations were always ready to answer on his behalf. In December 1833 he wrote to his son Victor:

The copy of your reply to Mons Waterton is excellent; that from Swainson ought to prove a death blow to the Demerara gent! I hope that these letters are now before the world, for my mortification has been great enough respecting the blackguardism of G. Ord and others, and I yet I am heartily glad that I never paid personally any attention to them through the press or otherwise.[31]

The public quarrel came to an abrupt end that same year, when Mr Robert Bakewell, a distant relative of Audubon, wrote the following accusation:

> Mr Waterton travelled from his own rich plantations in Demerara, surrounded with his slaves and attendants, Mr Audubon was a solitary wanderer in the forests of America, often dependent on his gun for support. While Mr Audubon is exposed to dangers and privations and looks forward to patronage from the public as his sole support and reward, Mr Waterton is tranquilly seated in a magnificent English manor, surrounded by paternal acres.[32]

Waterton was deeply stung. He did reply, describing for the first time some of the sufferings he had endured in British Guiana, and explaining, 'I studiously avoided mentioning all this, and much more in the *Wanderings*, lest they should savour too strongly of self'; but basically the battle was lost. Bakewell, sensing his power, added another attack in which he asked the public to decide which of the two men was the more honest: Audubon, with his gun, his dog and the drama of nature all around him, or Waterton, barefoot and foolhardy, wrestling victoriously with a poisonous snake, riding undaunted on the back of a large thrashing crocodile? There was no doubt that although the public enjoyed Waterton's writing, they tended to be more convinced by what Audubon had to say about nature in the raw.

CHAPTER XII

A Brief Marriage

In 1826 the wall round the park at Walton Hall was completed. There was now a thick stone barricade, three miles long, and sometimes as much as sixteen feet high, separating the park from the landscape that surrounded it. The wall had taken over four years to build, and had cost Waterton £9,000; money which he could hardly afford, but which he said he had saved by not drinking wine all his life.

The foxes, including the ones who lived under the roots of the great oak trees by the lake, were trapped and released in some neighbouring fields. The badgers were removed as well, although Waterton often regretted their loss, and wondered if he should have let them stay. All the other animals were allowed to remain, and every variety of bird was encouraged to come and use some corner as a nesting site. By the following spring six pairs of herons had arrived, and they steadily increased their number until there was an established colony of forty-three breeding pairs. Such huge and lumbering birds were easy prey for a man with a gun, regardless of whether or not he had a fish pond to defend, and Waterton knew of only two other herons' nests in the West Riding of Yorkshire, both in the secluded monastic grounds of Nostell Priory, which lay some miles west of Walton Hall. In that first year, Waterton also recorded five nests of the windhover hawk, and later he counted twenty-four such nests, all with eggs in them which hatched successfully.

It must have been extraordinarily gratifying to see with what speed and determination the birds and animals made use of the sanctuary he offered them; as if they had long been waiting for just such a fortress where they might increase and multiply without danger. Who else could boast of 'droves' of unafraid hedgehogs, of weasels scampering in the dusk like so many happy rabbits, or of presuming to see at least a dozen owls in the space of a short evening's walk? It was only the hares

111

who could not tolerate the wide confines of their new prison. Occasionally Waterton would find one of them lying dead near the wall, and said that they seemed to die of despair.

The wall had a straightforward practical purpose in keeping out poachers and casual intruders, but it also had a more diffuse symbolic purpose. It was as if Waterton felt that once he had enclosed his huge garden, he might be able to contain his own restlessness, and to provide himself with a place where he felt at ease. The house, which his father had altered so drastically, was not important to him, what mattered was feeling at home in the land. The park, with its tall trees and its gentle creatures, was to be a peaceable kingdom, an earthly paradise where there was no need to learn fear. It was to have a profusion of life such as he had seen in the South American forests, but not the same fierceness. It was to have the sense of security which he had known as a child; magically kept just out of reach of the growing horrors of the modern world. And to make the image complete, Waterton was precipitated into the determination to find himself a wife; for if he was going to live at home, he could no longer live alone.

Over the years Waterton had often thought about getting himself a wife, especially because as the eldest son he had a duty to maintain the family line. He once wrote in a letter that were it not for this sense of duty he would have become a Jesuit missionary. Indeed, two of his brothers had joined the priesthood, while the third remained a bachelor, so it would seem as if there were something in their shared background that caused them to avoid women. Certainly the tight-laced femininity of most ladies of the English upper classes filled Waterton with a dull dread which he could hardly conceal. He had apparently found their counterparts in North America more approachable, and there is an odd reference to a widow in Guiana, who offered him her hand along with 20,000 head of cattle.[1] However he was only able to be enthusiastic about the beauties and charms of the Indian tribeswomen from the tropical rain forests, servant girls in England, or peasant women, like a group he once watched in Italy laughing uproariously as they drove a big black pig to market. From what he has written it would seem that he never pursued any of his pleasures to an act of consummation; it was his son Edmund who was to be the licentious one, surrounded by sexual scandals and rumours, while the father probably remained celibate throughout his life, apart from the first few weeks of his marriage.

He did find the wife that he wanted, but she was so very young and innocent that it is hard not to see her as a little wild animal, captured and transported into a strange new country, trembling and afraid. And just as Eve was said to have brought death into the first garden, so also this young woman brought death with her; because of her, one aspect of Waterton's tranquillity was shattered for ever.

It is impossible to know when Waterton decided to marry one of the daughters of his friend from British Guiana, Charles Edmonstone. It has been said[2] that when he accepted the role of godfather at Anne's christening in Demerara, he was already planning to be her future husband as soon as she came of age, but this is not at all true to character, although it is in keeping with the tendency of his biographers to make him into an eccentric in all the details of his life. Be that as it may, the first intimation of his plans came in January 1827, when he wrote a letter to Charles Edmonstone:

Perhaps I may come and see you early in February, as I shall have a week or two to myself; after which I shall be much occupied here with workmen. When I have done with them, which will be about the close of summer, I must be off again upon another adventure, probably to New Holland. I find that I cannot live with any comfort at home unless I were married, and I have not courage enough to look for a wife . . .[3]

He did go to Scotland in February, and while he was there he became engaged to Edmonstone's second eldest daughter, Anne. She was timid and delicate, just fifteen years old: a girl who had not yet had the time or the experience to become a woman. Waterton never went to New Holland, in fact he never again travelled outside Europe, apart from a brief two-day visit to Madeira in 1845. His wanderings were over, at least on the scale that he had known them before, and he began to make the necessary preparations for his marriage.

Ever since coming to Scotland in 1817, the Edmonstones had been uprooted and uneasy. Charles Edmonstone had spent more than twenty uninterrupted years in British Guiana, and most of that time he had been deep in the forests and far from the civilized comforts that were enjoyed in Georgetown. When he left his homeland he had been a poor man with no prospects, but when he returned he was wealthy enough to buy back what had once been the family mansion of Cardross Park, near Glasgow. He was also thoroughly unwell, tormented by headaches, and the Scottish climate seems to have made him much worse. Apart from his wealth, and stories about his mysterious colonial adventures as Chief Protector of the Indians, he also brought with him a tall dark wife, four daughters and two sons. The youngest, Bethia, was born in the year of their arrival, the eldest,

Charles, was in his teens. Although his daughters had been cautiously described[4] as dark-complexioned Scottish ladies, his wife Helen was unmistakably of Indian descent. In one way or another, every member of the family must have felt out of place in the cold grey climate and the solemn presbyterianism of their new surroundings. Certainly within a few years of their homecoming the wealth had almost gone, and Edmonstone was on the edge of bankruptcy; his wife was desperately thin and being helped through some unknown illness with doses of laudanum, and his daughters were all in poor health, with backaches, headaches, leg aches and general malaises.

In many ways Charles Edmonstone must have welcomed the marriage proposition for his daughter, not only because of his long-standing friendship with Waterton, but also because it lifted some responsibility from his shoulders at a time when he felt weighed down by debts and uncertainties. It is curious to see how in the few surviving letters between these two men Waterton's role changed as he realized the need to advise and reassure the man he had once treated as a hero, a father-figure, and 'the best friend I ever had'.

The only practical obstacle to be overcome was religion, since the Edmonstones were Protestant, and Waterton would need to marry a Catholic. It was therefore agreed that Anne, along with her elder sister Eliza, should be sent to the English Convent at Bruges over which Waterton's formidable great-aunt, Mary Augustine More, had presided. There they could complete their schooling while being received into the Catholic faith, and within two years Anne would be considered ready for her marriage.

It says something about the character of the two Edmonstone girls that after a few months of 'saying we were happy before we were', they began to delight in the carefully ordered and regimented life of their new school, and were highly praised as models of piety and good behaviour. At that time the convent housed twenty pupils and thirty nuns, but only five of the nuns were in contact with the girls, while the rest lived a private contemplative life, floating through the days of their years in prayer and meditation and the simple tasks involved in running such a small and self-sufficient community. The rooftops and spires of the city of Bruges could be glimpsed from the dormitory windows; the life of the street could be heard but not seen. In the garden the Stations of the Cross were marked out on the high brick wall; a crucifix stood at the end of an interlaced avenue of lime trees, and there was an enclosed cemetery where the nuns could bury their own dead. The convent building was spacious and quiet, with black and white chequered floors stretching along the cloistered corridors;

silent at all times except for the soft chiming of bells. Only the chapel, with its gold-starred ceiling in a bright blue dome and its vivid images of saints and angels, was a place of colour and visual movement. Obedience and docility were considered the two most important virtues, and the girls were carefully steered through every hour of the day from the moment that they were woken with a prayer, 'My God, I give you my heart', to the moment when they were told to sleep. Here Eliza and Anne remained without interruption for two years, and although they never had any family visits, they did write home regularly, describing the cautious pleasures of their new life.

While they were obediently conforming to their new life at the convent, their home at Cardross Park was becoming increasingly chaotic and despairing. In the spring of 1828, Charles Edmonstone entered into a strange dotage: he became fixated on his daughter Helen, insisted that she remain with him at all times, and even that she slept with him in his room at night. He finally died towards the end of the year, and then there were confusions about his will, the family jewels were stolen by a servant, and a number of bitter quarrels erupted. The young Helen confined herself to her bed, withdrawing from all contact with the family, and when she was summoned to some legal appearance had to be carried into the courtroom. Mrs Edmonstone was 'reduced to a mere skeleton', unable to walk without assistance, and so severely overwhelmed by laudanum that she had no power of authority.[5] Many years later, when Helen and Eliza were confronted with Waterton's death, the confusion, the acrimony and the legal battles for rights of inheritance must have had a sharp familiarity for them, and perhaps that is why they were flung into such a hopeless and despairing passivity.

It was against this background, and surely not entirely oblivious of it, that Anne was preparing for her marriage. There is the image of an untamed and timid creature, and in all of her letters it is fear which dominates her thoughts. On one occasion she wrote to her father, 'I once intended to write to Mr Waterton, but write I cannot for my hand shakes so much.'[6] A few days before the arrival of her future bridegroom she said in a letter to her sister, 'The time of my marriage approaches very quickly. I tremble when I think of it. One happiness is that it will be very private.'[7] There is never a suggestion that she disliked Waterton, or felt that she was being forced into something against her will. She always expressed herself 'confident of his love', but simply, and overwhelmingly, she was afraid.

On 18 May 1829, a little before five in the morning, Charles Waterton arrived at the convent in Bruges. He was accompanied by

John Gordon, a Scottish priest who had taken on the role of spiritual guardian to the Edmonstone girls since their father's death, and who was to officiate at the ceremony. The wedding was held under the blue sky and the gold stars of the convent chapel, and it was all over well before the bells summoned the girls and the nuns for the first service of the day. After a short breakfast with the mother superior, the bride and groom, along with the bride's sister and the Scottish priest, were all on a barge that was to carry them to Ghent.

Waterton and his young wife continued on a honeymoon journey through Belgium, France and Italy. John Gordon went directly home to Scotland, while Eliza paid a visit to Walton Hall, in order to become acquainted with Waterton's sister and brother-in-law, Mr and Mrs Carr, who lived in Wakefield and were preparing a welcome for the new mistress of the house. Eliza quickly wrote to reassure her sister, 'I found Walton Lake quite beyond description . . . Lay aside your fears, Annie dear, Mrs Carr spoke in the kindest manner, and said she longed very much for your arrival in England.'[8]

By June 1829 Anne was already pregnant and feeling very unwell. She arrived at Walton Hall in August, but she hardly had a chance to appreciate the house, and still less the park, for she was ordered by her doctor to keep as quiet and still as possible, in order to avoid a possible miscarriage. The slightest exertion resulted in backache followed by the 'most unpleasant consequences', and she was sometimes sick five or six times in a day. She was deeply ashamed of the fact of being pregnant, and shocked by the physical suffering that her state caused her. It was not until October that she confessed her condition to her sister Eliza, in a letter that is written first down the page and then across it, making a spidery network of her delicate sloping handwriting:

I am now going to enter on a subject rather delicate to a young lady, but you being my eldest sister, I apply in preference to you . . . I am between three and four months gone in the family way, and I have been so ill until the last fortnight, that the doctors and all the married ladies with whom I am intimate strongly advise me to keep as quiet as possible . . . I beg you not to let any person know I am in that way, I am always ashamed when it is mentioned to me.[9]

It was not until the following February that she dared to write to her sister Helen and the nuns at the convent, and then she mentioned only that she had been ill but was now better.

In the vast solitude of Walton Hall, a place where there 'is every opportunity of keeping quiet', as she once said, though without apparent irony, the winter and the spring went by. Mrs Carr was a regular visitor, and a few house guests came to stay, but Anne spent most of her time confined to her room, writing letters, sewing little caps and shawls for her new baby, or embroidering gifts for her sisters. The preoccupation with baby clothes became something of an obsession as the months moved on, and her letters were increasingly filled with talk of cambric and lace, of how many caps can be made from a yard and whether the cloth of Scotland was superior to the cloth of Yorkshire. In a letter to Helen, written a few days before her confinement, she was trying to finish a cap, but could not do so because her pains were already upon her, and 'it is impossible for me to work much under such circumstances'.[10]

On 19 April 1830, Anne gave birth to a healthy boy, but she herself never recovered. She was physically weak, and contracted puerperal fever soon after the delivery; but even more crucial was the fact that from the moment when her child was released from her body she seemed to have no will to live. She died shortly after midnight, on the morning of 27 April. The priest whose task it was to inform her family and friends of her death explained, 'she requested that you might be informed that she died—"*most happy*". She had a deep-seated conviction that she should die and this did not at all discompose her.'[11]

Throughout the week of her dying Waterton sat at his wife's bedside. The priest, the doctors and Mrs Carr came and went, but he stayed there without interruption, watching the gradual departure of his tropic bird, the rare creature which he had only so recently acquired. Regardless of what his rational mind might have tried to tell him, he must have felt that by impregnating Anne with a child, he had brought about her death. Eighteen years later a visitor to Walton Hall wrote, 'It was impossible to be in Mr Waterton's company without being seriously impressed by the conviction that a cause of early grief (the death of his estimable lady), still dwells heavily on his heart, and still renders him the constant though silent mourner over an irreparable loss.'[12] Right up to the last years of his life the tears would come to his eyes at the mention of his wife's name.

When Anne died, Waterton's natural instinct was to escape from the house and the country as soon as possible, but he was held back by the realization that he must look after his son. Throughout the month of May he was in such a state of grief that his doctors thought he might never recover, and then in June he began to make contact with the outside world. He wrote to his friend George Ord, telling him what had happened.

Oh my dear Mr Ord, You will be sorry to hear that my angel of a wife is no more . . . Her loss to me can never be repaired—for she was indeed all gentleness and elegance and virtue and dignity. I am now desolate and forlorn and I can barely keep myself from sinking under the heartbreaking weight of grief and sorrow . . . My heart is full of grief, full to overflowing.[13]

He also wrote to Charles Edmonstone's nephew, Archibald, who was now the legal guardian of the Edmonstone girls. He begged that he might be made responsible for both Eliza and Helen, and asked for Eliza to be sent to Walton Hall immediately, and for Helen to be sent as soon as her education was completed. The request was granted: in that same month Eliza travelled down from Scotland to come and live at Walton Hall, and in October her sister Helen came to join her. They had both been instructed to 'soothe Mr Waterton's grief with sisterly and affectionate conduct',[14] and to the best of their ability, that was what they did for the next thirty-three years.

And so instead of a wife to share his garden with him, Waterton had two sisters and a son. Eliza and Helen became the joint mothers of his child, they kept house for him, loved him and tolerated him in their own way, but still their presence must have nurtured his sadness every time he looked into their faces and caught a glimpse of his wife. And in spite of all his determination to be fair and generous in his love for his son, his ambivalence could sometimes hardly be hidden, for in him Waterton saw an accomplice who had also played a part in bringing about Anne's death.

CHAPTER XIII

The Two Young Ladies

When they arrived at Walton Hall—Eliza twenty-three years old and Helen just turned seventeen—the Edmonstone girls were described as being tall, dark and beautiful. Then as the years moved on they became 'prim, kind and stately', young maidens who grew old without ever losing their maidenliness. There was an incident in 1854, when the 'machinations of an abandoned drunkard' caused Eliza immense but unspecified distress, and it seems that as a result of these machinations, she and Helen were planning to leave their adopted home for ever. On a little scrap of paper Waterton wrote them a final farewell,

> I have been a kind brother to you for four and twenty years. Whether on our travels abroad, or in our park at home, my constant wish has been to make you happy.
>
> I feel that I am not responsible in any point of view for what has taken place; but I deplore the occurrence with unfeigned sorrow; and I am prey to melancholy forebodings.
>
> But my pen gives way. God bless you both, my dearest sisters Eliza and Helen, wherever you go. I will not be here to see you depart: but I ask a parting favour. Oh, do not write to me. The sight of your handwriting would be more than I could bear. Again farewell, and believe me your afflicted and still ever affectionate brother.[1]

Apart from this one brief drama, a floating story without a beginning or an end, there is no evidence in the surviving family letters of anything that ever disturbed the placidity of existence for as long as Waterton was alive.

Because of the darkness of their skins, Eliza and Helen were marked as outsiders; like their sister, they would always appear to belong to another country, a different world than the one in which they found themselves. One visitor remarked that they reminded him of the native Indians he had seen in a district of Canada, while Charles Darwin described having tea with 'that amusing strange fellow Waterton' along with two Catholic priests and 'two mulatresses'.[2] As well as their obvious foreignness, they were isolated by endless ill-health, and either together or in turns they recovered from one sickness after another, or expected the worst that was still to come. Helen had trouble with her kidneys, Eliza with her lungs, and both were regularly afflicted by violent headaches. Often they were confined to their rooms for weeks on end; often they went with Waterton in search of some relief by taking the medicinal waters of Aix-la-Chapelle or Baden-Baden, or enjoying the warm winter sun of Italy, or going from one church to another praying to the saints and to the Blessed Virgin, consulting miracle workers, attending holy-day festivals in villages and towns.

The two ladies were inseparable. Together they were the mothering aunts for Waterton's son Edmund, and together they were the joint mistresses of his house, and, because there were always the two of them, there was little danger of any intimacy, either real or imagined. Apart from a short visit to Austria in the year of the death of his wife, and a trip to Madeira that Eliza made in the hope of alleviating a lung condition, this curious triumvirate was rarely separated. On the occasions when they were forced to be apart for a short time, as when Waterton went to stay in the exclusively male compound of Stonyhurst College, they wrote frequent, sometimes daily letters to each other, filled with quiet and comforting chatter:

My dear Eliza,
My health is excellent: the hiccoughs slight ... Yesterday the morning was bright: but rain fell at noon, and we had showers in the evening. No grass has yet been cut, but the crops are immense ... If anything fresh turns up, you shall have it, as the post is not closed until five. The weather is very cold, but we have famous fires. There have been some good swarms of bees here. I have just got your letters ...[3]

This bonding between the three of them was established very quickly, when they first lived together at Walton Hall, each weighed down by a private sadness which they could not communicate directly but still shared. In 1832, when the sisters were supposed to go to Scotland to settle some last details of their family affairs, Waterton wrote with undisguised gloom, 'I shall be so lonely without Eliza and Helen, who have been the greatest consolation and comfort to me, and I think I shall not be able to stay in this great house without them. Probably I may take a trip to the United States.'[4]

Later he was able to refer to 'my sisters and I' in one breath with talk about himself. 'My sisters and I shall be glad to welcome you . . . my sisters and I keep Spanish hours. We breakfast at eight, dine at one, and take tea and coffee at six . . . We are so close that we are like three branches on a single stem.'[5]

Eliza was the dominant one. It was she who dealt with all the practical aspects of running a large house, she who supervised Edmund's education, and almost always it was she who wrote to her 'dear brother', adding affectionate greetings from Helen. It was also she who came to be hated and resented by Edmund when Waterton was a very old man and his son was eager to take possession of his house, his land and his goods, along with the status of being the twenty-eighth male heir in an ancient family. Finally it was she alone who was named as the guilty party when Edmund contested the validity of his father's will.

It was not just the difference of age which established her as the stronger of the two. Helen was her sister's shadow, but as well as that she seems to have inhabited a shadowy world. When she was still in the convent, waiting to be shipped over to Yorkshire, the mother superior tried to describe the state of mind of her young charge. She was confined to 'what we call the purple room', and slept through much of the day as well as the night.

> You must not expect that Helen can make much progress in the scholastic way. She is often unable to apply, and we can never have the cruelty to force her to do something when we know how she is suffering. I think she is perfectly happy, and will leave us with regret. At this moment she is not in her best fashion respecting her health.[6]

There is little else to go by. The sisters kept journals for many years, but these have all disappeared. Their portraits were painted, but these were sold in an auction long ago and are lost. There were photographs showing them dimly in the distance, but these have now also been lost. In retrospect they only exist in the company of Waterton, quiet, obedient and waiting to be told what to do, passive and still, watching his boundless activity. Maybe in the daily reality of their lives they also existed only in his company, and that would explain why, with his death, they were so immediately thrown into confusion, lost and helpless even before they had to leave Walton Hall.

But that was at the end. In the first years when they were young, uneasy and uprooted, Waterton dedicated himself to acclimatizing them to their new home, determined that he would not let them slip away from him, as Anne had done. And in doing so, in worrying about them, sheltering them and trying his best to please them, he himself benefited. They provided a centre to his life, and enabled him finally to be able to stay at home for uninterrupted stretches of time. In a way, although it is hard to say quite how, they seemed to make him able to develop his own character, to become more odd, more outspoken, and in some respects more gentle.

Only three of Waterton's numerous notebooks and journals have survived the scattering of his possessions which took place shortly after his death. One of these, a small half-quarto book bound in red leather, spans a huge stretch of time. It begins with a series of meticulous entries concerning the Linnaean classification of zoology, written when Waterton was still a young man, perhaps even before he set out for Spain in 1802. Then, abruptly, the student abandons his lessons on the three orders of water fowl, the seven orders of insects, the teeth of mammals, the feet of birds; the handwriting becomes smaller and less formal, the Latin names disappear and Waterton begins to keep a personal record of the birds and other creatures seen around Walton Hall, along with occasional anecdotes and reminiscences of his visits to South America. The last pages of the book were written when he was in his eighties. The handwriting is unmistakably that of an old man, the letters large, erratic and sometimes shaking with effort.

17 April 1863
I was weighed by Mr Hardisty at Walton Hall, nine stone twelve pounds, again on the 2nd of May, ten stone one pound and a half, and again at Scarboro', ten stone.
5 Febr 1864
Counted here this morning more than fifteen hundred wild ducks.
9 March 1865
On this morning the French Giant, Monsieur Brice, his wife and Interpreter, paid me a visit. Monsieur Brice is exactly eight feet in height, stout and well made . . . his wife is Irish, very pretty, and below the ordinary size . . .[7]

Roughly at the mid-point of the notebook can be found a reference to the time when Anne Edmonstone lived with her husband at Walton Hall, and the years immediately after her death when her sisters were learning how to take her place as well as they were able to. When in

October 1829 she was confined to her room because of her pains, making baby clothes out of cambric and lace, and writing letters to Eliza and Helen in her delicate spidery script, Waterton recorded that he once heard a mistle thrush singing in the park. In November it sang again, on the 13th and the 20th. Fifty-two wild swans appeared on the lake in December, but nothing is said about how long they stayed. Sometime in March the sandmartins and wagtails returned, and by then Anne had only until April to complete her pregnancy. Still she was confined to her room, sewing, writing and worrying about her body.

The next entry in the little notebook is dated from the spring of the following year, 1831. Waterton does not start a new page, or even leave a gap after the arrival of the sandmartins and the wagtails; there is nothing to indicate the passage of time, or the changes that time has brought with it. By now Anne has been buried almost a year; her son Edmund is no longer a baby; her two sisters are growing accustomed to their new way of life; and Waterton notes that he has seen a windhover hawk, and that the white owls are again nesting in the old ivy tower on the island, but the redwing fieldfares have not come back, and he wonders if that is perhaps because of the deficiency of hawthorn berries during the last winter. From here the seasons in the notebook move on steadily for a number of years. The owls in the ivy tower begin raising three families, in June, September and November, and they become increasingly confident, 'He often comes into my room, and after flitting to and fro on wings so soft and silent that he is scarcely heard, he takes his departure from the same window at which he entered.'[8] During the winter months cormorants preen themselves on the terrace in front of the dining room window: 'Could they but perceive that there is safety for them here, and great danger elsewhere, they would remain with me while the water is unfrozen.'[9] There was an ox-eye titmouse (bluetit) with a nest fifty feet high in an old ash tree, and she grew so accustomed to having Waterton sitting perched on a branch beside her that he could stroke the feathers on her back without her showing the least sign of alarm.

He bought a large twenty-eight-guinea telescope and set it up in the drawing room. From there his sisters-in-law, and anyone else who was interested, could observe his peaceable kingdom and participate in his fascination with a minimum of effort. The two ladies were not naturalists, but they were content to watch from the windows after breakfast to help estimate the numbers in a new flock of birds, and to accept Waterton's way of life. They were unperturbed by the sight of him barefoot chasing a hare across a turnip field and catching it; they stood formally, one on either side of him, as he welcomed a party of lunatics from the local asylum, who in later years came regularly to enjoy the park and were also invited to make use of the telescope.[10]

With the death of his young wife, it was as if certain doors in Waterton banged shut, and could never open again, but as he became increasingly secure with his new family, he was able to develop in other ways. As a simple statement of the change that had taken place, and also to assert his need for separateness and privacy, he moved his sleeping quarters up into the attic of the house, and for the rest of his life he used this room as his study and slept there as well, lying on the bare wooden floor with a cloak as his only covering and a carved piece of mahogany wood as a pillow for his head. He established a small private chapel in the adjoining attic room where he would always pray at midnight. Summer and winter alike, he awoke between three and four in the morning to pray again before he began the day's work. Many of his essays on natural history came to be written in the deep silent time before the dawn, 'when all is still and my time is entirely my own'.

But before the new patterns could be established, the blank stretch of mourning had to be passed through. Eliza arrived at Walton Hall in the May of 1830, and two months later, having organized a wet nurse for the baby and a private maid for the young lady, Waterton set out for Europe. 'I shall leave this [place] about the middle of July for Flanders, and from thence I know not which way I shall bend my steps.'[11] He stopped off at Bruges to visit Helen, who was now at the convent, made arrangements for her journey to England, and then travelled down to Huttenheim in Bavaria to visit a friend. This was a certain Mr Fletcher, who acted as secretary to a strange and charismatic Jesuit priest, part of whose enormous and Germanic name was Prince Hohenlohe-Waldenburg-Shillingsfurst. He had become famous as a miracle worker when he cured a princess stricken with paralysis, and since then he had been inundated by visitors and letters begging for his prayers of intercession. Maybe Waterton asked the prince to pray for Helen in her purple room, or for Eliza with her responsibilities, or for the baby Edmund; certainly he felt that here he could find some spiritual comfort which would help to restore him. Maybe it was the prince or Mr Fletcher who, with an odd practical insight, advised him to make a small detour on his return journey in order to visit an old banker called Mr Berwind and ask to see his collection of paintings.

Waterton duly met the old man, and spent a whole day looking at his paintings. He learned to his surprise that they were being offered for sale, and decided to buy the lot: 156 old masters. And so, for an undisclosed sum of money, he became the owner of works attributed to Rembrandt and Rubens, to the Flemish school, the Spanish school and the school of Caravaggio. There were images of fruit and flowers and dead game; landscapes in Tuscany, in Holland and Germany; a beaver by the water, a wild boar in a forest, snails on a leaf, and numerous representations of saints and scenes from the Bible. It has been suggested[12] that Waterton bought all the paintings just so that he could become the owner of one in particular: a portrait of Saint Catherine of Alexandria painted by Carlo Maratti. It was true that the face of the saint bore a remarkable resemblance to the face of Anne. It was hung over the fireplace in the dining room at Walton Hall and Waterton often stared at it. Hopefully it was only the face of the maiden, and not the facts of her brief life which reminded him of his lost love, for she earned her sanctity when she refused to be seduced by an ageing emperor who, to punish her coldness, ordered her to be tied to a spinning spiked wheel, the Catherine Wheel.

The paintings were transported from the old man's home in Wurzburg to Rotterdam, and then over the Channel and up to Yorkshire, where they arrived shortly after their new owner. Just deciding where to put them all must have brought a wave of energy into the house, and involved Eliza and Helen in the need to decide where a particular saint or landscape would look its best. Dozens of canvases joined the museum of natural history which was slowly spreading through the downstairs entrance hall and up the wide staircase. There is a very faded photograph of the staircase, which shows the walls thick with paintings, and every available flat surface holding cases and cabinets, while objects of curiosity or natural history hang suspended from wires in the ceiling.

Waterton had no interest in Latin classification, nor did he care for an ordered and systematic display of his treasures:

Two pairs of horns of the Chamois, bought by me in Switzerland in 1841. On these horns is placed the tail of the smaller Cayman, killed by me in Mibiri Creek, Guiana, in 1812, and from them hangs a stone war club from New Zealand. On the architrave of the door, close to the horn of the Rhinoceros, is a hunting whip—a present to me from the good nuns of St Mary's, near Waterford in Ireland.

In the first angle of the Staircase is the head of Pero, the favourite pointer of my friend Tom Ikin . . . the head of Pero rests on a very fine tooth of the Hippopotamus, bought by me in Aix-la-Chapelle in 1836.[13]

125

At the time when he returned from his visit to the prince and set up house with Eliza, Helen and Edmund, Waterton was becoming a much more public figure. His *Wanderings in South America* had made him both famous and notorious. His manner of writing, his way of life, and his gentle and yet provocative personality angered some people, delighted others, and caused many to refuse to take him seriously no matter what he had to say. When someone did recognize his integrity, or the importance of his way of thinking, and tried with great courtesy to invite him to participate in a wider world than the one he inhabited, the chances were that either he would refuse the opportunity, or if he accepted he would do something to upset his hosts: '. . . there is to be an immense meeting of Naturalists and Philosophers from all parts of England and many parts of the continent, at York. I got an invitation from the Yorkshire Philosophical Society, but declined accepting it, under the plea that I had other engagements. The fact is I do not like the bother.'[14]

But although he was not prepared to go through the bother of public meetings, which would probably only bring him face to face with a crowd of 'closet naturalists' ('I would much rather stay here and listen to the cuckoo,' he wrote after another prestigious invitation), he did begin to write a number of essays, which appeared regularly in Loudon's *Magazine of Natural History* between 1831 and 1836. He wrote meticulously and lovingly about the observations of 'one in the habit of inspecting birds' nests in banks, in bushes, in trees, in ruins and on precipices, for nearly forty years'.[15] He mentioned how he would regularly visit the nests of his magpies and crows, how he would sit next to his owls as they slept in the ivy tower, and how in a single day he had observed a pair of bluetits coming to the nest to feed their young 475 times. He explained why it was important to let birds live, this one because it eats mice and rats, that one because it eats insects, the magpie for its tropical beauty, the starling, 'whom I protect for its wild and varied song, and defend for its innocence'.

In the same year that Waterton was writing his defence of the jackdaw and the carrion crow, an article appeared in Loudon's called *Something About Sea Birds*. The author described the excitement and the pleasure to be had from shooting sea birds at their coastal breeding grounds. It was becoming a popular sport; most shot the birds indiscriminately, although some collected feathers for the 'plume trade', with one prize shot claiming 10,000 kittiwakes in a single season. In 1834 Waterton decided that he would go and study the nesting habits of sea birds in the area around Flamborough Head on the east coast of Yorkshire. This was not as simple as it might sound.

The cliffs were a sheer face of chalk and loose flint, rising perpendicularly out of the sea to a height of 400 feet. It was easy to shoot at the birds from a fishing boat, but to get close to their nests needed a great deal of skill. The men and women who knew how to do this were the local 'climmers', or egg gatherers. Climming had been practised along this stretch of coast since the early eighteenth century, with different families covering different stretches of the cliff and giving it their name or a name that told something of its history: Broken Head, Katy Robson, Duggleby Corner, Shitt'n Shelf and White Breadloaf. Usually two men worked together: one held the rope at the top of the cliff, while the other swung and kicked his way down the rock face. The climmer wore a strong hat to protect his head from falling rocks, a cloth bag to collect the eggs, and carried little bundles of dried grass to stop the rope from cutting through his hands. In Waterton's time they would expect to collect upward of 130,000 eggs in a season, and these were sold in local markets to be eaten, or sent to the West Riding of Yorkshire where the whites of the eggs were used in the making of patent leather. Although it was a heavy culling, it was also a careful one, and the climmers tended their birds like shepherds with a flock of sheep, recognizing the faces of old birds who returned to the same site year after year, and always leaving an area of rock 'fallow' for a season if it became too thinly populated.

Waterton stayed at a country inn called the North Star, 'good accommodation for man and horse, but a lady would feel ill at ease in it'. He made friends with the climmers, and persuaded them to teach him their art.

> He who is to descend now puts his legs through a pair of hempen braces which meet around his middle and there form a waistband ... A man now holds the rope firmly in his hand, and gradually lowers his comrade down the precipice. While he is descending he has hold of the other rope, and, with this assistance, he passes from ledge to ledge, and from rock to rock ... It requires considerable address on the part of the descending climber to save himself from being hit by fragments of the rock, which are broken off by the rope coming into contact with them. He avoids the danger by moving sideways when the stone is falling ...[16]

Forgetting the 'little unpleasant sensations which arose on the score of danger', Waterton was delighted by the experience of descending like a spider, past layer upon layer of rock thick with nests and eggs, fledglings and stubborn parent birds; the stink of fish and guano; the

127

air around him deafening with the guttural cries of puffins, the groans and moans of cormorants and the varied screaming of countless other sea birds.

> The sea was roaring at the base of this stupendous wall of rocks; thousands and tens of thousands of wildfowl were in an instant on the wing; the kittiwakes and jackdaws rose in circling flight; while most of the guillemots, razorbills und puffins left the ledges of the rocks in a straight and downward line, with a peculiar quick motion of the pinions, till they plunged into the ocean . . . The nests of the kittiwakes were close to each other, on every part of the rocks that was capable of holding them, and they were so numerous as totally to defy any attempt to count them . . . You might see nine or ten or sometimes twelve old guillemots in a line, so near to each other that their wings seemed to touch those of their neighbours.[17]

Eleven times he made the descent, first at Flamborough Head, and then a little further along the coast at Buckton where the cormorants had their colonies and he could examine at his precarious leisure their huge stinking nests made of thick sticks, rock plants, ketlocks and bits of wool, and peer at the grotesque unfledged birds, who peered back at him.

As a result of these expeditions he wrote two essays which appeared in Loudon's magazine in January 1835. He tried to communicate the splendour and frenzy of what he had seen when he hung suspended above the sea, with a cloth bag on his shoulder, a spy glass in his pocket and perhaps a notebook if he could use it in such a position. He also tried to put into words his revulsion at the idea of going with guns to such a place, shooting into a mass of birds in order to count their corpses floating on the water.

> He who rejoices when he sees all nature smiling around him, and who takes an interest in contemplating the birds of heaven . . . will feel sad at heart on learning the unmerited persecution to which these harmless seafowl are exposed. Parties of sportsmen from all quarters of the kingdom visit Flamborough and its vicinity during the summer months and spread sad devastation around them. No profit attends the carnage, the poor unfortunate birds serve merely as marks to aim at, and they are generally left where they fall. Did these heartless gunmen reflect but for one moment how many innocent birds their shot destroys . . . they would, methinks, adopt some other plan to try their skill, or cheat the lingering hour.[18]

As well as writing his essays on natural history, Waterton used the pages of Loudon's magazine as a stage for some of his battles with those naturalists he considered to be fools or liars or innocents. 'Professor Rennie's errors can only be accounted for on the score that a professor, like many other naturalists of high note and consideration, has spent more of his time in books than in bogs. His deficiency in bog education is to be lamented; for such an education would have been a great help to his ornithological writings.'[19] In this particular instance he was stung into the attack by the fact that the professor had referred to him dismissively as 'the eccentric Waterton': 'As he has held me up as the *eccentric* Waterton, I make bold to hold him up as the *erroneous* Rennie.' Usually he was correct in his criticisms, but he did enjoy pointing out the mistakes of others with an extraordinarily blunt rudeness: 'His reverence could no more see the gland of a duck through this down, than I could see his own heart through the folds of his cassock.'[20] Whether consciously or not, he built up the image of his own eccentricity, telling comic stories when he should have been holding tight to a dry theory for the sake of proving a scientific point: 'I myself have actually swarmed with ornithological lice, for after applying alcohol and sublimate to the skin of the bird which I was dissecting, they would take the alarm, and, passing up my sleeve, would be in my hair in a trice. After finishing the bird, I used to take to the river, and there I startled the little fugitives into the stream by scrubbing my head and body with a lemon.'[21]

His enemies increased in number, closed their ranks, and answered him in kind, and so instead of earnest discussions about the function of the oil gland, or the appearance of a bird's beak, one personal attack followed another, and if Waterton observed that his crows did not cover their eggs when they left the nest, then it was because the crows were as eccentric as the man who owned the trees in which they sat. The last round of these battles appeared in Loudon's magazine in 1836, when Waterton was accused of being not only an eccentric self-indulgent Catholic aristocrat, but also a liar. The Reverend F. O. Morris had the last word: 'Let me only add that, while you were *wandering* in *South America,* I was acquiring an experimental knowledge in *England* on its *native* birds which you will never possess.'[22]

After this Waterton gave up contributing to magazines. His essays were published in book form the following year, along with a rambling account of his life, and two further volumes with additional instalments of his autobiography appeared in 1844 and 1857.

It was also in the 1830s that Waterton decided to open his park and his museum to the public. The curious and the incredulous could arrange to visit the museum and see for themselves the ancient and tragical face of the three-toed sloth, the grotesque bust of the Nondescript, 'The fierce ill-looking cayman or crocodile, on whose back Mr Waterton fearlessly mounted . . . the snake of gigantic size, which nearly cost the intrepid traveller his life when he grappled with it; splendidly plumaged species of birds, numerous other animals preserved in such a manner as to give them an appearance of life, which one can see in no other museum of natural history.'[23]

There was no entrance fee, visitors were given a catalogue, and if Waterton was in a sociable mood he might show them round himself. The park was also open for most of the year, and anyone could simply come to the main gate and be let in, so long as they had neither a gun nor a dog with them; large parties were however advised to make advance bookings. Everyone was welcome, but Waterton had a special preference for seeing local farming people, factory workers, coal miners and children on his land. By the early 1840s he estimated that 17,000 people had visited Walton Hall in a single year.

In spite of the invasion, Waterton apparently never felt that his privacy was being threatened. He could talk to people if he wished to, or he could hide himself in his attic room, or up in the branches of a tree, or he could carry on with his regular work on the land, and no one would suspect that such a rough-looking individual was the owner of the house and the land that encircled it. In return Waterton had what was for him the immense satisfaction of seeing people marvelling at the size of a crocodile and the sharpness of the spines of a porcupine; seeing them standing quietly to watch the herons by the water or the sandmartins in their little artificial nesting wall. 'Often, on a fine summer's evening, with delight I see the villagers loitering under the sycamore trees [by the house], longer than they would otherwise do, to have a peep at the barn owl as it leaves the ivy-mantled tower: fortunate for it, if, in lieu of exposing itself to danger by mixing with the world at large, it only knew the advantage of passing its nights at home.'[24]

CHAPTER XIV

Sentimental Journeys

Helen's health became 'more promising' once she was established at Walton Hall, but Eliza continued to suffer from troubles with her breathing and her legs, as well as other unspecified ailments which swept over her relentlessly. The mother superior at the convent in Bruges wrote to reassure her of the happier life to come; told her to accept her suffering with patience and resignation, and advised her 'not to dwell on the cause and object of her pain', presumably with the idea that despair and illness together made for a dangerous combination. Waterton, for his part, decided that what was needed was the warmer climate of Europe, combined with some of the medicinal cures that could be had at the hot-water springs of Germany. And so, after several delays, in the summer of 1833 he packed his two servants, his two sisters-in-law, his young son and himself into a carriage, and they set off for Dover and the Channel crossing to Ostend.

According to the travel books of the period Ostend was a dismal little town, and a few hours spent there was a tediously long time: 'The only thing worth seeing . . . is the sea wall, 40 ft high, and half a mile long, extending between the sea and the ramparts, faced with stone and paved with bricks.'[1] But in spite of this bleakness, Helen and Eliza became very attached to it, maybe because it was associated in their minds with the first stage of so many European travels. Much later, when they were homeless, it was one of the places where they tried, albeit unsuccessfully, to settle down. However on this occasion they did not stay long, but proceeded directly by carriage to Bruges. There the nuns at the convent were eager to welcome their dear sisters, their dear Mr Waterton, and their own 'dear and darling little grandson', for whom they had already laid in a supply of comfits and cakes.

After a few days at Bruges the party followed the same route that Waterton had taken not so very long ago with his new bride: to Ghent,

Brussels, Waterloo, Liège, and finally to 'the best of all places for stomach complaints', Aix-la-Chapelle. The ladies took the usual four-week course of bathing in the waters and drinking them, all under the supervision of a doctor. They could pass the rest of their time in the public gardens, the coffee houses and the Assembly Rooms where crowds gathered to shake off boredom with the aid of billiards, roulette and 'much more gaiety and more avowed vice' than was to be found at similar places in England.

Waterton quickly established his own pattern. He took a hot bath before five in the morning, went for long walks, and set up a dissecting table in the hotel sitting room used by himself and the ladies. On one occasion he spent several hours preparing a fresh-water crayfish and then, while he was out, the hotel proprietor threw away the perfect shell, leaving a little heap of dissected meat amongst the scalpels and preserving fluids, the needles, threads and bundles of cotton.

Eliza and Helen were favourably impressed by the curative powers of the waters and their brother-in-law brought them to Aix-la-Chapelle quite regularly. Over the years many changes took place: a railway line sliced its way through a quiet landscape, and tall trees were slowly replaced by tall chimneys whose smoke blackened the vegetation. Already in the 1830s the eagle and the raven were rarely to be seen, and then they were driven away for ever, and 'to their wild notes has succeeded the tiresome hum of modern machinery'.[2] In one of his later essays Waterton describes a ruined hunting fortress built by Charlemagne, which stood some two miles distant from the outskirts of the city. Its ancient walls guarded a derelict park and garden; the moat was stagnant, and the giant oak trees had been cut down and replaced by straggling and neglected pine saplings. With each year the factory chimneys grew closer, until by the 1850s they almost reached the moat itself, and the building was nothing more than a prime site, soon to be swallowed up and then quickly forgotten. There is a weary resignation in the way that Waterton writes about this fortress; its fate echoed what he clearly saw happening everywhere, and what he knew could also happen to his own walled territory, once he was dead and could not defend it.

From Aix-la-Chapelle they went on to try the baths of Baden-Baden and Wiesbaden in Bavaria, and it seems likely that they also visited Prince Hohenlohe in Huttenheim, so that his prayers for the miracle of a stronger body could be added to the medicinal value of hot-water springs.

Wherever they went they travelled comfortably because of Eliza's 'delicate condition'. They took a private carriage, although Waterton would have much preferred to travel in a public diligence. However, he often set out on foot before the dawn and long before the carriage was ready, so that he could enjoy the quiet and get a better idea of the bird life in the area. He was equally ambivalent about the presence of their servants, John Ireland and Mary Day, but again he accepted the irritation for the sake of the ladies.

> A servant is of very little use. I took one to be sure, but could have done just as well without him. Just be civil to the waiters, and do not grudge them their little perquisites, as most of the English do, and everything will go well.[3]

They stayed in good hotels, always hiring two bedrooms and a sitting room whenever possible. Waterton had his black cloak and his wooden pillow with him, so he had no need to compare the cleanliness and the comfort of the different beds that were offered to them, a subject which apparently caused much distress to English travellers —'One of the first complaints of an Englishman arriving in Germany will be directed against the beds,' says Murray's *Handbook*. He was impressed by the lack of fleas and bugs throughout Belgium and Germany, as well as by the absence of public drunkenness, and the fact that, 'No obscene sentences are ever to be seen written on the walls. No mice or rats in the bedrooms . . . no nits in the hair of the women.'[4] He was also impressed and deeply shocked by the scarcity of wild birds, even in the most remote areas.

Before departing Waterton consulted the standard guidebooks. There was John Murray's *Handbook for Travellers on the Continent*, with numbered routes, skeleton tours and a 'matter-of-fact description of what ought to be seen in each place'. A separate book of *Travel Talk*, also by John Murray, describes in four different languages how the horse is seen to run against the post, the bridge, the precipice; the coachman is drunk, impertinent, foolhardy; and a lady wishes that someone would dust her shoes, lace her stays and bring her a silver bodkin. There was also the more flamboyant style of Mrs Starke's *Travels in Europe*, filled with ominous advice for invalids and large families, and seemingly endless lists of the essential requisites for travellers, 'Leather sheets made of sheep skin or doe skin; pillows; blankets; callico sheets . . . a travelling chamber lock (always to be met with in London, and easily fixed on any door within five minutes); . . . a silver tea pot, tea and sugar canister, the last three made so as to fit into the kettle . . .'[5] Even if Waterton ignored most of the instructions ('it is wise to line the crown of the hat with writing paper, several times doubled'), and avoided as much luggage as possible, they were still a heavily laden company, accumulating books, souvenirs, religious relics and specimens of natural history as they went along.

The 1833 trip was judged to have been a success. The ladies were sure they had benefited, either because their health was better, or because they had been able to forget the cold weather and the boredom of a long Yorkshire winter; and in spite of a certain number of restrictions to his freedom of movement and behaviour, Waterton obviously enjoyed travelling with his new family. In 1835 and in 1838 they again visited Aix-la-Chapelle, and then in the summer of 1839 they were preparing to go to southern Italy. In July Waterton wrote to his friend George Ord:

> Winter still reigns in this cold and dreary climate. Yesterday we thought we had got into November ... The frosty nights have destroyed nearly all our cherries and the insect has gnawed the apple in the bud. However, I shall soon be able to bask in fine weather ...
>
> On Wednesday week we sail from Hull to Rotterdam, and thence we proceed to Flanders and expect to reach my dear Aix-la-Chapelle in the first week of August ... After this we shall go southwards, and visit the finest parts of Italy and saunter up and down in the countries bordering on the Mediterranean.[6]

And so they set out for Rome, a city which Mrs Starke considered 'ideal in consumptive cases'. They were gone for two years, returning to Walton Hall in the August of 1841. They went on another year-long jaunt to Italy in 1844, and in 1846 Eliza was sent off with her sister to the island of Madeira in a final attempt to strengthen her health. After that her troubles did not diminish, but the idea of finding relief or a cure was relinquished, as with many prayers and sighs she steered herself into middle age.

It has been said that the ladies kept 'very correct journals' of all their travels. No doubt like two obedient schoolgirls they sat straight-backed side by side, recording the events of the previous day: the hawk that only Helen's sharp eyes could see in the distance; the shipwreck in which they lost everything including their bonnets; the miracle they witnessed at a church in Naples; the behaviour of the little Edmund. Waterton mentions that Eliza copied into her journal a letter which gave 'a most terrible account' of a person possessed by the devil. Perhaps she also tried to put words to the occasion when she was in a church and the man who was lighting the candles fell from a great height and landed on an old lady, killing the two of them outright. All that is left from the sisters' impressions of their foreign travels is a fragment of a letter from Eliza, which stands in very sharp contrast to Waterton's humorous and easy-going accounts.

> Edmund was very ill in Freiburg, and I was up two nights with him. As usual when ill he was very docile and very pious. As yet I am a little disappointed in Italy, but must own that I am frequently so tired that I can scarcely get up stairs, and my knees are so stiff that I dread entering a church, for if I get down on my knees I cannot easily get up again.[7]

Certainly for the ladies the pleasures of seeing new cities and landscapes and meeting new people were often offset by the effort of travelling long distances, the responsibility of looking after Edmund, and the heat, the filth and the fleas which met them once they had crossed the border into Italy. They survived a number of accidents, dramas and illnesses. Near Rimini, where 'The oxen are docile, large and beautiful, and nearly all of a dun colour. Fat white pigs, some of them with red faces, might be seen in curiously shaped carts as we passed along',[8] the horses suddenly bolted, the carriage crashed into a ditch, and Helen and Eliza somehow got pinned under a broken wheel. Waterton was very favourably impressed by their self-composure: 'My sisters behaved nobly. Although exposed to immense shock, not a sigh, not a shriek escaped them . . . When we released them from their prison, they retired to a little distance to await the results.'[9] When they were all involved in a shipwreck not far from the island of Elba he was equally delighted by their lack of hysteria. They were on a steamer making its way from Civita Vecchia to Leghorn. During the night the captain and his steersman filled themselves with wine and fell asleep, leaving the boat to find its own way home as if it were a horse accustomed to carrying a drunken master on its back. Unfortunately their path crossed with that of a much larger vessel, the steamer was badly damaged and began to sink. In the confusion that followed, a fat Neapolitan, with gold coins sewn into a belt around his waist, plopped overboard and sank beneath the water with such speed that no one could rescue him; but apart from that one loss there were no casualties. Waterton wrote proudly of how the ten-year-old Edmund prayed to the Virgin Mary to come to their aid, and how Eliza kept crying out, 'in a tone of deep anxiety, "Oh save the poor boy and never mind me!"' The ladies lost their dresses and their jewels, their books and their papers, and there was a great deal of confusion about getting new passports so that they could continue on their journey. Most of

Waterton's collection of specimens of natural history were travelling by a separate route and so as far as he was concerned the accident was dramatic but not serious. He did, however, develop a fever shortly afterwards, which in turn became a severe case of dysentery, so that instead of being able to protect and guide his little family on the return journey, they were made responsible for getting a sick and delirious man home to England as quickly and as safely as possible.

There is always the impression that Waterton enjoyed horrible accidents and sudden encounters with danger. Not that he wanted to suffer, or to see other people suffering, but he liked the excitement of an emergency, and when it involved his own body he seemed to take the part of a keen spectator in watching the battles which took place when the virulence of a fever or the nastiness of a wound was set against the toughness of his constitution. Maybe it was a way of testing destiny to see if he really was supposed to go on living. Be that as it may, all the troubles they met are described with a rather disconcerting relish, whether they involve major disasters, or such casual inconveniences as the mice in the beds, the filth in the streets, the droves of fleas jumping up to welcome them from the hotel carpet, or the occasion when the cook was seen preparing an omelette in the hotel chamber pot.

As far as Waterton was concerned, he was in Europe for the sake of the health of his two sisters-in-law, and for the sake of his own idle curiosity. He would have preferred to be back in the wilds of Guiana, or some other wilds, but now that he was tethered by responsibility, he would make the best of it. He travelled in search of birds, alive if possible, but if that presented a problem, then he would look for them in market stalls and in hotel kitchens: 'seeing a blazing fire in the kitchen, I went in to warm myself, and there I saw some very fat ring ouzels and fieldfares, under the depluming hand of the cook.'[10] He also wanted to see the way that specimens of natural history were displayed in the museums of Europe, partly from a professional point of view, but also to confirm his belief that no one had mastered the skill of taxidermy as well as he.

He took pleasure in being in Catholic countries where he was not despised for his faith and where he could get his fill of saints' days and processions, and even the occasional miracle. There was always a sadness in him, but it was easily pushed to one side by the sight of a flock of birds, or of a group of laughing women and black pigs working together at collecting acorns from the ground. 'What could be better,' he said, 'than walking out on a fine Sunday evening singing *"Viva la joia, fidon la tristessa"*? . . . to tell the truth, I have no real science in me. I merely look at art and nature as I pass along; and I pen down that which gives me most delight.'[11]

From the pages of his autobiography, from some of his essays, and from the faint pencilled script of a journal that he kept when travelling from Hull to Rome in the late summer of 1844, it is possible to see the sights that attracted him as he passed through Europe, and when he stayed in Rome and 'sauntered along the Mediterranean'. Holland was interesting because it reminded him of Demerara, because the people were gentle and hospitable, because the waterfowl were still plentiful and the stork was not persecuted. In Antwerp he met up with his old friend, Mr Kats the naturalist, who had just succeeded in hatching and rearing a Carolina duck and kept a most intelligent African baboon on a chain.

The men in Bavaria all wore black boots and the women had high pyramid caps and short petticoats—'excellent fashion'. They buried their potatoes in long trenches close to the road; their geese were fine and plentiful; their dogs large and their cats scarce. The pigs were white and ochre red, with long curved backs and stiff bristles. The trees along the avenue approaching Munich were ill-conditioned and ill-trimmed. The porter at the picture gallery was a giant with something wrong with his knees. Since leaving England he had seen only two birds' nests; everywhere wild birds were terribly scarce, and he noted down each one that he saw: a single magpie, a crow, a finch or two, no hawks.

The Alps were disappointing, not because of the scenery, 'I am not easily captivated by European scenery, be it ever so magnificent,' but because here at least he was expecting to see some of the rarer birds of passage, as well as a good number of hawks and eagles, but he saw almost no life at all, even though he made a point of travelling on foot ahead of the coach. 'The earth appeared one huge barren waste, and the heavens produced not a single inhabitant of the air to break the monotony around us.'[12]

At Innsbruck in Austria he was assured that golden eagles were plentiful, and believed what he was told because he saw so many ornaments made from the legs of golden eagles and sold in all the shops. He got a glimpse of the glaciers, but saw not a single bird except for two finches. In the cultivated valleys at the foot of the Alps they passed the edge of a swamp, but that also was 'as barren of feathers as our exchequer is of real money. A few carrion crows, a finch or two, and three wagtails was all I saw.'

They knew they were entering the south because the stink of human excrement became more overwhelming, and the women were busy combing the lice out of each other's long hair. Rats increased in number and in Venice he saw an especially well-fed Hanoverian.

> . . .which stared at me full in the face. It was sitting contentedly on a ledge at the base of a house about a foot from the water. How well this little intrusive brute thrives both in cold and hot climates! Bats were plentiful over our heads as we passed along, and in the course of the evening in my ramble amongst the shops I could see that this city is well supplied with woodcocks and the small kinds of birds.[13]

They crossed the Apennines without seeing a single hawk, buzzard or eagle, and it was only as they approached Rome that the countryside began to come alive.

> . . . flocks of finches and sparrows, crows and larks and wagtails plentiful, and beetles and bumblebees have been perpetually flying on the wing. Miss Helen drew my attention to another buxom Italian damsel, astraddle assback, she had a red shawl on, nice white cotton stockings, and polished shoes. The day is summerlike and sunny. A flock of starlings passed over us just as the sun was going down in the west, with all the golden glory of a tropical brilliance. Our journey is now at its close.[14]

During the first expedition to Rome they were accompanied for some of the way by Mr Fletcher, the secretary to Prince Hohenlohe. The two men decided to walk the last twenty miles from Baccano to the celestial city. They set out at four in the morning on a road covered with hard frost and under a black sky pitted with stars. Waterton, for reasons best known to himself, decided to go barefoot. He had gone 'merrily along' for some time, when he noticed blood on the pavement; only then did he realize that he had damaged both his feet, and lacerated one of them very severely, but apparently the cold had numbed the pain. He refused to stop walking, but put his shoes on and they resumed their journey. This meant that on arrival he was at once confined to a sofa and needed to remain on it for the next two months. It also resulted in a rumour which grew in strength and colour, and which told of a devout and penitent Catholic gentleman who had walked on bleeding feet to the holy city, 'a reputation by no means merited on my part'.

Waterton decided that Rome was the quietest city he had ever visited. He liked the people and the churches, but best of all he liked one particular market: 'I fear the world will rebuke me when I tell it that instead of ferreting out antiquities and visiting modern schools of sculpture and painting, I passed a considerable portion of my time in the extensive bird markets.'[15] It would seem that here, in a cluster of stalls near to the Pantheon, or Rotunda as it was also called, all the birds of passage which had failed to reach the Alps and the Apennines, all the song birds which had never eaten the berries of the rowan trees of Austria, the water fowl, the eagles, were to be found, freshly killed, and carefully displayed.

Nothing astonishes me more than the quantities of birds which were daily exposed for sale during the season; I could often count four hundred thrushes and blackbirds, and often a hundred robin red-breasts in one quarter of it; with twice as many larks and other small birds in vast profusion. In the course of one day seventeen thousand quails have passed the Roman custom-house; these pretty vernal travellers are taken in nets of prodigious extent on the shores of the Mediterranean. In the spring of the year and at the close of summer, cartloads of ringdoves arrive at the stalls.[16]

Everything is good food with these people, from the wren to the eagle. Hawks, owls, and crows are regularly plucked and sold for the spit . . . The roebuck and wild boar are very plentiful and to be had every day during the season. I have counted four kinds of snail on sale in the market; and the red worms from dunghills and sewers are considered very good food.[17]

Every day he went to first mass at four thirty in the morning, and then straight on to the Rotunda. He became friendly with the rough-looking men who worked there, and they learnt to put interesting birds on one side for him. Between May and June he watched the boys catching swifts and housemartins which came to the city in multitudes.

They procure a silken line of sufficient length to reach above the eaves of the houses. To one end of this they attach a small curled feather or two, and behind this is formed a running noose. This apparatus is thrown up into the air by the current of wind blowing through the street; and as the poor birds are on the look out for material wherewith to line their nests, they strike at the floating feathers, and get their necks into the fatal snare, and are taken to the market at the Rotunda for sale.[18]

139

It was from the market that he obtained a fine specimen of an eagle owl and, in order to catch its stance and its expression, he went on alternate days to visit a tame one that was kept in the gardens of the Colonna Palace.

> I became thoroughly acquainted with all its bearings. I observed that when I peeped at it from behind a tree, and it did not see me, it would raise the feathers of its body, wings and head, ever and anon . . . but the moment it got sight of me, down went the long feathers at the ears, and the size of the body became instantly much reduced.[19]

In Rome also there was the fascination of the great slaughterhouse, where upward of 700 or 800 pigs were killed every Friday during the winter season. Like an onlooker at a public bullfight, he went regularly to watch the scene of carnage. 'About thirty of these large and fat black pigs are driven into a commodious pen, followed by three or four men, each with a sharp skewer in his hand . . . On entering the pen, these performers, who put you vastly in mind of assassins, make a rush at the pigs, each seizing one by the leg, amid a general yell of horror on the part of the victims.'[20]

It can be difficult to disentangle Waterton's interest in the spectacle of a slaughterhouse or a market place from the spectacle of a religious procession or a public miracle with people shouting and crying with joy at the proof of the strength of an almighty God. Maybe there is no need to bother about the disentangling: he was simply attracted to displays of all kinds, and particularly to anything that had a bizarre or theatrical element to it. If he saw a giant or a dwarf he was quick to stare and ask questions. If he was told of a mermaid or a two-headed calf, he was quick to go and examine it, to see if it was a genuine production of nature or a fake. Without disrespect it can be said that he visited shrines, watched processions, and waited patiently for miracles with this same spirit of enthusiasm and curiosity. He had no difficulty in believing that the painted eyes of a portrait of the Virgin Mary had been seen to blink; no doubt in the healing magic contained within a fragment of the True Cross. As far as he was concerned, miracles of all sizes and strengths were a regular occurrence, and he was eager to be in the vicinity of any that he heard about.

Waterton and his family went to Naples in September 1840, in order to practise the 'sauntering along the Mediterranean' that they had been planning, and also because they wanted to witness a religious event known as the 'Liquification' of the Blood of Saint Januarius. The saint was said to have been martyred in AD 305, and samples of his blood had been preserved since that time in a richly decorated glass phial. On certain holy days this phial was displayed before a tense congregation and, amid the fervent chanting of the women, the dried blood was suddenly transformed into a bright red liquid. The event could not simply be explained away with scientific reasoning. Sometimes the liquefaction was slow to occur, sometimes it took place almost at once. It has been reported that when it all took too long the women would begin to insult the saint, calling him a pig and a yellow-faced dog and worse, and then apologizing to him afterwards.

The first time that Waterton witnessed this miracle he was at the cathedral with his patient entourage at eight in the morning. The blood did not liquefy until two in the afternoon, but he stayed on until after five, kissing the phial at regular intervals in order to get a clear and objective look at its contents. Goodness knows how long Helen, Eliza and the boy lasted during this day, it cannot have been for the full nine hours. The miracle was repeated three days later, and this time it was all over in little more than an hour. Waterton concluded, 'Nothing in the whole course of my life has struck me so forcibly as this occurrence. Everything else in the shape of adventures now appears to me trivial and of no account . . . the liquification of the blood of St Januarius is miraculous beyond the shadow of a doubt.'[21]

In Sicily they witnessed a very different demonstration of the triumph of life over time and the grave. On the Day of the Dead the people in the Palermo region fetched the mummified bodies of a large number of their relatives out of the nearby catacombs, where generations of the dead were preserved in a wizened but intact state, and paraded them through the streets, decked out in their brightest and most colourful clothes. The scene upset Waterton painfully, maybe partly because he looked on with the trained eye of a taxidermist, and partly because he had a great respect for the mummified bodies of the saints, who often had an equally gruesome but less festive appearance.

We saw what had once been fine young ladies, and elderly matrons, and fathers of families, in dresses fit for a convivial dance; and we might have imagined that they were enjoying an hour of repose till the arrival of the festive time, but when our eyes caught the parts not veiled by the gorgeous raiment, oh Heavens! there indeed appeared death in all its terrors . . . These shrunk and withered exhibitions of former bloom and beauty brought to my mind the exhibitions of monkeys which we see in our museums.[22]

But surely the encounter with the powers of the supernatural which most impressed him and his sisters was a visit they made to a young lady called Maria Mörl who was known as the Ecstatic Virgin of the Tyrol. This was in 1844 when they were on their second visit to Rome. They had read accounts of the lady, and managed to obtain special permission to visit her. She was kept—'lived' somehow seems too vigorous a word—in a convent in the mountains near Innsbruck. They were met by a gentle and cordial priest who acted as her confessor and guardian and, along with their two servants, they were led into a small, almost dark room. They could distinguish a bed with a crucifix at either end of it; a number of religious pictures on the wall; a Barbadoes dove in a cage which hung by the shuttered window. Beside the bed, the virgin was kneeling in a state of trance. She was dressed in a white robe, with a tight cord tied around her waist. Waterton asked respectfully if some candles could be lit so that they could see her face more clearly. 'We were all lost in utter astonishment at the angelic countenance of the Estatica, who was kneeling with her eyes immovably fixed on the crucifix before her, and her body as unmoving as a statue.'[23]

When they had stared at her long enough to satisfy their curiosity, the Father gently requested her to come out of her trance. She obeyed immediately, climbed on to the bed, and lay there, with a smile on her lips. The Father told them that they should take hold of her left hand, which was stretched out towards them. While they were doing so she suddenly jumped up on to her knees 'in a motion so sudden that I cannot describe it', and fell once more into her ecstasy with her eyes on the crucifix. Waterton had managed to feel the 'holy wound' or cicatrix on the palm of her left hand, but her right hand was too far away from him to see it clearly, and although he would have liked to examine the wounds on her feet as well, he felt that it was not right to do so.

The virgin kept slipping in and out of her trancelike state. She entered the real world long enough to be able to give everyone some little leaflets about herself, but she never looked at them and never spoke. After staying on for a further twenty minutes in that strange and claustrophobic room, they crept away.

The meeting impressed them all. They discussed in detail the positioning of the wound on the virgin's hand; the beauty of her face; the extraordinary way that she had sprung on to her knees. Then with regret they left the convent and resumed their journey. On the following day Waterton noted in his journal, 'The road to Trent is nearly level . . . The scenery is astonishingly magnificent. I saw only one crow and a small flock of finches, but it has rained from morning to night, so the birds in this district might have thought it prudent not to expose themselves.'[24]

CHAPTER XV

The Soapworks

As the years moved on, the tall chimneys of industry grew taller and more numerous. Clusters of brick towers carried billows of smoke and gas—black, sulphur yellow, grey and tinged with ochre red—up into the sky to a height of 100, 200, 300 feet. The smoke poured out, floated, hung motionless, was blown about and sank back to the earth. Combined with certain atmospheric conditions, it could blot out the light of the sun. If it contained certain chemicals it stank and could induce dizziness and vomiting. People told how the leaves of the trees over which such air had passed were burnt and withered, and the trees began to die. A man giving evidence at a government inquiry into the effects of 'noxious vapours' evolved in 'certain manufacturing processes' described how the landscape around his farm had been affected:

> It is one scene of desolation. You might look around for a mile and not see a tree with any foliage on whatever . . . some have fallen down entirely and at present lie upon the ground, but the forty or fifty trees which are left standing are like so many stems, and I think it would be difficult for anybody to say that there is a vestige of vegetation left for anyone to see in the shape of grass or anything else.[1]

The chimneys belonged to the factories where this, that or the other was produced in vast and seemingly endless quantities, and one of the new industries which was enjoying a sudden burst of commercial activity was centred around the production of soap and its numerous chemical by-products. For several years Waterton concentrated his horror of the modern age in a battle he waged against one particular soap boiler: a man who erected his chimneys on a little plot of land

144

which shared a boundary with the Walton Hall estate, and was also conveniently close to the Barnsley Canal, the new North Midland Railway, and a small stream which ran through the nearby water meadows, amongst the trees of the park, and into the lake at the point where the herons nested in the tall elms.

It has been said that the civilization of a country can be judged by its consumption of soap. It could just as well be said that the filth of a country, and a country's shame for the filth it produces, can be judged by its need to consume soap. When fresh water and sunlight are scarce, then soap and bleach together provide people with cheap cleanliness and cheap brightness. With a neat irony in which the uroborous quietly swallows its own tail, it must be added that the production of soap, according to the methods of the mid-nineteenth century, was one of the smelliest and nastiest processes imaginable. It would take much more than simple washing to clean up the acids that were released into the air, the rivers and the soil; the fats that thickened the waters with a stinking scum; and the soda wastes, that nobody knew what to do with, and which were left to accumulate in huge sterile hills: '. . . they deposit this stuff wherever they can get a place to deposit it in immense heaps; in fact they have made railway embankments of it. This contains a large amount of sulphates, and when the water comes upon it, there is a very offensive matter flows from it; a yellowish creamy matter, sometimes nearly black; this flows into the streams . . .'[2]

Basically soap is made from boiling a fat with an alkali and a salt. Any greasy matter, mutton suet, whale blubber, bone grease, palm oil, could be used for the fat, but the important revolution in the whole business came in the early nineteenth century with the development of man-made alkalis. A soap boiler could easily learn to save on his costs by producing his own alkali from common salt and sulphuric acid. It was then a logical step for him to produce his own sulphuric acid; a process which in turn resulted in him having large quantities of hydrochloric acid, some of which could be used in the manufacture of bleaching powders. In this way, almost inadvertently, many soap boilers became involved with the central core of the heavy chemical industry, with each stage dependent on the following one, and almost every effort to use up the wasted chemicals necessitated the manufacture of some other product. If one was to try to picture the whole process in one of those awkward educational diagrams, then soap would appear in the central bubble, and arrows would be shown pointing to and from the centre, carrying sulphuric acid, hydrochloric acid, epsom salts, chloride, sulphur, artificial fertilizers, soda ash, caustic soda, lime, and a number of other items, most of them dangerous or at least very unpleasant.

In those early days the first of the modern soap kings were almost exclusively preoccupied with the speed at which their industry was advancing and their profits accumulating. Safety precautions were a secondary consideration which evolved in a rather slow and tortuous manner as a result of such private lawsuits as Waterton's, and finally in response to flimsy government legislation. It was possible, but it was not easy or financially rewarding, to minimize the release of hydrochloric acid into the air and the water, but it was not until the 1860s that the manufacturers were forced to make serious attempts to do this. It was always difficult to know what to do with the thousands of tons of useless soda waste, and the obvious solution was simply to acquire stretches of land on which to dump it. Many manufacturers chose to concentrate all their inventive efforts on finding ways in which they could release their acids secretly, dump their wastes privately, and hide the true source of the damage by every available means. As a rule it proved far cheaper to pay for the cost of legal battles with individuals and compensation where this was necessary, rather than slow down the growth of the industry while trying to improve its technology.

Part of the problem was the emergence of specialization. Only a few people had a proper understanding of the chemical processes involved, and it took a very determined solicitor or individual to prove that what the manufacturers were doing was directly responsible for killing off the vegetation or giving the local inhabitants severe headaches. But in spite of this general ignorance, already by the early 1840s it was becoming painfully obvious to anyone living near a soapworks that hydrochloric acid was responsible for devastating whole stretches of the countryside:

Farms recently well wooded, and with hedges in good condition, have now neither tree nor hedge left alive; whole fields of corn are destroyed in a single night, especially when the vapour falls on them while in bloom; orchards and gardens have not a fruit tree left alive; pastures are so deteriorated that graziers refuse to place stock on them; and some witnesses have attributed to the poisonous nature of the grass the fact that their sheep and cattle cast their young in considerable numbers.[3]

But it was still difficult to pinpoint the blame. One solicitor who had followed a number of such cases explained that 'a great deal of mischief is found to be done at night', for when the acids were released in the dark nobody could prove where they came from or where they went to. He also explained, with a world-weary tolerance, that the tall chimneys of the trade had absolutely no practical function, '. . . but that they were very convenient, because the vapours were thus spread so far that there was little chance of knowing where any mischief came from'.[4]

Even if the evidence of the destruction being caused was overwhelming, there was still in the background the fact of the huge commercial value of the industry; the fact that it brought work, albeit dangerous and unhealthy, to areas where people were often poor and desperate; and the fact that the owners were fast becoming extremely wealthy and therefore extremely powerful individuals. Waterton, in the battle that he fought against one quite small soap boiler, was involved in four years of persistent litigation. In the end he told himself that he had won his case, but the victory was only relative. He had lost hedgerows and trees, birds, animals and fish, as well as a good deal of time and money; his water had been badly contaminated, his health and the health of his family had been affected, and he had made a number of new enemies. His opponent was never once forced to stop the production of soap, but at a certain stage in the proceedings he was persuaded to move to a much better appointed site, some six miles away from Walton Hall, in the little village of Thornes. There he quickly set up a similar but larger establishment, and, as another government inquiry noted, '. . . soon after the Thornes Soap Works were begun, many stones of fish, which had come to the river to spawn, were to be seen floating dead upon the surface. During that year all the fish forsook the stream as regular inhabitants . . . for some time after, however, a fish was occasionally to be seen as a curiosity . . .'[5] The steady march of progress had simply made a small and, as it happened, a temporary detour around Walton Hall, and then it went on, unabated in its strength and in its ferocity.

The first soap boiler to come to Waterton's village was a man called William Thornhill Hodgson. There seems to be something rather sympathetic about him, but that might simply be because he was dead before anyone could challenge him to a fight in the courts of law. Certainly he was more of a chemist than a businessman, and just at the point when the demand for bars of soap, bleach and artificial fertilizers was on the increase, he went bankrupt, and shortly afterwards committed suicide in his own soap-boiling house where the great vats of fat were boiled up with the salt and the alkali.

Hodgson was a north Yorkshireman who arrived in Walton in

1815. By 1818 he had obtained a licence for a small soapworks, and he must have done quite well since by 1836 he had taken on one of his young workers as a business partner and also as his unofficial adopted son. This was Edward Thornhill Simpson—the Thornhill was added in deference to his senior partner, and Waterton sometimes mocked his assumed middle name by referring to him as Edward Vitriol Simpson; but that was later, once the legal battle was under way and the mutual hatred well established.

The firm of Hodgson and Simpson grew in size and ambition, and in 1839 they acquired for themselves a new site: a triangle of land which had somehow become separated from one of Waterton's meadows. Waterton had tried to buy this little acre on several occasions, but when the sale was being arranged he was not consulted or informed. He resented the intrusion of another 'hideous long chimney' so close to his estate, but he had no initial fear of the factory since he got on quite well with old Hodgson, who had 'solemnly promised' that he would never produce his own acids. Then in 1840 the works were expanded, a second chimney was erected, and shortly afterwards a furnace was built for the decomposition of salted cake and the manufacture of sulphuric acid. For some reason, in the middle of all this apparent commercial optimism, Hodgson went bankrupt and killed himself, Simpson promptly acquired his ex-partner's share, and the soap business began to flourish. Simpson balanced the speedy rise of his fortunes with a rise up the ladder of respectability and over the following years he became an important member of the local community, a town councillor, and a leading partner in the Wakefield and Barnsley Union Bank. He built himself a new chimney 286 feet high, he acquired several elegant houses and sent his sons to the best schools. Already in the 1840s his annual turnover was said to be upward of £60,000 a year, and by the time of his death in the 1870s his effects alone were valued at more than £250,000.

In trying to tell the story of the battle between Waterton and Simpson, the most difficult element to describe is the bitterness it released. Behind each of the two men there was an army of friends and lawyers, advisers and sympathizers, who hurled abuse at each other. On a wider circle there were the angry and contradictory opinions which were regularly published in the newspapers and magazines of the day for as long as the legal proceedings lasted. Officially the battle was brought to a close in 1852, but it went on smouldering like a half-stifled fire long after the death of the two main protagonists.

Waterton took Simpson to court in the spring of 1847. He and his neighbour Sir William Pilkington decided to work together in proving

7 Waterton counted the American naturalist George Ord as one of his closest friends although they only met briefly on three occasions.

8 Norman Moore was still in his teens when he became a friend of Waterton and was with him when he died.

9 The celebrated illustrator and naturalist J. J. Audubon was said to combine the 'traits of a French courtier and an American salesman'.

10 In 1839 a soapworks was set up on the edge of Walton Hall Park. It released chemicals which severely damaged the environment. Waterton fought the manufacturer in the law courts and eventually the factory was forced to move to a site at Thornes, near Wakefield, where this photograph was taken in the 1870s.

11 A view of the old gateway seen from the island. The crescent of yew trees offered protection 'little inferior to that of the house itself'. The starling tower with its sixty nesting holes was designed so that an observer could watch the occupants without disturbing them.

the damage that was being done to their land by 'those mischievious bastions which are incessantly pouring forth torrents of destruction'. Confident that 'alkali works are universally acknowledged to be destructive', they began their case in a mood of angry elation. Simpson was seen as an insignificant petty businessman, who had taken too many liberties in the name of free enterprise, and who must now be put in his place. They presumed that as local landowners and members of the upper classes they had immense power, 'We are prosecuting the fellow, and we shall thrash him soundly' was how Waterton described his intentions.

It would be interesting to know whether at this stage Waterton was fully aware of the case of Sir John Gerard, a very wealthy landowner from Lancashire, who had been trying to 'thrash' one of the young kings of industry since 1839, and who went on with his battle until his death some twenty years later. There was no doubt that Sir John's estate was being slowly and inexorably destroyed by the acid vapours emitted from a cluster of local factories. Many times he proved his case before judges, juries and arbitrators, and many times he was awarded damages for the loss of his trees and the pollution of his water and his air. But the point was that the trees went on dying and, although the manufacturer paid his fines, he did not go away; he was doing very well indeed, and if need be he could afford to pay for several more estates equally grand and gracious as the one owned by Sir John Gerard. This was the harsh lesson that was having to be learnt by a number of people: a new sort of money was being made, and everything could be found to have its price, even the air they breathed, the land they owned and the good health that they wished to enjoy.

In 1845 the garden was in such a condition that I never saw anything like it . . . we had arbitration over it at that time, and Mr Gamble who was living at that period said I ought to be very thankful . . . I said that damages would not repay me, because I wanted something to gratify the eye, and I did not look upon it as a money question; there is now not a tree alive on the place, except where sheltered from the works; I had intended to live and die there, and I should have lived there all my life, but for the injury to the place from the works.[6]

However one looks at it, by the year 1847 Simpson, his lawyers, his land surveyors, his scientists and his learned professors all knew, and they must have known without any doubt, that a factory such as the one on the edge of the Walton Hall estate was responsible for the dead hedgerows, the trees with bare antlered branches and the sick animals. When the air stank, and 'labouring men and others swore that sometimes, especially in damp heavy weather, the stench from the works was so offensive as to make them sick'[7] they knew from where the stench was emanating. When a drainage cover was lifted to reveal the 'foetid matter' that was making its way towards Waterton's lake, they knew what it was composed of, and where it had come from. When work went on all through the night they knew the power of the stuff that was belching out of the mouths of the tall chimneys. But Simpson also knew that on his own account, and for the sake of the industry, he had to fight the battle inch by inch, and those who worked for him knew that they must back him up, and had the added encouragement of knowing that when they stood in the witness box they would be paid substantial sums of money to strengthen their determination.

In the series of law suits that followed, the differences in the attitudes of the two sides were clearly stated. Waterton, and those who supported him, adopted a tragic stance in which they mourned for the loss of whole stretches of countryside and for the other fearful changes that the machine age was bringing about,

... the importance [of this subject] cannot be overrated when it is recollected that every estate in this country may be ruined by the chimneys of chemical works.[8]

... the neighbourhood of Wakefield was chosen for the scene of devastation among gardens, fair meadows and richly wooded property ... ancient trees, inestimable for their beauty and historical associations, as well as valuable for their timber, were scorched, dried up and killed ... Of course the perpetrator of all this mischief found witnesses who swore that there was nothing in the appearance of the damaged trees beyond what might be ascribed to 'natural causes'.[9]

Here all nuisances are tolerated or even encouraged on the score of giving employment to the poor, who now swarm through the manufacturing districts like lice formerly did in Egypt.[10]

... Simpson's operatives are the very personification of death alive. There is not a single cherry-cheeked fresh or healthy looking man among them. They are all 'mere shreds and ends of men'.[11]

For their part, Simpson and his supporters wasted little effort in evocative speech making, and relatively little effort in trying to prove that the works did no damage. Instead they concentrated on undermining the credibility of the plaintiff, and in working to swing the innate power of public opinion over to their side. Two local farmers who were trying to prove that damage had been caused to their land and their cattle at the same time as Waterton's first case were accused of being motivated by 'bad feelings and a desire to oppress', rather than from any wish to see justice done. A selection of witnesses who could prove that the water was pure were called in, and as an added precaution Simpson's solicitor managed to obtain a jury list: 'I have got notice of the special juries and their names, if you can run over tomorrow I would go over the names with you, and see who we ought to strike out and who retain . . . I shall have plans ready in a day or two.'[12] The farmers lost their case and had to pay a fine of £700 or face going to jail.

Waterton, the author of the *Wanderings*, a man unnaturally fond of the bat, the jackdaw and the owl, as well as old and hollow trees, was ridiculed as a false romantic and a teller of tall stories.

> Mr Waterton, a lover of natural objects, allows trees to stand which on all other estates would have been taken down half a century ago; he sees these, and the tall chimneys, and he imagines the one produces the other, as the Goodwin sands were affirmed to be caused by the Tenterden steeple.[13]

> That Mr Waterton is a bold man there can be no doubt, if all he has written about himself be true . . .
> Mr Waterton should adhere to the truth. If [the story he told] about Widow Lumb, Mr Simpson, Mr Waterton and myself, be a fair sample of his productions, the opinion I formed whilst reading the *Wanderings* is confirmed, *for it is not true*.[14]

When, in the summer of 1848, Simpson and his party had reason to expect that they would win the next case, Waterton described to Eliza how they '. . . were so sure of triumph that they talked of a procession to Wakefield; louder in their abuse of me and Sir William—louder and more inveterate, I am told, than at any other period.'[15] In the following year this abuse took on a further dimension. The porter's lodge on the edge of the estate was fired at, a neighbouring farmer had his foal shot in the shoulder, and 'I myself have had the most revolting and indecent message sent to me: so indecent that it must not appear in print. One

Daniel Wilson sent this message to me by my gardener. Twice did someone attempt to set my hay rick on fire . . .'[16]

The case first came up at the York Assizes in the winter of 1847. In spite of Waterton's initial confidence in being able to 'smash our antagonist to atoms', there is in everything he wrote at that time a sense of foreboding and unease. The winter was extremely cold and cruel, with black frosts and fogs and no berries on the holly trees. The potato crops had been ravaged by disease, there were outbreaks of cholera in the cities, and industrial growth was producing industrial poverty and despair:

> Long chimneys and railroads are now beginning to produce their anticipated mischief. Last Monday I met thirty men on the highway. They looked like skeletons risen from the grave. They told me that they had come from beyond Huddersfield, to see if they could beg for bread, for there was none to be got in their own country, where trade was sunk to nothing, and where mills (oh those curses of a community!) were stopping in all directions.[17]

The failure of the potato harvest in 1846 was followed by a failure of the bean harvest in the following summer, with the surreal image of fields in full bloom suddenly enveloped by a plague of blackfly.

> Nothing could surpass the beautiful blossoms of all the bean fields in the neighbourhood, when all of a sudden myriads of little black insects attached themselves to the stalks and leaves. All the beans have fallen under this tremendous and unforeseen attack, and the farmers in all directions are mowing down the dead and black stalks, and carting them off into the fold to make manure of them.[18]

Around the end of 1847 the case was given its first hearing, but instead of reaching a verdict the judge referred it to arbitration, 'a very slow, tedious and expensive mode of terminating disputes'. Waterton had to wait another year before the matter was settled. By an odd coincidence a bundle of seventeen letters from Waterton to his solicitor, Mr Robert Pashley, was handed over to Stonyhurst College tied up with a blue ribbon; another smaller batch of letters and papers, addressed to Simpson by his lawyer John Middleton, was rescued from an old trunk in the stable buildings of Walton Hall. And so, in a rather lopsided manner, it is possible to follow some aspects of this long and painful struggle.

Waterton worked as hard as he knew how in preparing his evidence.

He sent off to a Mr Brett of Liverpool, ordering some more samples of a recent invention:

> I think they call it 'Litmus' (but I never studied divinity, being a poor and ignorant man in everything but birds) . . . I tried the last piece of your blue paper and the water changed to red instantly.
>
> It is my intention to test the water, down by the covered slough, twice every week, until the arbitrator shall graciously condescend to close our far too long delayed and most expensive case. In the meantime our trees are suffering dismally.[19]

In July 1848, a month before the arbitrator was due to consider the evidence, he prepared a detailed report, in which under headed sections he described 'The Smoke', 'The Vegetation' and 'The State of the Brook', as well as explaining the history of the soapworks, and his opinion of the value of Simpson's scientific evidence and the unscrupulous way that he had behaved up until now. He concluded, still hopeful and still trusting in the natural supremacy of justice and good sense, '. . . we feel ourselves authorised to request that the Arbitrator will put a stop to the evils so justly complained of, by bringing the affair to a final close at the approaching sitting.'[20]

Simpson on his part produced no fewer than eighty witnesses: local men who 'swore that they could neither see the smoke nor smell it', and learned men like Professor Johnson, author of a book called *The Economy of the Coal Field*, who sought to prove scientifically that the acid and sulphur in the brook were natural deposits which had nothing to do with Simpson's effluents. 'Insects, old age, wet tenacious soil, high winds, frosts, bad land, recent transplantations were, we understand, assigned by the defendant's witnesses as causes sufficient to explain the appearance of the Walton vegetation,' said an article in the *Gardener's Chronicle* of August 1848.

The arbitrator, 'a Leeds lawyer who can thrive in smoke', pondered the matter until October when he found Simpson guilty of negligence and awarded Waterton the sum of £1,100 as compensation; but at the same time he ordered Waterton to pay a share of the legal costs of the case which pretty well discounted his award. Simpson's punishment was a stern warning that he must always be as careful as possible with his safety precautions.

Within four months Waterton and his solicitor were preparing for a second case. In February he wrote to Pashley, 'Simpson goes on worse than ever . . . I have written to warn him of another prosecution. In his whining and methodistical answer he declares that his works are not, and never have been a nuisance . . . We must beat him again and give him no breathing time.'[21] More land surveyors were called in to assess the extent of the latest damage. Notes were made about the diminishing value of the crops, including a field of hay that was declared unfit for cattle, and which was finally sold to an iron foundry to be used for packing iron castings. Basically the evidence was unchanged, except that another year had passed and more trees had died and more birds, animals and fish had been affected. It was a question of weighing up the credibility of one man's word against another's; and it was a question of money.

Simpson called in eighty-nine witnesses. The manager of the vitriol works (the one who had sent the indecent message), the manager of the sulphur works and several scientists were each paid more than £70 for their trouble, and this at a time when a working man could expect to receive £1 a week in wages. Land agents, chemists and others were also paid very substantial sums; the tavern bill for meetings with witnesses came to £70. 12s. 4d., and it would appear that a number of local people were receiving small but regular sums of money to make up for any inconvenience caused by the works. Simpson's solicitor sent in the balance of costs in August 1848 which stood at over £2,000. Along with his detailed accounts, the solicitor also sent Simpson several rather ominous letters, such as the one in which he warns that a government inspector was due to come and visit the premises: 'You will be so good as to keep the works in such order as they were in when Mr Hall was over before. I merely mention this as he was much pleased with the clean appearance they had before, but Mr Nettleton thought proper to say that it were [sic] not always so, and that the premises were put in order knowing that Mr Hall was coming.'[22]

In August the second case was given a hearing, and on this occasion Waterton was given no financial redress, while Simpson was encouraged to maintain his high standards of safety. So, in October of that same year, Waterton began his third action. With a newly acquired practical cynicism, he adopted a different approach to the problem. He had learnt that Simpson was anxious to obtain a larger stretch of land, so that he could expand his business still further and, realizing that he could neither thrash nor smash his enemy, he decided to try to lure him away from the immediate vicinity of Walton Hall. Eliza was the owner of an abandoned dye works on the River Calder—quite why this property was in her name is not at all clear, it seems an odd investment, and might have been bought secretly to be used as bait for Simpson. Be that as it may, Simpson was informed that if he were to sell his one acre and close down the Walton Soap Works, then he could become the owner of a 'prime site, supplied with power and an abundance of excellent water'. It was offered to him for the very modest sum of £5,000 which included not only the industrial complex, but also a nearby 'residence fit for a nobleman'. Finally a light could be seen at the end of a long tunnel, and Waterton's solicitor turned poetic in his enthusiasm.

There was a final court hearing, but now with the means of resolving the problem, the arbitrator saw reason at last: Simpson was ordered to move, and had to pay for this round of legal costs. The two solicitors then came to an understanding on behalf of their two clients, and in April 1850 an agreement was drawn up and signed. Simpson officially denied that he had ever caused a nuisance, and Waterton officially asserted that such a nuisance had been caused. Simpson agreed to close down his works in a very leisurely manner, and swore that by April 1853, he would have taken away the vats, the steam engines, the furnaces and the tall chimneys. Waterton signed a declaration promising that he and his heirs would 'refrain from the manufacture of soap at Walton'.

In the same month, when the last of Simpson's machinery was being removed or moved on and one of the broken chimneys was sold at auction for £8, Waterton learnt that his trusted solicitor Robert Pashley had taken on another soapworks battle, but that this time he was going to represent the cause of the manufacturer. Waterton was surprised, but he did not apparently feel that this was a betrayal of a cause, it was simply the way of the world.

> Knowing, as I do, your unrivalled prowess in attacking long chimneys, I am quite at a loss to conceive how you will manage to defend those of the notorious Muspratt. However, as Sancho Panza says, 'There is a remedy for everything but death'—and thus I conclude that as lawyers' consciences are said to take wide ranges, you will find dry fustballs enough to enable you to throw a good handfull of their dust in the eyes of your opponents . . .
>
> Believe me, my dear sir, ever most sincerely yours,
> Charles Waterton.[23]

CHAPTER XVI

Father and Son

Waterton never let go of the vividness of his own childhood. He clung to the boy he had once been with a tenacity which grew fiercer as he grew older: climbing the same trees he had always climbed; playing truant to hide from unwelcome visitors; demonstrating how he could stand on his head, and how he could jump over the table in one brave leap. Sometimes the imagination is confronted by a person whose charm and strange innocence pushes all other impressions to one side; but there can be a fleeting and almost sinister image of an old man capering wildly on the edge of his own grave.

And if it was true that Waterton was fixated upon himself as a child, then where did that place his own son Edmund? Was he ever allowed to enter the charmed landscape which his father inhabited, or was the door always kept closed to him? And if his father concentrated so much energy on playing, then what was Edmund supposed to do to fill the hours of the days?

There is no way of knowing how Waterton treated his son when the boy was still young, simply because nobody bothered to do more than mention him in passing. For the first eleven years of his life the 'poor dear child' went everywhere with his aunts and his father. The nuns of Bruges asked after his health, the Jesuits of Rome called him 'the English angel' and instructed him in the Catholic faith. George Ord, who was supposed to detest all children, spent a contented summer at Walton Hall in 1835, and never forgot how the two of them gorged themselves on cherries. Everyone declared themselves very satisfied with his obedience, his piety and his golden curls. There is no indication that he ever defied his elders, or ran away, or made a joke. While his father bobbed up and down in an attempt to communicate with an eagle owl, or sang a little song as he pottered along the dusty roads of Italy in his bare feet, Edmund was silent and solemn, and must often have been filled with acute embarrassment at the spectacle of his aged and unconcerned parent.

But no matter how good Edmund aspired to be, and how pleased everyone was with the way he behaved, there were always a number of submerged facts floating around him that he must have found confusing. There was the far-distant figure of the naked Arawak Indian woman, Princess Minda, who had been his great-grandmother; the Scottish Presbyterian woodcutter in the rain forests of Guiana who had been his grandfather; and the very young convent girl who had given birth to him and had died in the process. And always to remind him of this side of his dislocated family history, there was the constant hovering presence of his two dark and maidenly aunts. On the other side there were the Watertons, with their powerful lineage spanning the centuries and culminating in the present Lord of Walton Hall, who dressed like a poor farm labourer and was apparently immune to the demands of his position in the social hierarchy.

At the age of eleven, immediately after the little family had made its hurried retreat from Rome, Edmund was sent to Stonyhurst College. Waterton was still suffering from the dysentery and fever which had set in after they were shipwrecked near Elba, but he was determined that he must go with his son on this important journey: 'The time had now arrived when duty called upon me to place my poor boy under another tuition; and sick as I was, I determined to accompany him to the place selected for his education.'[1]

He provided Edmund with the first volume of the *Essays on Natural History*, along with a copy of the *Wanderings*, and a letter of paternal advice, or 'short instructions' as he called it, written on the first blank pages. Edmund is told always to rise early, to take part with enthusiasm in outdoor sports, to avoid forbidden books, to shun 'particular friendships', and above all else to love and obey his teachers, 'you will find a father at every step in the good Jesuits'. If he follows these instructions carefully then life, according to Waterton, should not present any real problems.

With an odd need to make such a private document into public property, Waterton included the text of this letter as part of the autobiographical essay which preceded the second volume of his *Essays* published in 1844, when Edmund was fourteen, and had been at his school for three years: 'Perhaps the reader will not refuse to cast his eye over this. I have nothing else to show him how much I love my darling boy, and how deep an interest I take in his future welfare.'[2]

Edmund remained at Stonyhurst until he had turned twenty. The little angel with the golden curls became a dark-haired giant, who was called Tom Slaughter or Long Tom by his friends, and was said to 'much resemble an ape'. His closest friend was a fellow pupil called Percy Hetherington Fitzgerald, who later wrote two books about his schooldays (and a further thirty books on a variety of other subjects) in which Edmund makes frequent appearances. Fitzgerald was intrigued by Edmund's combination of confidence and unease, and by his many 'strange antics' such as the way he would pick a quarrel merely for the sake of making it up afterwards, or 'would take you aside mysteriously, catching you by the button, and tell you some surprising circumstance about his best and bosom friend with whom he had been walking only five minutes before'. He never looked anyone in the face when he was talking to them, and his eyes would wander up and down from the boots to the collar, pausing to stare at a button or a pocket, and then continuing in their restless search. 'It gave a most disagreeable feeling.'[3]

Edmund was good at outdoor sports, but showed no particular interest in academic studies, although seemingly without effort he was often first in his class. Like an old man counting and recounting a string of worry beads, he had evolved his own system for keeping his thoughts at bay. He was an obsessive collector of objects:

> The interior of his desk was a strange knick-knackery of beads, little altar crosses and piles of old rare religious books ... His favourite occupation was making chain work for beads with silver wire, and nothing could be more finished than his workmanship. He was always busy with some fad or hobby, and had really good taste in matters of art. One of his feats was filling an entire prayer book with his own exquisite handwriting ... He devoted some hours of the day in making a new translation of the *Imitation of Christ*, and designing for it a tasteful and elaborate marginal illustration.[4]

Apparently Edmund was extremely popular both among the other boys and with the masters. Fitzgerald gives a rather vague account of the qualities which were so attractive and which included 'an excellent heart, free and easy ways, a great good nature and a public spirit'. He was fond of playing elaborate tricks on people, but 'because he was held in such high esteem by the authorities' he was never suspected.

There was a darker side to him as well and already in his earliest letters there are indications of the way that his mood would sometimes swing from a listless boredom into what he later called his 'old enemy, hysteria'. Throughout his life he had an obstinate stammer, although according to Fitzgerald this was 'no hindrance to his progress', he was also spasmodically a compulsive eater and was sometimes immensely fat.

Throughout his life Waterton maintained a regular contact with Stonyhurst. So long as he was in England he went to the Christmas festivities, and often took a comic part in the school plays. He was perfectly at home, and everyone joined in 'doing him honour', but in spite of his years he persisted in being 'at school', eating with the other boys and avoiding the company of too many adults. The fact of his son being there did little to change his habits, but there are occasional glimpses of his growing irritation with this rival presence. He sends Eliza greetings 'from your enormous nephew', who is apparently too busy with antiquarian matters to find the time to write to her himself. In one particularly vivid account he tells Eliza, 'Edmund is all laugh and activity; and to see the way he stretches his huge limbs across these long corridors, you would fancy him lord of the whole establishment.'[5]

From 1841 until he finished his schooling in 1850, Edmund would come home only occasionally. When his education was complete he set off at once for Rome, and a combination of his own qualities and his father's strong Jesuit connections gave him access to the top hierarchy of the Papacy. In 1851 he helped with a papal inquiry into attitudes in England towards the Immaculate Conception of the Virgin, and following this he became a member of Pope Pius XI's immediate entourage which culminated in 1857 with his appointment as the Pope's Privy Chamberlain. His services continued spasmodically up until the time of his father's death, but it was not a profession, and he had to cover his considerable costs from his own pocket.

In 1854 Edmund was temporarily staying at Walton Hall. His father had recently made over to him certain aspects of the management of the family estate, and he had come to learn what his new duties entailed. Waterton and his two aunts were away when a letter arrived from George Ord which he decided to answer himself. It is the only occasion on which Edmund can be heard making an assessment of his own character and explaining his ambitions. Typically the letter opens with an apology for having let 'day after day slip without replying', and it ends with an apology for the 'rather unconnected' information that he provides.

You will be sorry to hear that I have not much taste for Natural History. My natural inclinations lead me to the study of Archaeology, in which I take great pleasure and interest. I have for some years been a fellow of the Society of Archaeologists which ranks second only to the Royal. I have derived much advantage from the opportunity of meeting with the principal savants of the day.

When I say I have no taste for Natural History, I would not have you understand that I dislike it. On the contrary I only regret that I cannot take the same interest in it that my father does, I can, however, sufficiently appreciate his invaluable collection of birds.

My father has now given over to me the management of the estate. This gives me much pleasure, amusement and exercise. I am anxious to settle down quietly and lead the life of an English squire. I am now fitting up my room as a library. Since I left Stonyhurst some 4 years ago I have collected nearly 1,000 volumes of useful and interesting books . . . and I have also got several objects of antiquity, and some carved ivories which I am going to expose in my room. I am fond of shooting, but have not much fancy for hunting although it is one of our national sports.[6]

Waterton for his part rarely mentioned his son to Ord, or to anyone else, but in letters to Eliza and to Edmund himself, his feelings often erupted in brief, dismissive comments. Only on one occasion did he indicate how much he was disappointed in Edmund's lack of interest in natural history which was in a letter he wrote to him in 1863 to congratulate him on the birth of his first child, Charlie: 'Would that one could know beforehand if he is to have a touch of the field naturalist in him. He will soon begin to show whether birds or boudoirs are most to his taste. "Just as the twig is bent, so is the branch inclined." '[7]

It would seem that in 1854 Edmund first began to fully establish his own territory at Walton Hall, with his father gazing incredulously at the way that the branch was inclined. Perhaps it is possible to begin to understand the full extent of the antagonism in the relationship between the father and the son by looking at the private apartments that each made for himself.

Ever since the tragic circumstances of Edmund's birth, Waterton had chosen to sleep upstairs in the attic. Throughout the year the window was kept open so that he could see the stars and listen to the birds, and the owls could fly above his head if they wished to. Maybe bats also came to hunt around him in the darkness, just as they had done long ago in the deserted house on Mibiri Creek.

With the roof open to the rafters and the window open at night, the room was often bitterly cold. During the winter the water in the little wash basin would freeze into a solid block of ice, and yet even in his eighty-third year when he was 'labouring under a cold more severe than my pen can describe', a cold that no amount of purging or blood-letting would shift, Waterton persisted in sleeping on the bare wooden floor, wrapped up in his Italian cloak, having 'long learned that a bed is an absolutely useless luxury'. The cloak became thin and threadbare, and the block of mahogany on which he placed his head was polished and worn. On his travels he always took his cloak with him, but he was able to leave the wooden pillow behind, since he had found that his portmanteau served the purpose just as well.

When the cloak was not in use it was thrown over a rope stretched from one side of the room to the other. This rope also served as a wardrobe, and carried a limited assortment of clothes, 'coarse, thick, sailor-looking dress, only changed for the very best company', and an old apron with a big front pocket. The room also contained a plain kitchen table, a high, old-fashioned chest of drawers, a cupboard and three kitchen chairs. On one of these chairs was placed 'a cracked red pan, glazed white inside, and a square of yellow soap which seemed to live in a broken white earthenware saucer lay beside it. A hard, rough Jack-towel, hung from a roller behind the door.'[8] On the wall there were a few old engravings, and a large map of South America, with the intricate pattern of the wanderings marked out in red ink. A selection of books occupied one shelf, and on the other there was 'an assortment of bottles, oil, varnish, spirits etc ... and little jars containing pigments, pins, nails, beeswax and pieces of cork'.[9]

Only here in this bare little room that was both a monk's cell and a schoolboy's secret den, did Waterton feel truly at home in his own house: 'Here I play and here I work, for work and play are with me convertible, and my best recreation is my work.'[10]

Although several visitors described Waterton's attic, only one felt it relevant to describe also the part of the house occupied by Edmund. This was a lady called Julia Pitte-Byrne, a successful journalist who wrote several books based on her studies of social injustice and one book based on her encounters with people; a compendium of recollections which was given the daunting title of *Social Hours with Celebrities*. Her description of Waterton and his son was based on the occasion when she went to stay at Walton Hall for several weeks in 1861, but it can be presumed that although Edmund's apartments might have grown larger and more cluttered over the years, his 'boudoir' style was established when he was first setting his rooms in order in 1854.

While Waterton rolled himself up into a bundle on the bare floor, Edmund trod across thick carpets, 'in which the feet were embedded'. While Waterton sat perched on the edge of a hard chair, Edmund reclined like an oriental princeling among draperies and cushions, pillows and *portières*, all of the richest, the softest, the most costly material. The walls were heavy with hangings, tapestries and gilded mirrors. The bedroom was lined with medieval panelling, and an ornate Elizabethan fireplace had been specially fitted. In one of the drawing rooms the chimneypiece was dominated by a life-size portrait of himself, dressed in what he described as the 'becoming costume' of the Italian papal order of the Cameriere Segreto. In the adjacent drawing room he appeared in another portrait, equally large and flamboyant, in full Highland dress, presumably as an allusion to the Scottish side of his mother's disjointed ancestry.

Waterton was always up before the dawn and, unless the weather was too bad, he was out in the park with the first light, busying himself with his trees, his birds and his animals. If it was very cold then he would light a fire in a clearing, so that he could stand before it and take the numbness from his hands. The rain never bothered him and he would come in dripping like a dog, and then sit on a stool in front of the drawing room fire, 'almost lost in the cloud of steam drawn from his wet clothes by the heat'.

Edmund tended to sleep late, and his day began with a slow and elaborate toilet. He dressed with extreme elegance and correctness; he was fond of wearing silks and satins and he loved jewellery, especially rings, which he bought 'compulsively and entirely reckless of cost'. He drank a lot of wine, he was an inveterate smoker of pipes and cigars, he gambled, and he was able to get rid of money at remarkable speed.

Somehow one has to try to imagine these two unlikely men meeting each other at various times of the day. They must have sat together at the punctual mealtimes in the dining room, with Eliza in her place at the head of the table and her African parrot sitting near her in its brass cage and shouting 'Oh Polly!' at random intervals. The windows were always open for the sake of the necessary current of fresh air, and a fire would be roaring in the hearth even in the summer. At mealtimes Waterton's huge cat Whity would leave the cat room where a fire was also kept burning throughout the year and where the feline population of Walton Hall had all learnt to drink milk by dipping their paws into a jug, and it would come and sit on its master's lap to be fed with cream and sugar. Waterton himself took a piece of toast and a cup of hot water with a thimbleful of tea for breakfast, bread and watercress for lunch, and often stood with his back to the fire telling stories while everyone else was busy with the 'hot, much roasted fare' that was served at supper. At the best of times he ate enough, according to the keeper at the Regent's Park Zoo, to 'sustain a blackbird and two white mice'. During Lent he did what he called 'putting a padlock on my grinders' which meant that he survived for seven uninterrupted weeks on nothing but black tea and dry bread. This regime delighted him. As he explained in a letter of 1856 to George Ord, 'My bowels are in the most perfect state, my brain so clear and free from all confusion that I scarcely know it exists on my shoulders; and my frame becomes so elastic that I can knock off twelve to fourteen miles without feeling weary, and climb a tree as if I were twenty years old.'[11] His weight would then drop from more than ten stone to a little over nine stone, which was not a great deal for a man six foot tall, with 'enormous and beautifully formed legs'. This must be contrasted with Edmund who suffered from gout and digestive troubles from an early age, and who once wrote proudly to the family solicitor telling him that he had lost forty-one pounds in weight in the short span of a few months.

On several occasions Percy Hetherington Fitzgerald came to stay at Walton Hall, and he also wrote his impressions of the place and its occupants. Although he was Edmund's guest, he was obviously fascinated by Waterton himself. 'I have him completely before me now, with his shrivelled head and wizened mouth, and his blue coat and brass buttons and grey hair. He would deal out droll observations and curt sayings from a distance, in a sort of country tone as if he was munching walnuts.'[12] His descriptions are interesting for the way in which he tries to understand his own feelings towards Waterton whom he found ridiculous and yet immensely dignified, 'I have a wonderful admiration for this curious man, and a reverence too; he is truly one with "man-stuff" in him, and his high principle is shown in the most trifling act.'[13]

Edmund was not able to view his father with such a dispassionate eye. Perhaps he admired him for a variety of reasons, but the man also distressed him and filled him with embarrassment, especially whenever he chose to make a public spectacle of himself. Mrs Pitte-Byrne explained, 'a marked annoyance for him was his father's indifference to dress and appearance. Nothing irritated him more than to witness the *naif* amusement of the old man when mistaken for a son of the soil.'[14]

This was a reference to Waterton's particular pleasure at being addressed as a farm labourer or a tramp, especially if the stranger wanted to ask prying questions about the eccentric Wanderer. 'He's as queer as my hatband. He's not on show exactly, but ye might catch a sight of him somewhere's about. Perhaps ye'd better go round to the front door and perhaps the butler might help ye.'[15] If he was offered a small coin of money for his advice then he would tip his cap and bow his wizened head and mutter a 'thank ee kindly zur'. On several occasions he went visiting his grand friends and was firmly taken to the servants' quarters and told to wait while it was decided what should be done with him.

Even Waterton's numerous and often near-fatal accidents had an edge of theatricality to them which Edmund obviously found disconcerting and irritating. He was standing on the topmost rung of a high ladder and pruning a pear tree when the ladder 'swerved in a lateral direction' and the two of them crashed to the ground together. Waterton declared himself very pleased with the way that he bounced when he landed—he had been on a fast, and his body was, as it were, quite hollow—but nevertheless he suffered partial concussion of the brain, his whole side from foot to shoulder felt as though it had been 'pounded in a mill' and his arm was broken in several places. There was only one remedy to be considered:

> In the course of the afternoon I took blood from my arm to the amount of thirty ounces, and followed the affair up the next day with a strong aperient. I believe that, with these necessary precautions all would have gone right again (saving the arm), had not a second misfortune followed on the heels of the first; and it was of so alarming a nature as to induce me to take thirty ounces more of blood by the lancet.[16]

This other misfortune occurred when he sat down just as a servant was moving his chair back, and he fell so heavily to the floor that he suffered a second partial concussion of the brain. The doctor was summoned and added leeches and blisters to Waterton's own methods, but the arm caused him such pain that he could hardly sleep at night, and when he did it was only to have vivid nightmares.

> I was eternally fighting wild beasts, with a club in one hand, the other being bound up at my breast. Nine bull-dogs one night attacked me on the highroad, some of them having the head of a crocodile. I had now serious thoughts of having the arm amputated.[17]

Luckily help came in the form of a very old man called Joseph Crowther, a bone-setter, the last in a line of bone-setters who, by means of '. . . potent embrocations, stretching, pulling, twisting, and jerking, forced the shoulder and the wrist to obey him, and to perform their healthy movements'.[18] He then moved on to the elbow, which he cured by 'smashing to atoms' the callus which had formed on the joint. Eliza, seeing what was about to happen, felt her spirits sinking and retired to her room, just as she did ten years later when Waterton really was dying.

Even in his description of the 'unmitigating severity' of the bone-setter's work, Waterton maintained his curiosity, as if he enjoyed experimenting with the furthest limits of pain which his body could be made to endure. As well as showing his visitors how he could scratch the back of his head with his toe, he would also roll up his sleeves and expose his arms which were pitted with scars caused by searching for a vein with the lancet. For him the fainting, the fasting, the pain and the deliriums were all a means of learning more about death and acquiescence and his own particular religious faith.

Edmund, for his part, looked on with dismay. Illness and pain filled him with panic, and panic could easily be overrun by hysteria. Yet, poor man, when he was in his late thirties his health was already failing, and hypochondria was being replaced by real symptoms. Towards the end of his life his doctor wrote to a family friend, 'Make as light of Mr Waterton's illness to him as you can. He is very much alarmed by himself, and I have heard his late wife saying that whenever anything was the matter he got so alarmed that it was best to make light of it.'[19] In Edmund's last letter, written only a few days before he died in 1887, he was suddenly wondering whether his father's drastic remedies might indeed help him; but he had no lancet, and no little pills of jalap and calomel.

CHAPTER XVII

A Way of Life

Waterton is long since dead. His house is a modern hotel which caters especially for groups of travelling businessmen. His park wall survives only in a few derelict and broken sections, which no longer keep anything in or anything out. There have been speedboats on the lake, and the sandmartins' wall with its fifty-six nesting holes has been broken up and used as ballast in the construction of a squash court. There is no trace of the holly and yew trees which were planted in wide crescents, in rings and in clumps to give shelter to the birds. The gently undulating valley, that was once thick with ancient trees, is now mostly stripped to its bones and used as grazing land and grain fields divided by short and tightly-clipped hedges. One old man, who until recently lived in the stable cottage near where the sandmartins' wall had stood, said that 15,000 trees had been cut down during the last few years. Another old man, a house-painter by trade, remembered that as a child he had seen tropical birds flying around the park, birds of paradise and such like, unmistakable because of their brilliant metallic plumage and the long sweep of their tails. He was sure that they had learnt to adapt themselves to the alien weather and the long chimneys, and had gone on breeding, in spite of the death of their benefactor. But it was true that he had only seen them when he was a child, even though he had often searched for them later.

Much has been lost, but all memory of the park as it once was has not been annihilated. Waterton's grave is there by the water's edge, with a stone cross and a rusting metal fence around it, although the two huge oak trees which once guarded it closely, one on either side, have disappeared. In the patches of unkempt woods that still remain, it is possible to come across the hollow stump of a tree that has been carefully roofed over to provide a nesting site for an owl, or a little chamber cut into the flank of a wall, or the remains of a nesting box.

Waterton used to place cut-out wooden silhouettes of roosting pheasants in the trees that stood at the border of his territory to waste the shot of any poachers who might be prowling around the wall, and some of these dark and weather-stained shapes are still clinging to their perches over a hundred years later. Given a space of time and quiet the birds and the animals would undoubtedly try to return to their old home; living things prefer not to die, and will fight hard to ensure that a new generation is allowed to succeed them, binding the links of a chain which stretches out towards an uncertain future.

What Waterton did with his park was simply to make it secure. He enclosed a stretch of land that was no bigger than five of today's modern fields of wheat, and within that contained area he worked at providing numerous and varied sites where birds and animals could build their nests and raise their young in safety. But still it is hard with the mind's eye to understand the full extent and complexity of his achievement. There was no one to study the Walton Hall estate as a 'conservation area' set in the heart of nineteenth-century industrial England, and no one attempted to provide a thorough documentation of the quantity and variety of wild life that was sheltered behind the high walls of the park. In the 1850s, when the place was in its prime, Waterton mentioned that there was not another country house throughout the whole extent of Great Britain that could boast such a huge show of waterfowl as he had on his twenty-four acres of lake, and he was also convinced, probably quite rightly, that were it not for his efforts, several species of native birds would have been banished entirely from the West Riding of Yorkshire.

In order to try to get closer to the reality of how the place once was, to get a sense of the quite extraordinary profusion of creatures that lived in such close proximity to each other, it is necessary to gather the fragmentary and scattered comments and descriptions, the few drawings and even fewer photographs, as well as Waterton's own essays and letters, and let the words, the pictures and the occasional numerical estimates, settle into a series of images.

From contemporary drawings made of the park it is possible to see that the hedges of yew and holly were high and dense, the trees numerous, the lake wide, and the little bridge to the island on which the house was built surprisingly narrow and delicate. There are some charming sketches of the decoy silhouettes; the starling tower looking like the castle from a game of chess; the ruins of the old water gate surmounted by a cross and thick with ivy; the sandmartins' wall; the stump of a tree adapted for the especial use of owls; but everything is stiff and isolated, like diagrams of apparatus that is to be used in a scientific experiment. There were some photographs taken shortly before Waterton's death, but these have all been mislaid recently and, who knows, perhaps they were yellow and faded, holding only the ghosts of trees, the faintest reflections of water, the dim shadows of figures in a far-away world. There is one later photograph which does manage to transcend the passing of time, and which shows a man in a top hat, sitting before the squire's grave, with the huge and vaulting architecture of the two oak trees towering above him, and a dense forest behind him and stretching out along the curved shore of the lake.

All, except perhaps the last of these images, fail to capture the wildness of the Walton Hall estate; the fact that it had been turned into a sort of Western jungle, with ancient hollow trees allowed to die slowly and undisturbed, with dense bushes, trailing ivy, crumbling walls, swamps and marshes, and endless possible hiding places for birds and animals. What Waterton understood so clearly was the need for his creatures always to have access to the safety of shelter: all the vegetation he planted and fostered over the years was inspired by this need. When in 1817 he had visited the Cascini pheasant garden in Tuscany, what had impressed him there was the sight of 'our common pheasant roving through its walks with a confidence little inferior to our own domestic poultry. As the evening closed in upon us, I observed multitudes of the smaller birds resorting to the "ivy-mantled" trees, in order to enjoy the proffered convenience of nocturnal rest and safety.'[1]

By the 1850s he had ivy growing up the trunks of countless trees, sometimes with the twisted stems stretching out along the branches to a length of seven feet, so that it looked as if two trees had merged together. He had ivy festooning the trunks of trees long since dead, he had ivy over the walls and towers and as ground cover. Not only did it offer protection, it also provided berries for the birds at 'a season of the year when the ordinary food of the field is far from being plentiful'.

He planted quantities of yew and holly with the same motive. Not far from the bridge there was a high yew-tree crescent, 300 feet long, 'It has already repaid me for the pains which I have taken in its cultivation, and when I resort to my usual evening stand, in order to watch the flocks of sparrows, finches and starlings, whilst they are dropping in upon the neighbouring hollies, I feel not the wintry blast . . . the yew trees offer me a protection little inferior to that of the house itself.'[2] Most of all he respected the holly tree because it offered not only food and shelter, but also an 'impenetrable retreat' throughout the year. There was a wide circular clump of hollies where the pheasants came to be fed, and where, '. . . throughout the whole of the winter, a vast number of sparrows, green linnets, buntings, blackbirds, and some starlings resort, to take their nocturnal repose in peace and quiet.'[3]

Waterton cared for his trees as if he were a shepherd tending his flock, and his gamekeeper John Ogden once said that a single broken branch could never pass unnoticed for more than a few days. Throughout the park there were trees with hollow trunks and hollow branches that had been sealed, made weather-proof, bricked up, roofed over, and at the same time carefully adapted so that an owl, a jackdaw or some other bird would find it an ideal nesting site. For his own satisfaction Waterton ensured that there was some way that he could spy on the hidden nest and its occupants. He might have a loose brick which could be lifted out or, when dealing with much smaller birds, a pebble that could be pushed to one side to reveal a little spy hole.

The most flamboyantly successful of all these nesting sites in the park was the ruin of the old water gate, which stood on the island overlooking the lake. To make this crumbling edifice all the more sheltered and private, Waterton planted a thick crescent of yew trees around it. Here in one single year, '... seven pairs of jackdaws, twenty-four pairs of starlings, four pairs of ringdoves, the barn owl, the blackbird, the robin, the redstart, the house sparrow, the chaffinch, have their nests ... The barn owl has had two broods; and while I am writing this there are half-fledged young ones in the nest.'[4]

Behind the water gate he built a starling tower, setting it on a tall stone pedestal to make it inaccessible to Hanoverian rats. It had about sixty nesting chambers, each one set behind a loose stone which could be removed. A second starling tower was erected further from the house, and the birds rewarded Waterton by coming every day in huge noisy gatherings, and feeding on the lawn in front of the house. Although the old water gate was always especially crowded, it was not unique in the variety of species it held, and there are several references to equally cosmopolitan gatherings of birds: 'I examined the inside of a large old oak tree stump, on the hill near the hunting gate at the water's side. In it I found a jackdaw's nest containing five eggs, a barn owl's nest with young ones, and several dead mice, and a half-grown rat, and also a redstart's nest with six eggs in it.'[5]

It was not only the birds that Waterton was fostering. He paid sixpence a piece for each live hedgehog that was brought to him, and in the late afternoon little droves of about twenty of these creatures could be seen nosing about for grubs and insects. For weasels he had set up little heaps of stones or broken bricks in secluded corners which proved to be all that was required as a 'safe retreat and a pleasant dwelling'. If he wanted to watch weasels hunting or playing, he had a choice of several places where on a sunny morning he would be bound to see them. He was also, inevitably, fond of snakes:

> . . . adders are plentiful within the park wall, where I encourage and protect them. I love to see them basking on a dunghill, or catching the meridian rays of our short summer's sun, on the southern bank of a hawthorn hedge. Sometimes they will ascend into the trees to a height of twenty feet.[6]

Visitors to Walton Hall could hardly ignore the almost absurd super-abundance of wild life that was to be seen, and the disconcerting tameness of certain creatures which were supposed to be terrified by the slightest indication that a human being was near. Cormorants preened themselves in front of the dining room window; owls flew through the attic bedroom. Although it might be that Mrs Pitte-Byrne was too enthusiastic when she spoke of birds coming out of the woods to meet the old man, and flying around his head as he walked, still when he pottered amongst the trees, his pockets bulging with dried bread, grain and nuts, there was no need for them to show signs of alarm, and perhaps the more gregarious ones did fly towards him and offer some form of greeting. All the creatures in the park had grown accustomed to his presence and his watchful eye: 'If you approach the nest of any bird with gentleness and silence, and allow the owner to slip off without being flustered, you may take the eggs out of the nest, and blow upon them, and put them in your mouth if you choose, or change their original position, notwithstanding which, the bird will come back to them, and continue to sit on them as attentively as before.'[7]

It is odd to realize from the distant vantage point of this present time that the majority of Waterton's visitors considered the park and its wild inhabitants as little more than the fanciful creation of its owner. People were truly amazed by the sight of a seventy-year-old, even an eighty-year-old man, kicking off his slippers and clambering barefoot up a tall tree so that he could pay his daily visit to some precariously placed nest, but they were not especially interested in the fact that the parent bird was obviously unperturbed by such visits, or by the intimate knowledge of bird behaviour that Waterton was thus able to accumulate. Only very few were able to understand and share the quiet joy which he felt when he was watching a nestful of fledgling birds, or when, with each new year, more sandmartins, more herons, more owls and more woodpeckers chose to come and live with him.

In spite of the inevitable dryness of figures, the numbers that are available can help to give some idea of the quantity of life that was to be found in the park. In 1832 Waterton had bought himself a telescope and, with the aid of its keen eye, it was possible to count the birds that could be seen from the house. During the summer months in the 1850s and 1860s, there were between 3,000 and 5,000 waterfowl in sight. This included pochards and mergansers, teal and wigeon, wild geese and wild swan, grebes and cormorants, coots and moorhens, and many of them had learnt to be so tame that they would gather on the lawn in front of the house. There were 90 adult herons in the heronry, and 5,000 wood pigeons, 800 rooks, and 100 carrion crows, 'I turn loose on the public from my park about three score carrion crows per annum; which no doubt are considered as a dangerous lot of rascals by the good folks of the neighbourhood.'[8] There were enough owls— barn owls, tawny owls and the little owl or *civetta* which Waterton had imported from Italy—for the hooting and the screeching to be heard throughout the night, with never an interval of longer than five minutes. There was an estimated 100 windhover hawks, although this number included the fledglings who would later have moved to a new territory. There were over 100 sandmartins, which arrived in the same year that Waterton built them a special nesting wall, and in spite of the fact that because of Wakefield's tall chimneys they had avoided this part of the country for several years. There were also kingfishers, nightjars, woodpeckers and many more.

Although Waterton did all that he could to persuade the birds to breed and take shelter in the park, he could not stop them from flying over a much wider area, often paying the penalty for their lack of fear. Through opening the park to the public, through his published essays, and also presumably through talking and arguing with farmers, gamekeepers and anyone else who cared to listen, he tried to extend his protecting arm much further, but he could do little:

Five cormorants came here this day. At night they went to New-millerdam and the brute of a keeper managed to kill two of them. The remaining three returned to Walton Hall, and remained some months with me.[9]

Considering how secure and sheltered the herons are, the number of nests ought to be much larger; but in freezing weather, the birds are apt to frequent the neighbouring brooks, and there they are shot down by heartless gunmen and gamekeepers who try their utmost to exterminate from our Yorkshire Fauna this last large bird, so pleasing to the sight and so ornamental to the scenery.[10]

A flock of fifty or so Canada geese had been coming to the park every year since the 1830s, and some of them learnt to stay there throughout the seasons. In order to try to protect them, Waterton paid the local farmers an annual rent which was to cover the cost of the birds taking corn at harvest time, and grazing on the young shoots of corn during the early spring. For many years the flock was unscathed, but during the severe winter of 1855 their numbers were decimated by 'fellows prowling up and down with guns, in quest of whatever might start up in the path before them', and by April he was reduced to only two pairs.

Although he was always honoured when a bird or an animal chose to make the park into its home, and grew accustomed to his presence and showed fewer and fewer signs of fear, Waterton had no wish to turn wild creatures into tame ones. He could easily have trained a hawk, caged an owl, or studied his hedgehogs in a fenced-off area, but that would have given him no pleasure. In the early days of his South American wanderings he had tried occasionally to keep tropical birds in aviary cages, but when they did not breed and died young because of their captivity, he found it too distressing and gave up any further attempts. True there was the wild Marjay cat from Guiana which proved such a ferocious ratter; and there was once a raven called Marco, which he bought from some local people at Flamborough Head and which became 'as playful as a kitten and showed great aptitude in learning to talk', and loved to lie on its back and wriggle in snow or dry sand. But once Marco was dead, killed in a quarrel with the coachman, Waterton refused to consider taking on a replacement. In one letter, dated 1850, he mentions enigmatically, 'you must come and see my lions'. This most probably meant that one of his menagerist friends had recently sent him the bodies of some lion cubs, or even a pair of adults, since he was in the habit of receiving all kinds of exotic dead creatures which would arrive on his doorstep suitably packaged in a trunk or a cask, and ready for the laborious process that would turn them into a museum exhibit.

The delight for Waterton was always in giving freedom to a wild creature and watching it enjoy that freedom. He once said that the story which impressed him most when he was a child was Lawrence Sterne's account of a starling in a cage, endlessly repeating the words, 'I can't get out! I can't get out!' The sight of a bird singing in a cage, especially a blinded songbird, seemed to him like a contradiction in terms which he could hardly bear to witness. In Aix-la-Chapelle he once saw fourteen such cages, hung along a wall not far from the cathedral, and all the little prisoners singing in 'apparent ecstasy'.

In most of his observations of wild creatures, Waterton's role is that of a silent and passive witness, who watches, and then describes what he has seen.

> I was sitting quite still at the time, and could easily have despatched either the rabbit or the weasel, but I did not interfere until the affair was concluded, and then I took the rabbit for my share, and allowed the weasel to go in search of another supper, when and where it might think fit.[11]

> In the afternoon a bat was hawking for flies in the boathouse, dipping his mouth to the water. After a while the bat appeared exhausted, and it alighted on a plank which was close to me, and I took it in my hand and then turned it loose. It came a second time, and I took it up, gave it its liberty, and it again hawked for flies, and continued to do so until I was called away and lost sight of it.[12]

> The toad, that poor, despised, and harmless reptile, is admirable in its proportions, and has an eye of such transcendent beauty, that when I find one, I place it on my hand, to view it more minutely.[13]

When he did perform experiments, they tended to be rather haphazard and inconsequential, simply because he was not prepared to disrupt the pattern of life of the creature involved.

> This day I took up a flower pot which I had buried in the ground. In it I had incarcerated three toads amongst a little soil. I found all three alive. Two of them were much bleached, the other was black. I gave them their liberty, and told them to enjoy the spring . . .[14]

> This season I have made jackdaws hatch magpies and magpies jackdaws; carrion crows have brought up rooks, and rooks carrion crows. It is quite laughable to see a brood of young jackdaws following an old magpie, and *vice versa*![15]

> The magpie (and we may include all other birds) shows not that intensity of feeling for its eggs which it is known to have for its young. Thus, if you take the eggs from the nest and place them on the ground, the magpie will abandon them for ever; but if you remove the young to a place to which the parent bird can have access, she will regularly bring a supply of food.[16]

Nevertheless, over the years Waterton did provide very thorough and accurate accounts of the way that a large number of birds built their nests, raised their young and what they chose to eat. The food of birds was for him an especially important topic, since he was always adding new evidence to prove that most indigenous birds and animals were a positive asset for the farmer, the gardener and the gamekeeper, and should not be exterminated. Only for the Hanoverian rat was no punishment considered too severe.

CHAPTER XVIII

Other People

Waterton had always been childlike in his erratic spontaneity, but this became all the more disconcerting as he grew older: a rumpled, clownish figure in unlikely clothes, stooped and wrinkled, his hair snow-white and 'as erect as a brush all over his head', his complexion 'perfectly colourless', no matter what the season. He could be extremely sociable, inviting friends to stay at Walton Hall for as long as they wished, and encouraging an endless stream of strangers to visit the park and the museum, but always there was the sense that he was encapsulated in a private labyrinth of association and memory, and the best that he could do in the way of communicating with others was to provide a running commentary on the images and associations that went through his head. If his thoughts drifted to a subject that saddened him—the death of his wife so many years ago, the fear of what might happen to his estate when he was no longer there to protect it—then he would cry, silently and unashamedly, with the tears streaming down his face. If he felt suddenly good-humoured, he would sing a favourite song or perform an acrobatic trick, not caring who was with him or what they might think. And always there were the stories, told in the soft and lilting blur of a rich Yorkshire accent, stories in which he relived the adventures of his past with such an intense concentration that he seemed to return to distant countries, and talk once more with friends who were long-since dead.

> One night I lay very ill in my hammock, and I called my boy to me, 'Daddy, do you think I shall live?'
> 'No massa, you go dead at midnight!'
> 'Well pitch my body anywhere and go as fast as you can to the nearest settlement, and let my friends know.'
> Oh, I was very far gone in the dysentery, but I got through.[1]

One day, walking along the Via Flaminia in Rome, I met a fellow
with a badger on his back.

'Hello friend,' says I, 'what are you going to do with that?'

'I am going to take it home and eat it,' replies the man.

'Then I will give you this coin for it, sir,' says I. And the man
accepted the coin and I got my badger.[2]

Many people anticipated a meeting with Waterton with mixed feelings
of 'pleasure and uncertainty', one such was the London physician
George Harley. The two men had been in correspondence about the
uses of curare, and in the spring of 1856 Harley accepted an invitation
to stay at the home of someone 'whom even his friends had taught me
to regard as an interesting curiosity'. He arrived at the front door and
was politely ushered into the drawing room by a servant and, as he was
gazing out at the lake through the telescope, the window was heaved
open, and Harley was suddenly 'face to face with the famous naturalist
and traveller'. In spite of the unexpected form of this encounter, his
first impressions were extremely positive, 'No one could catch a sight
of his beaming smile, or receive a glance from his speaking eye,
without feeling that, no matter how *bizarre* might be the appearance of
the outer man, the inner was lit up by a genial, highly-cultivated mind
and sympathetic heart.'[3]

Without bothering about any formalities, Waterton asked if Harley
would perhaps like to look at some of his curios. He led him through
the collection which lined the staircase, and Harley paused to compli-
ment him on the way that his specimens of natural history were
stuffed.

'What do you mean? *Stuffed*, did you say? Allow me to inform you
that there are no stuffed animals in this house.' Then thrusting his
fingers into his waistcoat pocket, he drew from it a key, and
unlocking the door of the case opposite him, extracted from it a
finely preserved polecat. Extending it somewhat brusquely towards
me, he said in a piqued, yet commanding tone of voice, 'Take hold of
the head, and hold it firmly.'

I did so when he immediately gave the specimen a sudden jerk and
left the head in my hand. Astonished and dismayed, I immediately
began to stammer an apology. But instead of paying any attention to
what I said, he cut my speech short by saying, 'Look at the
head—what do you see?'

'Nothing,' was my answer.

'Then put your fingers into it, and tell me what you feel.'

'Nothing,' was again my reply. No stuffing, no bones, no skull could I either see or feel. It was simply empty. It contained *nothing*.

'Now then, can you dare to say my animals are stuffed! Have you never heard of my method of preserving them?'

'No.'

'Then sir, I will show you; you shan't leave this house until you have not only seen, but learned the whole process. Give me back my head please.'

On returning the head to him, to my still further astonishment —which he evidently thoroughly enjoyed—he gave it a half twist and twirled it immediately on to the neck, just as if it had merely been the lid of a box.[4]

They reached Waterton's attic bedroom, where the first thing that caught Harley's eye was the big baboon strung from the ceiling. 'No sooner was the door shut behind us, than, walking round to the off-side of the baboon, he placed a hand beneath it, gave it a smart tap, when the creature bounded into the air like a child's balloon. Then with a smiling face he said, "Do that, and tell me what you think it is filled with."'[5]

Waterton proceeded to fling open the drawers of a cupboard, pulling out a bundle of clean white baboon bones which he threw to the floor with a clatter, and an unmounted cockerel, which he pitched across the room for his guest to catch. Finally he invited Harley to sit down with him before the little table, where he set to work on another specimen, explaining the stages of the process as he went along, and extolling the virtues of his beloved bichloride of mercury, which protected all his creations from a butterfly to an alligator against the ravages of time. When the dinner bell rang, the two men interrupted their work, and cleaned their hands at the little sink. Waterton offered Harley the use of an excellent nailbrush, cut from the shank of one of his old toothbrushes, but this Harley declined. They joined the ladies downstairs, and after a good meal they talked of curare and 'other matters', and Harley was presented with some samples of curare, carefully contained in a lump of beeswax, and as powerful as it had been almost forty years previously. At eight o'clock Waterton announced that he was going to bed, 'I shall be up tomorrow by three. I leave you in good hands with my sisters-in-law. Goodnight.'

George Harley grew to be very fond of Waterton, and from that first meeting he learnt to accept him wholeheartedly and without prejudice. If before he had been uncertain about the veracity of some of the exploits described in the *Wanderings*, his mind was now made up: 'I could never doubt him again; if he were to tell me that he walked from Walton Hall to London on his head, without either using his hands or his feet, I should believe him, for I am sure he would not tell a lie.'[6]

Waterton regularly sent little presents to him and members of his family: a bow and arrow which he had used to shoot a fish on the lake at Walton Hall; a complete set of Guianese poisoned weapons; and for Christmas, in the last year of his life, a bundle containing a dozen blowpipe spikes, wrapped in an Indian cloth and with their lethal points tipped with beeswax.

There were a number of other friendships such as this one, with Waterton in the role of host and entertainer: cordial, welcoming and generous, but always maintaining his distance. He was definitely more at ease with those who were prepared to watch and listen, rather than with those who wanted to share ideas, or argue over topics of mutual interest, and there is the impression that whenever he was confronted by a particularly important individual he made a special effort to be difficult and unapproachable. There were many brief encounters, but few close friendships. Although in his letters to his sisters-in-law and to George Ord, Waterton never failed to remark on such events as the visit of the French giant and his diminutive wife, the Yankee rattle-snake dealer, or the dwarfs on show in Bloomsbury, he made no mention of his contact with Dickens, Darwin and Thackeray, or that extraordinary naturalist Frank Buckland who was addicted to cooking bits of every animal he obtained and served his guests with such delicacies as mice on toast and stewed rhinoceros.

The story of Darwin's visit must in that way have been typical. The two men had met briefly in Edinburgh in 1826, when Darwin was only seventeen and wanting to learn the art of taxidermy. There is no way of knowing how long they spent together, or whether they got along well, but twenty years later Darwin decided to see Waterton at Walton Hall. It is known that he admired the *Essays*, saying that such 'discussions and observations' on what 'the world would call trifling points of Natural History' were in his mind very important, and yet, when he met the author, it would seem that there was little opportunity of discussing this point or anything else of interest, and instead he felt himself to be a guest at some sort of Mad Hatter's tea party.

Visited Waterton at Walton Hall, and was extremely amused by my visit there. He is an amusing strange fellow; at our early dinner our party consisted of two Catholic priests and two Mulatresses! He is past sixty years old, and the day before ran down and caught a leveret in a turnip field. It is a fine old house and the lake swarms with wild fowl.[7]

Charles Dickens was also known to have been 'partial' to the *Essays*, and he corresponded with Waterton when he was writing about the raven called Grip who played such an important role in *Barnaby Rudge*. If Dickens did visit Walton Hall to talk further and to see Waterton's own pet raven, then the occasion was never considered notable enough to be mentioned. Similarly Thackeray was an acquaintance of the Watertons when they were in Rome, and wrote what has always been supposed to be a sketch of the 'good kind W', a saintly man, '. . . who dines on a crust, lives as chastely as a monk and gives his all to the poor'.[8] But there were no further meetings in England, and when Waterton was questioned on the subject all that he had to say was, 'I knew Thackeray in Rome. He is a clever man.'

The obstacles which anyone must have faced when trying to approach Waterton on a professional basis can be seen quite clearly from a few letters between him and Sir Richard Owen, Curator of the Hunter Museum at the Royal College of Surgeons, and in later life the highly successful, albeit highly pedantic, Superintendent of the Natural History Department of the British Museum. In 1850 Richard Owen and his wife came to stay at Walton Hall. He was at that time preparing the Natural History Section for the Great Exhibition at the Crystal Palace, and presumably the underlying motive for his visit was that he wanted to see Waterton's collection and arrange to borrow certain items. The two men apparently got on well enough, and it is tempting to imagine their respective ladies discussing the inconveniences of having large dead animals arriving unannounced on the front doorstep in barrels and boxes. Mrs Owen once complains feebly in her diary about the presence of the corpse of a rhinoceros for a few days during a hot summer, and perhaps Eliza and Helen mentioned that the smell of pickling rum, along with the object that was being pickled, sometimes lingered in the dining room and travelled along the corridors.

Not long after this meeting, Owen wrote a courteous letter to Waterton, making the expected request: 'I trust therefore, that for your own justly-earned reputation, as well as for the honour of our common Country, you will send a few of your choice specimens of Birds and Quadrupeds, of Insects and Crustacea to the Exhibition.'[9]

It took Waterton five months before he sent a reply, along with an explanation as to why he did not want his work to be put on show: 'Being aware that not one man in ten thousand of those who shall pass through the Crystal Palace has ever paid sufficient attention to preserved specimens . . . it struck me forcibly that my specimens, done upon a principle never before contemplated, would be merely looked at with a nod of approbation, and that would be all.'[10] He did, however, reach a certain compromise by announcing that at some as yet unspecified date he would personally bring to London a quadruped, a bird, a reptile and an insect, that would 'set all competition at defiance', and these would be contained in '. . . a box two feet long and a half wide, and one ditto long. You will only have to open it and to shut it. When opened, it will instantly exhibit to view, on the inside of the *lid*, the specimens which it contains.'[11]

Although Waterton was condescending about the Great Exhibition, fondly quoting Eliza's comment of it having 'great magnificence and much insignificance', he nevertheless thought it worth while to send a series of very rude letters to the *Illustrated London News*, in which he criticized the appearance of one particular peacock, with its 'shrivelled legs and toes', the 'sad confusion of its feathers', its 'sickly thighs' and other faults which made 'a mockery of nature'. It could hardly have been a coincidence that in the following year, the spring of 1852, he was suddenly preoccupied with the 'gigantic work' of entirely rearranging and expanding his own staircase exhibition, his private Crystal Palace over which he had complete control.

With regard to his achievements as a taxidermist, and also his observations on matters of natural history, Waterton became increasingly pedantic, complacent in his own convictions, and truculent when faced with opposition of any sort. When Owen asked for his opinion of the exhibits at the Crystal Palace, 'I said that when the medal is awarded the words ought to run thus, "to the least bad".'[12] In the early 1860s he donated a giant anteater to the British Museum, saying that they ought to have, '. . . at least one specimen in its collection of which it is not ashamed'. Throughout the last decade of his life he insisted that he had seen all that there was to be seen, with regard to the behaviour of certain creatures. Since he had never witnessed a cuckoo push another fledgling out of the nest, such an event never had, and never would occur. Because he had observed the apes of Gibraltar in 1803, had watched howler monkeys in the tropical rain forests some forty years ago, and had studied a few apes in captivity, he felt that he could stand as an authority on the characteristics of a newly discovered beast called the pongo or gorilla, whose existence and behaviour suddenly became of great interest when the idea of the evolutionary descent of man was simmering in so many minds. The gorilla was, as it were, introduced to England by Paul

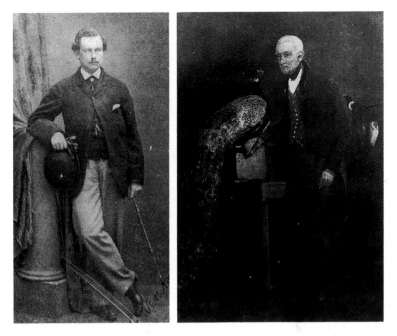

12 Waterton's only child, Edmund, in a photograph taken in the 1860s. In sharp contrast to his father he was 'addicted to every kind of fashionable entertainment'.

13 Waterton with a peacock. He disliked being either painted or photographed, and this portrait was made some years after his death.

14 Looking 'like an old spider' after a long winter, Waterton in a sketch by the writer, Percy Hetherington Fitzgerald, who stayed at Walton Hall in the late 1850s.

15 Waterton's coffin on its floating bier was towed across the lake accompanied by boats draped in the black cloth of mourning. People present said that a flock of birds followed the procession.

16 Waterton chose to be buried in a place of 'solitude and abandonment' between two great oak trees. The grave, which can still be seen, was marked with a simple cross.

Belloni du Chaillu, a Frenchman with a flair for vivid journalism, who had written a book called *Explorations and Adventures in Equatorial Africa* in which he claimed to have had hair-breadth escapes from this murderous, 'hellish dream-creature, . . . half man half beast'.[13] He came to England in 1861 to promote his book and to give a series of lectures on all that he had seen. To prove the veracity of what he had to say, he brought with him a battered and moth-eaten collection of twenty stuffed gorillas and an assortment of skulls and skins.

For Waterton it was like being confronted with Audubon all over again, and he at once determined to expose the 'inconsistencies, exaggerations and consummate ignorance' which were being put about. As with Audubon, and indeed with all his battles, his manner was so rough that he irritated and exasperated a number of people:

> It is really astonishing that our learned doctors in zoology should have been so gulled. Du Chaillu makes his gorilla a man in every-thing but speech . . . I am quite convinced, in my own mind, that du Chaillu's adventures in the land of the gorilla are nothing but impudent fables. He always meets the gorilla on the ground. It ought to have been in trees. I suspect strongly that the traveller has been nothing but a trader on the western coast of Africa, possibly engaged in kidnapping negroes, and that he has bought his skins off negro-merchants from the interior.[14]

When Richard Owen became persuaded that the gorillas were genuine, even if du Chaillu was over-fond of blood-thirsty stories, Waterton was quick to round on him as well: 'I myself never boggle at "yes" or "no" where the good of natural history is concerned.' After Waterton's death Eliza noted with obvious relief that Owen had sent a surprisingly friendly letter of condolence, 'a much nicer one than I expected,' so at least that difference of opinion was allowed to be laid at rest.

Exactly who Waterton considered to be his closest friends, and whose friendship really mattered to him, can never really be known, since the letters and papers which have survived are an ill-assorted bundle which seem to have escaped destruction more by accident than by design. There was apparently a large metal trunk in which he kept all the papers he considered important and worth saving. However Edmund, with his disorderly but determined instinct to get rid of everything connected with his late father, managed after a bit of effort to separate himself from this small but crucial item of family property. First he placed it, locked and without a key, in an auction of books and furniture held at Walton Hall not long after Waterton's death, but the auctioneers insisted on forcing it open, and when they discovered the contents they returned it to its rightful owner. He then deposited it in a warehouse in London, and there, in 1868, a fire consumed the trunk and whatever it was that it contained. What has been left is a haphazard collection of papers, many of which were in the possession of Eliza and Helen, and an extraordinary correspondence, complete in its voluminous entirety, between Waterton and the American zoologist George Ord, which managed to avoid Edmund's destructive net.

The initial bond between Waterton and Ord was their shared admiration for the ornithologist Alexander Wilson and their growing resentment of Audubon with his bold stories about his dealings with birds, animals and influential people. They had met briefly in Philadelphia in 1824, and Ord came to visit Waterton in 1831 and again in 1835, anticipating his return with typical trepidation, 'I tremble to think of revisiting Walton Hall, lest I should be disappointed.'[15] However there was no need for the danger of further disappointments for they never saw each other again. Instead, they went on writing, regularly and at great length, and the result was a correspondence that functions like two journals running along parallel lines from both sides of the Atlantic. The letters provide a commentary on current affairs and the weather, along with any recent observations in the field of natural history, or any recent arrivals among the ranks of the closet naturalists. There was also a brief account of what the author had been doing and, as the years moved on, an ever more detailed account of his state of health.

Ord, who had been a 'puny infant, destined during childhood to be the prey of various diseases', was a natural hypochondriac, always expecting to be struck down by sudden and painful mortality, in spite of the fact that he pottered along without too many physical inconveniences until his eighty-fifth year.

I myself have been ailing. As one who has renounced all the active pleasures of the world, and whose only solace is derived from the pursuit of literature and the exercise of the pen . . .[16]

My excellent friend's letter has been lying before me for nearly two months unanswered. This seeming neglect has proceeded from various causes: first I am troubled by chilblains . . . In the second place my eyesight has become very feeble, insomuch as I read with difficulty my own handwriting; and lastly, truth compels me to confess, what the aged are very loath to do, that my intellectual powers are in the decline.[17]

Waterton responded to Ord's fears about his failing mind and suffering body with a confident indifference, combined with personal medical advice:

By the description which you give of your state of health, and especially as you suddenly found yourself much better on the changing of the weather, I would fain conclude that you have been labouring under a severe attack of lumbago and nothing more. Many labourers in this vicinity . . . are subject to lumbago, and when they apply to me for relief I use the lancet freely and the disorder disappears in the course of a day.[18]

Should a second [fainting fit] occur, steep your feet in hot water and open your bowels immediately . . .[19]

There is no indication that Ord ever paid attention to such instructions, or that he was comforted by Waterton's reassurances. He became increasingly bitter and withdrawn, 'lost most of his old friends and made no new ones',[20] and when he died in 1871 he ignored the numerous members of his family and left a quite considerable fortune to the Pennsylvania Hospital for the Insane.

In contrast to Ord, Waterton never once doubted his mental faculties, and became ever more euphoric, dangerously so perhaps, about his wonderful good health and the youthful vigour of his body: '. . . [I am] as full of health and mettle as a fighting cock.'[21] 'My ankles are now as fine as those of a race horse, and I can walk twelve or fourteen miles without lassitude.'[22] This image of himself full of strength and mettle was very much at variance with the impression that others had of him. Everybody agreed that his body was strong and sinewy, and his calves 'remarkably fine', but the regular purging and blood-letting had left him pale and 'as dry as a quince', and although he was almost six feet tall, he always gave the impression of being a little man.

On the occasions when he teetered dangerously near the grave as a result of a bout of malaria, or because of one of his horrible accidents, he dismissed the experience lightly. 'Attacks of ague, botherments, and other nuisances, have prevented me from writing sooner. However, spring will be here soon, and then all will be right again.'[23] He did complain when he could not hold a pen easily, once because of the broken arm which was smashed back into order by the bone-setter, and again because of the stupidity of a 'rash' stonemason, who dropped a two-tonne slab of granite on his thumb, crushing it to a 'jelly'. In the last years of his life he decided to have a new set of teeth made for him by a dentist which did make him feel a victim to his own frailty.

> I myself have been ailing in a manner, although not dangerously, extremely annoying. And this has been caused by an officious race of men called Dentists. After depriving me of all my teeth in my upper jaw, they applied their artificial ones, which have never given me a moment's rest, so that I am now entirely without any masticators in the upper jaw, the want of which has deranged my stomach, and has caused perpetual hiccoughs when taking food.[24]

Although the correspondence between Ord and Waterton was maintained for more than thirty years and was brought to an end only a few weeks before Waterton's death, and although both men's letters were filled with declarations of their great friendship, it must be said that they studiously avoided all personal matters, and hardly ever confided a private thought or fear or expectation. When Anne died in 1830, Waterton had briefly communicated his despair, but later there was no indication of the confusion and wounding he suffered because of Edmund, indeed he even 'forgot to mention' Edmund's marriage, an event which took place in 1862 and about which he was not consulted. He was also silent about his growing dread about what would happen to his sisters-in-law, his park and his museum once he had departed from the world.

It would be interesting to know whether this transatlantic friendship would have persisted if the two ageing men had been confronted with one another. They had aspects of the study of natural history in common, but apart from that they held opposite views on almost everything. Ord was a staunch conservative, whereas Waterton declared blithely, 'Indeed, had I a vote, I would never give it, either to Whig, Tory or Radical.'[25] Ord was horrified by the abolition of slavery, and answered Waterton's enquiries about the true history of John Brown with an angry diatribe against that 'rebel, incendiary and murderer'. He had no comment to make on Waterton's observation: 'One way or other, we are all slaves. I am convinced that if a slave from the United States was placed in one of our own factories on Monday morning, and then told that he would have to work there for years to come; he would hang himself on the first Saturday night . . .'[26] Nor, for that matter, did he ever bother to respond to Waterton's religious enthusiasms, such as his long and detailed account of a recent miracle in Italy, when all the paintings of the Blessed Virgin in the town of Rimini began to flutter their eyelids. In return Waterton was silent on Ord's opinion on vermin: 'You English philosophers are more tolerant of *vermin* than we Yankees are: you sit calmly by and watch a whole brood of ducklings torn to pieces by a Carrion Crow . . . damn the whole tribe I say!'[27]

In fact there is never an indication that either of them could be persuaded to take a different view of any aspect of the world which they both inhabited, and there is the overriding impression that they learnt very little from each other over all those years. Stubbornness of will was perhaps what they held most firmly in common.

It was inevitable that someone like Waterton would be a natural target for mockery and sarcasm, and that during his lifetime he would accumulate many enemies, while making no attempt to establish or maintain friendships for the sake of his reputation. But his oddness, his qualities and his rare achievements might have been allowed to coexist in a relatively harmonious balance, had it not been for the literary efforts of one man, a Leeds physician called Richard Hobson.

Hobson acted as Waterton's doctor from the 1840s onwards, and perhaps from an earlier date. He himself claimed to have had 'an intimate and most confiding personal association for nearly thirty years', but he did have the habit of exaggeration. Certainly he tended Waterton during several dangerous illnesses, and certainly for twenty years the two men were on friendly terms and met quite regularly. In 1862 they had a serious quarrel. 'Hobson proved a false friend and tried to set Edmund and his father at variance',[28] wrote Lydia Edmonstone in a letter to George Ord which is the only account of what took place, but after that they never met again. It was on the eve of this quarrel that Hobson embarked on his book, *Charles Waterton: His Home, Habits and Handiwork*, which was published the year after Waterton's death, with a second edition following closely on its heels.

Richard Hobson was ten years younger than Waterton. He was said to be a kind, genial, hospitable man, generally held in esteem by all who knew him. He bred racehorses, enjoyed hunting fox and hare, collected stuffed birds, mosses and lichens and worked as the consulting physician at the Leeds Infirmary and the Hospital for Women and Children. Apart from his wonderfully titled book, he had published a paper on diabetes and another on 'The External Use of Croton Oil'. There are no surviving portraits of him, but there is the impression that he was short, rotund and always slightly ridiculous, especially when he meant to be dignified. This visual image is strengthened by the fact that Waterton had a duck with webless toes which he called Doctor Hobson.

As much as Waterton might praise the 'worthy doctor' for his medical skills, '. . . he executed his giant powers with wonderful precision, ordering the immediate application of leeches and blisters to the head,'[29] he also seemed to enjoy his company because here was the perfect audience: gullible and enthusiastic, and prepared to act as a buffer to whatever game Waterton chose to play. If he saw himself as Don Quixote, a man going in quest of one thing and finding another, a man doing battle with windmills and sheep and never learning to understand the way of the world, then Richard Hobson was cast in the role of Sancho Panza. When Waterton hid under a table and growled and bit him playfully on the leg, Hobson did not storm off in a rage of indignation, but tried to understand the joke and to appreciate it. He watched with a mixture of horror and delight the spectacle of an old man showing off:

> I have frequently, in painful suspense, and much against my own inclinations, seen the Squire, when beyond seventy years of age, hop on one leg along the brink of a rock forming the highest terrace in the grotto, whilst the other leg was dangling over the chasm below: and, when thus hopping at a rapid rate, he would return again by hopping on the contrary leg. On my cautioning him, he would reply: '*Non de ponti cadit qui cum sapientia vadit*'—He falls not from the bridge who walks with prudence.[30]

> Mr Waterton not only manufactured fictitious wings, but actually attached them to his arms and trunk, and also formed and fixed the remaining mechanism which he conceived was necessary . . . He arranged to make his first essay from the eaves of a roof of a building in the farm yard . . . from whence his flight, it is true, would be of limited extent in a forward direction, and where an abundance of litter would break the severity of a possible uncontrollable and rapid descent.[31]

> His remarkable suppleness of limb and elasticity of muscle, I have often seen marvellously and most amazingly displayed in his eighty-first year, by a variety of physical contortions. When Mr Waterton was seventy-seven years of age, I was witness to his scratching the back part of his head with the big toe of his right foot.[32]

186

If indeed Hobson was made the butt for so many private jokes, and if he sometimes had the disquieting impression that he appeared even more foolish than the old man who was hopping along on one leg, or considering whether to test his wings, then he got his revenge with a most complete thoroughness. However guileless and stupid he might have been, one suspects he must have sensed his own ambivalence towards his hero, and realized that spite was one of the inspirations which guided his work. But he said nothing of this when he explained why he had taken it upon himself to 'issue to the public this little Volume'. 'Another reason, and one which I am delighted and proud to entertain and express, is my absolute love for the Memory of the man who was so warmly, so faithfully attached, and so abiding a friend.'[33]

When Waterton heard that the book was being prepared for intended publication, he attempted to take action to suppress it. 'Somehow or other I had got an idea into my head, that it was to have appeared in a gazette of ordinary communications, which are read in the morning and then sink into everlasting oblivion as the shades of night set in . . . I could wish (most confidentially betwixt ourselves) that in your answer to the worthy doctor you could contrive, somehow or other, to give it a squeeze or two, so that it would never see daylight again.'[34] But the book was not given a squeeze, and after Waterton's death it was completed and submitted to a publisher. Eliza and Helen, for once united with Edmund, tried to take legal steps to stop publication, with Edmund declaring sanctimoniously, 'As my father's memory, and his every wish to me is sacred, I know that I am fulfilling a filial duty in making this protest.'[35] But nothing came of this either, and the detailed exposure of Waterton's home, habits and handiwork was presented to an eager public in 1866. The first edition sold out very quickly, and the second edition was ready in the following year, at a cheaper price, and with 'much additional matter'. 'On a careful re-perusal [the Author] was mortified to discover the omission of many temporarily forgotten incidents familiarly exhibiting the genuine characteristics of "the old Squire" which were apparently worthy of record.'[36]

Hobson's book, complete with its 'additional matter', was divided into eleven chapters. It was not a biography, and it made no attempt to tell the story of Waterton's life; rather it was an extraordinary study in free-association, with Hobson remembering one incident which reminded him of another, his thoughts rambling from one tangent to the next, unashamed of their circumnavigations and confusions. The headings for the sections in the chapters are a good indicator of the overall style.

- Special immunity in the Female Sex from Death by Lightning.
- The Author suspects that the Squire had a foreknowledge of the trees' suicidal termination when he trained them.
- The Ape searching the Squire's head reminds him of a Cambridge anecdote.
- Explanation why the Squire was able to make his Elbows meet.
- Visit of the Lunatics from Wakefield Asylum.
- Stone and Mortar Tower prepared specially for certain of the feathered Tribes.[37]

Many people were shocked by the book and did what they could to save Waterton's reputation and dignity. The *Westminster Gazette* described it:

> It is a tangled web of fact and fiction, and the clumsy dovetailing of truth and error, with opinions misrepresented, facts distorted, incidents inverted, circumstances misstated, the letters misdated or palpably 'cooked' . . .
>
> We hope that such a man, whose reputation as a naturalist was European, and whose excellent qualities of heart and mind endeared him more especially to his fellow countrymen, may find a biographer worthy to record, together with his virtues, the incidents in his remarkable and interesting life . . .[38]

But the damage was done. The public enjoyed this work in which mockery was presented as if it were praise, and it established a precedent for all the future accounts of Waterton, his life, and his achievements. The sad fact of the matter is that although Hobson undoubtedly exaggerated and even invented many of the anecdotes that he told, nevertheless, like Sancho Panza before him, he did have a certain intimate understanding of his master, and there was for a time a strong bond between this unlikely pair. It is even possible to presume that for Hobson the quarrel with Waterton had been a very painful event, and was the reason why he needed to hold up a distorting mirror in front of someone for whom he had once felt a great affection.

CHAPTER XIX

Strange Creatures

In the nineteenth century unfamiliar animals from far-away lands were gazed at with credulous amazement. The same crowd that went to see a bearded lady in a fairground booth, or a two-headed calf, or the shrivelled but nevertheless clearly recognizable body of a mermaid, turned its eager attention on each new specimen which managed to survive a long journey, an abrupt change of climate, and usually a very unsuitable diet. There were still a great number of creatures that were known only by their skins, their bones and the stories told by travellers. Obaysch, the first hippopotamus ever to be seen in England, arrived in great style in 1850, and during the six weeks that it took him to travel from Egypt to Regent's Park, he was, '. . . provided with all sorts of creature comforts; an army of cows and goats accompanied him to afford him milk; he had a huge portable bath to bathe in and, in fact, he travelled *en prince*.'[1]

More than 10,000 people were said to have visited this 'great overgrown dropsical baby' in a single day, and his popularity diminished only with the arrival of a baby elephant, and the brief appearance of a giant anteater.

Ever since it was opened to the public in 1828, the Zoological Society of London had seen a succession of apes, monkeys and sad-faced orang-utans, such as the one that Queen Victoria watched sipping tea, and being in every way 'painfully and disagreeably human' in 1842. However it was not until 1887 that they finally acquired a live gorilla, the most celebrated link between man and beast, but this gentle vegetarian's chances of survival were severely diminished by feeding him on sausages, beer, cheese sandwiches and boiled mutton.[2]

Waterton had several good contacts at the Zoological Societies of both London and Manchester, as well as among members of a family

189

of famous travelling menagerists with the wonderful name of Womb-well, and although he preferred to stay at home and listen to the cuckoo rather than attend a meeting of learned scientists and natural-ists, he was always prepared to make a special journey to visit a new monkey or a large snake. He got advance warning when something interesting was going to be put on show which was useful since the life of many of these uprooted creatures was very brief. He was also the willing recipient of corpses of various sizes and in various states of freshness, whether it was the huge and stinking carcass of an adult male gorilla which he struggled to restore to some semblance of life in 1865; 'an extraordinary young monster pig' which he must have acquired from a fairground; an ostrich most kindly presented to him by Mrs Wombwell; or the two toucans, which arrived unannounced in the post, and which he presumed had been sent to him by his good friend David Mitchell, the Secretary of the London Zoo. 'I have preserved two toucans which have been sent to me without a letter to say from whence they had come . . . I never thought to live to see the day in which I should have two dead toucans lying before me on the table.'[3]

For some reason Waterton missed the brief appearance of the giant anteater in 1853, and when it died its body was kept in London for dissection. But he was delighted that finally his description in the *Wanderings* of this ancient survivor of the Pleistocene Age, which walked on its knuckles, had a mouth like a hosepipe, and a tail which it spread over its recumbent body in 'the fashion of a counterpane' was proved to be entirely correct. A few years previously a live sloth had arrived, and once again his account of its unlikely upside-down habits was seen to be without exaggeration.

The story of the anteater is worth telling, simply because it is so typical of the age. Four giant anteaters were captured and brought back from Brazil by two impoverished German sailors. Two of them were taken to Paris, where their fate remains undocumented, one died on the journey, and the fourth was put on show in London. The sailors rented a room in a squalid street in Bloomsbury where they exhibited the living anteater, along with the bedraggled stuffed remains of its companion. A sign in the window proclaimed that for the price of sixpence (threepence for children), passers-by could

'*Step inside a see the great* ANTITA *heat a hegge*'

On opening the shop door we found ourselves, in proper showman fashion, shut from the sight of the inner mystery by a check curtain. Passing that, we came into the shop which was divided by a little wooden barrier, into a small space for spectators, and a small space for the proprietors of the animal itself . . . On the straw was a rough grey mat, of a circular form, or a heap of hair, which presently unrolled itself into the form of a magnificent tail, from under which the long nose of the living Ant-bear was aimed at us like a musket . . .

It is healthy, but thin and languid, as most exotic animals become when they are brought among us.[4]

Waterton's friend Mitchell arranged to acquire this important addition to the zoo's collection for the sum of £200, and during the six months of its existence it attracted a great deal of attention, in spite of the fact that it slept for most of that time.

During the early 1850s Waterton was working on a long essay which he called *A New History of the Monkey Family*. He combined his observations of monkeys in Gibraltar and South America with some recent encounters in zoos and travelling menageries and, fired by his recent success with the sloth and the anteater, he presented himself as the only reliable authority on the behaviour and characteristics of the whole monkey tribe. Scientifically the essay was not very sound, and it also brought out his most infuriating and presumptuous style, which reached an apotheosis in a conversation between Mr Ant-bear and Mr Howler Monkey, in which these two gentlemanly animals pour their scorn on all closet naturalists, and praise the accuracy of that 'eccentric writer' who, '. . . disdaining information acquired in the closet, dashed boldly into the heart of our tropical forests . . .'[5] It is however possible to ignore the scientific arguments put forward in this essay, and to concentrate instead on the anecdotes. Waterton remembers how in 1807 he went to see a creature which was said to be a cross between a domestic cow and a tapir, and how he was served with excellent tasting coffee on that occasion. In Georgetown in 1812 he had the opportunity of 'examining minutely, an entirely white negro', who went by the name of White Jemmy and was a tailor by trade. He mentions birds, rats, vampires, the north-west passage and the majesty of trees, and he tells how in recent years he has had, '. . . the good fortune, here in England, to have made the acquaintance of three different species of apes from their own warm regions in the tropics; two of which are now in high preservation at Walton Hall.'[6]

There was a chimpanzee with bronchial trouble who was exhibited at Scarborough by the Wombwells, and when this 'little African stranger' died, Waterton was offered her corpse. 'I suggested the idea, that, although his poor ape was dead, he would do well to take it with him, in order that the public in Huddersfield might be gratified in having an opportunity to inspect so singular an animal, so rarely seen in this country. I added that it might be forwarded to me when he had no more use for it, as the frosty state of the weather was all in its favour.'[7] Although this sounds macabre, dead animals were often exhibited, and George Wombwell once even presented an enthusiastic audience with the impressive spectacle of a deceased elephant which had died on its way to a fair in the north of England.

Waterton's chimpanzee suffered further delays when the man who was bringing it to Walton Hall spent two extra days in Leeds getting drunk with his cousin, but finally the work of the taxidermist could proceed: 'After seven weeks of application, I succeeded in restoring its form and features. Hollow to the very nails, it now sits upon a cocoa-nut (not by the way its correct position), which I brought with me from Guiana in the year 1817.'[8]

The second meeting was with an orang-utan at the London Zoo in September 1851. The animal had only recently arrived from Borneo, and when Waterton came to inspect it there was a crowd of curious onlookers peering through the bars of its cage. What impressed him most was the gentleness and sadness of this 'shaggy prisoner' and, feeling sure that it would not harm him, he asked to be allowed to enter the cage. The description of this event has often been quoted as an example of Waterton's eccentricity, although really it was a very typical encounter between a human being and a large ape, and something which has been documented many times in recent years.

As I approached the orang-utan, he met me about half way, and we soon entered into an examination of each other's persons. Nothing struck me more forcibly than the uncommon softness of the inside of his hands. Those of a delicate lady could not have shewn a finer texture. He took hold of my wrist and fingered the blue veins therein contained; whilst I myself was lost in admiration at the protuberance of his enormous mouth. He most obligingly let me open it, and thus, I had the best opportunity of examining his two fine rows of teeth.

We then placed our hands around each other's necks; and we kept them there awhile . . . It were loss of time in me, were I to pen down an account of the many gambols which took place betwixt us . . . the surrounding spectators seemed wonderfully amused at the solemn farce before them.[9]

Richard Hobson gave a very different version of this famous meeting in his book about Waterton's home, habits and handiwork, and here his manner of restructuring and altering information can be followed very simply and clearly. The date according to Hobson was 1861, and David Mitchell was still in attendance, in spite of the fact that the poor man had died in 'melancholy circumstances' some two years previously. The orang-utan, whose placid countenance had so impressed Waterton, was on this occasion filled with jungle savagery.

> After much entreaty on the part of Mr Waterton, he was permitted to pay his personal respects to a large orang-utan from Borneo, which was reputed to be very savage. Indeed the keepers one and all declared that 'he would worry the Squire and make short work of it', if he should enter his den, especially as he was just then in a horrid temper. Nothing daunted, the Squire, to the very great horror of the numerous spectators, entered the palisaded enclosure with a light heart. The meeting of these two celebrities was clearly a case of 'love at first sight', as the strangers embraced each other most affectionately, nay they positively hugged each other, and in their apparent uncontrollable joy, they kissed one another many times . . .[10]

Nine months later, in June 1852, the orang-utan expired and, much to his disappointment, Waterton missed the opportunity of adding it to his collection:

> Our astonishing orang-utan is dead, and unfortunately for me, it died when my friend Mitchell was out. He had determined to send it, when dead, down to me. But having left no instructions on this point before he left London, the under keepers knew nothing of his intentions, and, of course, Walton Hall was never thought of. What a loss for me.[11]

Throughout his time as secretary at the zoo, Mitchell took it upon himself to send regularly any specimens which he thought would be of interest to Waterton. He apparently also sent the sloughed skins of snakes, although what use these were put to is not at all clear.

> In poor Mitchell's day at the Zoological Gardens, I used, now and then, to get a snake's slough or two from the Keepers; and in return, I gave them a shilling to drink my health.
> Being in want, just now, of a dark coloured slough of the

Rattlesnake or the Egyptian viper, I wrote to Mr Bartlett for one or two, but I have received no answer to my letter, so, I conjecture that he is from home. Could you call at the gardens, before you leave London for Yorkshire, and procure a slough, and pay a shilling for me. Sloughs are of no value. Believe me, my dear sir,

Very truly yours,
Charles Waterton.

PS a slough of the rattlesnake would suit me best.[12]

The third ape that Waterton met was thought to be a particularly dark-coloured chimpanzee, but in fact it must have been a young gorilla. It had been captured on the bank of the River Congo, and when Waterton saw it, it was being kept in a stuffy attic room in a house in Scarborough. It belonged to the Royal Menagerie of Mrs Wombwell, and was being looked after by a 'young female' by the name of Miss Blight. If the anteater in a crate in Bloomsbury was an image of a pathetic creature trying to sleep its way through a nightmare, the description of Jenny the gorilla was not only sad but very disconcerting. The lady and the gorilla lived together in one room, along with a clutter of furniture and a 'pretty little dog' which Jenny loathed and bit whenever the opportunity arose. Crowds of spectators would pay their money and troop up the stairs to view this uneasy domestic scene, and Jenny, who was always kept dressed in human clothes, could be persuaded to hobble across the room, especially when tempted by a stick of celery.

Waterton visited Jenny on four occasions; he was fascinated by her, and filled with pity. Watching her make her way across the room, supporting her heavy torso with her clenched fists, he decided, wrongly as it happens, that in her natural state she would spend all her time among the branches of high trees. And when she clambered up his body and clung to him, he mistook her need for comfort as a fear of walking unaided:

. . . it managed to thread its way up and down the surrounding furniture; and on reaching me it climbed up to my neck, where it found a comfortable resting place . . . But when on the floor again, it seemed distressed, the countenance underwent a change, and we could not doubt its discontent . . .

Her skin is as black as a sloe in the hedge, whilst her fur appears curly and brown. Her eyes are beautiful; but there is no white in them; and her ears are as small in proportion as those of a negress.[13]

When Waterton paid his last visit to the attic room he had a sad final meeting with the gorilla, knowing that she would not be able to survive her captivity for much longer.

'Farewell, poor little prisoner,' said I. 'I fear that this cold and gloomy atmosphere of ours will tend to shorten thy days.'

Jenny shook her head, seemingly to say, there is nothing here to suit me. The little room is far too hot; the clothes which they force me to wear are quite insupportable, whilst the food which they give me is not like that upon which I used to feed, when I was healthy and free in my own native woods.[14]

Jenny was moved on from place to place, and finally arrived in Warrington in Lancashire, and there she died in February 1856. Miss Blight promptly wrapped her up in a linen winding sheet, put her in a little trunk and forwarded her to Walton Hall, where Waterton at once set about preserving her 'as though the cruel hand of death had never laid her low'. In spite of his assurances to Miss Blight that she would survive for ages to come, this particular item from the museum collection has disappeared without trace. However, it is known that Waterton decided to turn Jenny into one of his strange satirical creations. In her case what he did was quite simple: he gave her donkey's ears, and he called her Martin Luther.

Waterton's grotesque taxidermal jokes are very difficult to accept. There is something peculiarly sinister about a composite creature that is recognizable in its parts but not in its entirety, and the sense of distaste and unease gets in the way of any appreciation of the humour. In Jenny's case it was also a most unfortunate treatment of what was in fact the first specimen of a gorilla to have been seen alive in England. Just as the Nondescript with its sorrowful mongoloid features had shaken the credibility of the *Wanderings*, so too a succession of unlikely monsters made some of the display cases in the museum better suited to a fairground than to a place devoted to the study of natural history. The two toucans from Regent's Park ended up under a large glass dome, along with twenty-four scorpions, a monkey with horns called 'Martin Luther after his fall', and a cluster of creatures which bore the title of 'England's Reformation in its infancy, with Edward the 6th and his sister Betsy for lunch'. This evocative gathering of the Protestant community has been lost, so what creatures it was composed of can only be guessed at. It probably contained a number of reptilian parts, since Waterton was very busy with toads, lizards and fishes at that time.

Friends and acquaintances who felt that they understood this brand of humour were eager to contribute, and Waterton was showered with gifts, sent especially it would seem by ladies. There are several letters to such donors:

Mrs — kindly brought me a huge toad a few days ago, and her present has enabled me to finish off Martin Luther—so I have now Martin Luther and his Mother; and I trust that your handsome donation will shine conspicuously in the list of Reformers.

Had I been in the forest, free from the bother attendant on civilised life, your presents would have been most acceptable. But, under existing circumstances, I dare not attack the animal's head, as it would take me full five weeks to restore the form and features.

Whereupon, as you order me not to return it, I will consign it to Mother Earth.

I have now finished my specimen of the Spirit of the Dark Ages, and am anxious to have your opinion of it.

I remain, dear madam, respectfully yours.[15]

When Mrs Pitte-Byrne described these creations, she insisted that they were intended to cause amusement but not distress, and she told how Waterton shielded her from certain cases, saying, 'Ye needn't look at these if ye'd rather not.' Nevertheless, even if they were harmless jokes, it involved hours, even whole days of concentrated labour to produce them. Like the battles with the Hanoverian rats, it was a way of dealing with aspects of resentment, although even that explanation does not reconcile the mind with the image of an old man painstakingly turning a monkey into Martin Luther, or giving a tortoise the face of a worried man with hairy legs and calling it John Bull.

These publicized private jokes were extended into the park as well, but in a much more gentle fashion. There was an oak tree and a fir tree which had been persuaded to twine their trunks together, and which were known as Church and State. There was a cluster of thirteen willow trees all growing from one base, and when a strong wind blew one of them would creak and groan. This group was known as Judas and the Twelve Apostles. There was a nut tree which had grown up through the central shaft of an old mill stone, and had slowly heaved up this huge weight, until by the 1850s the stone was suspended eight inches above the ground. The tree was called John Bull and the National Debt, and when it finally died from its exertions, Waterton planted a new sapling in its place.

He was endlessly fascinated by freaks of all kinds, whether they were artificially created, or had occurred naturally. He considered himself an authority, which no doubt he was, in ascertaining whether something was a fake, or a genuine deformity of nature. He rushed to Leeds to examine a toad encapsulated in a lump of coal. He was delighted with the acquisition of

> . . . a curiosity most probably unique throughout the whole world. It is the head of an old sheep without horns from the cranium, but from its right ear, more than half way down, there proceeds a huge horn more than a foot in length, and six inches and a half in circumference at its thickest part . . . The appearance of such a horn, on such a place, is an astonishing phenomenon, and must put all our wise men to their last shifts to account for it. I long to show it to you. I need not say how happy I should be to see you here, especially when the cherry trees are in bloom, as they shortly will be.[16]

When a mermaid was sent to him in the post, he studied it carefully before returning it, along with his opinion of its origin.

> It is a compound animal, half monkey, half fish . . . The upper part of the Mermaid has been joined to the lower part by means of attenuating the two skins with considerable effect. Still, the junction has been so formed that it is perceptible to a knowing eye. The ears have been removed . . .[17]

In 1853 Waterton was in London to make a personal assessment of two dwarves, who were being put on show by some Americans, and were attracting a great deal of attention. They were said to be survivors of an ancient Mexican race; they lived in a mysterious city in the mountains, they were attended by Aztec priests, and, wonder of wonders, they had never learnt to use the power of speech. Queen Victoria was most impressed by them, or, as Waterton explained in a letter to George Ord, 'Our fat and foolish queen has swallowed every ounce of it, and this was quite sufficient to make the fabrication pass for gospel truth.'[18] While he was standing close to these two exotic creatures he did have the satisfaction of hearing them muttering in soft but distinct English to one of their American keepers, but he made no effort to try to expose the 'humbug' any further.

Another American, whose travelling show was much more to Waterton's taste, was a young blacksmith called Vangordon. He had the enterprising idea of capturing a heap of rattlesnakes, putting them into boxes, and then setting sail for Liverpool, where he hoped to make his fortune by showing them to a willing and curious crowd. However, shortly after he arrived in England, something went wrong with his plans and he found himself penniless and friendless, although still in possession of thirty to forty snakes. He had read and enjoyed the *Wanderings*, and he had the good sense to get in touch with their author, first by sending a dead snake in the post, by way of bait as it were, and then by asking directly for help. Waterton rushed to Liverpool and brought Vangordon back with him to Walton Hall, where the two men set about planning a way to make the show more successful. They were greatly helped in this task when a drunken keeper at the London Zoo, 'wishing to show the multitude how good he was in handling poisonous snakes', had the temerity to take hold of a *cobra de capello* and allow it to glide around his body. The snake grew exasperated with the man, bit him on the nose and he died that very same day. It was an event which at once made the public 'very curious about poisonous snakes, and will, no doubt, help our good Yankee in his journey onwards.'[19]

With the instinct of a natural showman, Waterton realized that Vangordon needed a better box in which he could display his 'speckled pets' to advantage, and offered to let him use a large glass case which had been specially made to house the giant anteater he had brought back with him from Guiana.

But then the question was, where could a mouse be found to hang the bell around the cat's neck? I volunteered, remembering well the plan I put into execution whilst I was in the forests of Guiana. Conscious that there was no danger, provided I preserved my presence of mind, I very calmly put my hand into the box, and then placed my finger and thumb exactly on each side of the neck, close to the head. By this simple process I transferred every snake from the boxes to my glass case. The sly little fellows rattled incessantly, as much as to say, 'Don't hurt us. Otherwise we will rebel!'[20]

Waterton arranged for a display to be held in Wakefield, and he followed this up by inviting a select gathering of professional gentlemen to come and witness the effects of curare on an animal already poisoned by rattlesnake venom. The meeting was held at Dr Hobson's house in Leeds, and Hobson arranged to procure a selection of rabbits and guinea-pigs for the occasion. The snakes were back in their original travelling boxes, and Waterton began the work of the evening by transferring them for a second time into his anteater box.

One of the serpents, wearied no doubt with its long imprisonment, glided about half its length through the opening before it. The company instantly rushed out of the room, as though the apparition of Death was present among them . . . In the meantime, Dr Hobson, with his wonted presence of mind, had gently pressed down the lid of the box, upon the back of the snake, which, with a little help on my part, was easily coaxed into the prison whence it had wished to escape.[21]

The remaining twenty-seven were shifted without incident. The rodents were all poisoned twice over, and when they had breathed their last the experiment was considered to have been successfully concluded and everyone went home. Presumably Waterton held a snake as it released its poison into a rabbit or a guinea-pig, although this detail is not explained very clearly in his account of the proceedings.

Hobson told the same story in very different terms. It was his idea to get in touch with Vangordon, and it was he who invited the medical men who came to watch this historic occasion. Even the curare-tipped spikes belonged to Doctor Hobson, although admittedly they had been given to him by Waterton. The Squire was also invited to come along, and, as it turned out, he proved to be 'the hero of the day, and in his genial element, every inch of him'. For some reason the group of victims included pigeons as well as rabbits and guinea-pigs.

It would seem that no one had anticipated the difficulty of extracting a snake from the box, but luckily the Squire fearlessly offered to do the deed. Boldly he thrust his hand amongst the snakes who, on this occasion, possibly because the boldness and the thrusting made them more unsettled, not only shook their rattles, but also hissed loudly. The horrified company watched in breathless silence. Everything went smoothly at first, but then they were precipitated into 'danger never before dreamt of'. One snake, who had just been persuaded to bite a rabbit and was being replaced in the box, 'angrily raised himself into an erect position, and, as quick as lightning, suddenly and rapidly darted forward'.[22] The audience rushed from the room, while the Squire and his steadfast companion managed between them to capture the snake.

Hobson concluded this account of Waterton's presence of mind and bravery with an unexpected reference to the celebrated occasion when he had ridden on the back of a crocodile in the waters of the Essequibo River. Here praise was quickly transformed into mockery and sarcasm:

Now the man who dared to put his unprotected hand amongst a host of the most venomous snakes in existence would not likely have refused a mount on a defenceless cayman, dragged by seven men, by means of a rope with a barbed hook in its extremity, and firmly fixed within the stomach of the animal. This mechanically restrained condition of the alligator, it must be admitted, rendered it totally incapable in a physical point of view, to give battle to any creature on earth.[23]

Vangordon eventually departed, presumably content with the success of his transatlantic enterprise, and Waterton had another close encounter at the London Zoo when he obtained permission to enter the cage of a leopard, and by 'playing his cards right' managed to examine its paws, and to see that indeed the claws were retractable.

In 1865, and only a few months before his death, Waterton had the pleasure of welcoming the French giant, Monsieur Brice, to his home. It has been said that giants are usually very unwilling to allow themselves to be measured, especially when, like Monsieur Brice, they made their living by putting themselves on show. But Waterton was obviously very persuasive, and he recorded proudly in his diary that without his shoes on Monsieur Brice was seven foot eight inches tall, and remarkably well made.

The image of an old man measuring a young giant. The image of an old man standing in a cage, admiring the teeth of an orang-utan. Or to go back fifty years in time, the image of Waterton in Georgetown, knocking on the door of an albino negro slave, and saying that, '. . . having heard much of his fair skin, I had come that morning to make acquaintance with him . . .'[24]

CHAPTER XX

There is a Remedy for Everything but Death

Quite near to the house, and sheltered by a dense crescent of yew trees, there was an area known as the Grotto by the Waterton family, and as Picnic by local people. The grotto itself was a natural cave, and a little pillared temple had been built next to it, with a conical roof, a stone table and stone benches. There was also a larger temple where the cotton workers, the farm workers, the lunatics and other regular picnicking parties would gather, play music and dance. There was a swing, a stream with steep banks thick with ferns, an avenue of fir trees, an Anglo-Saxon cross that Waterton had once found being used as a doorstep in a cottage in Walton village, a heap of stones which he had arranged in a good south-facing position for the convenience of the weasels, a second starling tower which was also the occasional home of a green woodpecker, and a little house with only one room where he spent many hours, especially during the winter. Sometimes he might come here to take tea with Eliza and Helen, but often he would sit here alone, with a fire blazing, and the door wide open so that he could watch the birds and animals outside, and listen to the endless crying, calling and rustling of life around him. Magpies and robins would come into the room for the grain and breadcrumbs he scattered on the floor, pecking around his feet, and hopping on to his shoes.

It was here, in the grotto and near to this little house, that Waterton at first thought he would like to be buried. Then he changed his mind. Maybe the place suddenly seemed too tame or too public, or maybe he had an ever stronger presentiment of the confusion that was going to follow his death, and preferred to be further away, out of sight of all the strangers. He decided instead that he would like to have his final resting place far from the house, under the huge oak trees from whose branches he had studied the foxes when he was a boy, and amongst whose branches he had so often settled himself, reading from the *Odes* of Horace or Ovid's *Metamorphoses*, and looking up to watch the kingfishers fishing in the Drain Beck River—the same river that had once carried Simpson's dangerous effluents down towards the lake, but which was now free of chemicals although silted with a thick black mud. This site could be reached by boat across the lake, or one could go over the iron bridge, and then skirt along the water's edge, past the Heronry, past Stubbs' Wood, and then make towards a point where the dark leaves of a yew could be distinguished from amongst the deciduous trees. There was a view out over the lake, and on the other side of the stream a stretch of marshland where the more rare and the more timid wading birds were sometimes to be seen. Even in Waterton's time it was a landscape where human beings seemed to have no place, and everyone who has described it since his death has been impressed by its 'utter solitude and abandonment', its 'sense of being forsaken'. But it did prove to be a wise choice, for although so much else has gone at Walton Hall the grave can still be seen: a little patch of ground thick with brambles and nettles, surrounded by rusting iron railings, and nearby a stone cross and a marble slab with the inscription eroded by the weather and hidden by moss.

Waterton was in the habit of rowing across the lake to this spot quite regularly, and he would take Eliza and Helen with him if their health and determination allowed them to accompany him. It was as if he were trying to teach these two querulous ladies to anticipate the time when he would no longer be with them; encouraging them to realize that their lives must not come to an end with his, and that the park and the house were their rightful home. Or, as he explained it in one of the several wills that he wrote and rewrote during those last years, should they remain unmarried it was to be hoped that 'nothing will ever persuade them to leave Walton Hall'. Perhaps it was as an aspect of this preparation that he decided, in January 1864, to remove the old stone cross that had for so long stood above the watergate on the island, and set it up by the oak trees, facing the lake. He had already decided on a Latin epitaph which was carved on a marble slab, waiting for the occasion when a second date could be added to the first, 'Pray for the soul of Charles Waterton, whose weary bones lie close to this cross. Born 1782. Died 18..'

And so, as quietly and as gently as possible, Waterton did his best to set things in order. He knew very well, sometimes painfully well, just how vulnerable his peaceable kingdom really was; with the outside world jostling around its fragile boundaries, waiting for an opportunity to enter. When in the 1850s he had visited that hunting fortress near Aix-la-Chapelle, built by the Emperor Charlemagne over a thousand years ago, he had been confronted by a distant mirror image of the possible fate of Walton Hall and its park once he was no longer there to hold it firm at its centre. That fortress had stood in forlorn incongruity, with factory chimneys mushrooming on all sides, and 'speculators, brokers and attorneys' all eager to pounce on the site itself, putting you in mind, said Waterton, 'of old Orpheus, the sweet musician, who was seen one day with his lyre, amid a group of monkeys and dancing dogs'.[1] But in his verdict he was as harsh as he was realistic: 'Its ancient walls, its moat, and huge massive tower, rising from above the other buildings, bespeak its former consequence and pride. But, if it were mine, it would soon disappear; for there is nothing left around it to tell the best part of its early story.'[2]

Waterton was a profoundly religious man, and for him it was crucial to be able to acquiesce to what he saw as the will of God; to accept that everything he loved and cherished could be abruptly swept away and lost without trace. He had to learn that delicate juxtaposition of caring and not caring in which he treasured his trees, his birds and his animals, his museum of curiosities, his sisters-in-law, everything for which he felt himself responsible, and yet could let them go and not be afraid for their sake. But that did not mean that he tried to hide himself from the fact that the two ladies were painfully uncertain; the hedge-hogs and the owls, the herons and the weasels had learnt to be recklessly unafraid of human beings; and all the old trees in the park needed such careful attention, such regular binding up of their wounds if they were to go on standing for future generations to marvel at their crooked hugeness.

As the years moved on it became inevitable that the rift between Waterton and Edmund would widen, since Edmund came to represent the personification of so many of the things that Waterton had carefully rejected and avoided. And yet this bulky, stuttering young man, with his silken clothes, his sparkling jewellery and his endless obsession with money and status, was the rightful inheritor of all that Waterton possessed, and the son of a young woman he had loved.

From the 1850s onwards the father and son learnt to avoid each other's company, although they did both try to get to Stonyhurst for the Christmas celebrations, and occasionally they spent a few uneasy weeks together at Walton Hall. Whereas Waterton's religious beliefs led him to private prayer and private acts of self-denial, Edmund was drawn to all the vivid displays and decorations of the Catholic Church, and welcomed every public opportunity of decking himself out in elaborate finery. In 1858 he received what he referred to as '. . . the most distinguished Order in Rome—the Order of Christ, which is a splendid decoration!' In that same year he went to join the Pope at Loreto, and accompanied him on a tour of the Papal States, an itinerary which lasted four or five months. He was invested with the Order of St John of Jerusalem which gave him the right to be presented at the royal courts of Europe.

Inevitably, all these duties and decorations cost him a huge amount of money. In order to receive the Order of St John he needed to pay £150.16s. and 6p. The trip to Bologna set him back £250 in travelling expenses alone, and then there was £30 for the 'undress uniform' of a chamberlain, and a further undisclosed sum for other costumes, including the 'Spanish chamberlain's one, with ruffles', which he wore for one of his many portrait sittings. Apparently the finished canvas was shipped over to England as a gift for his father. On top of all that there were papal fees, and the inevitably high cost of maintaining the standard of living of 'a person of my background and reputation'. Waterton meanwhile was running his entire estate on an income of between £650 to £750 a year, and whatever investments he and his two sisters-in-law might have had were soon used up.

Both in England and in Italy, Edmund was relentless in his search for antique rings and brooches, swords and fruit trenchers; early editions of the *Imitation of Christ* by Thomas à Kempis, and any books related to the devotion of Our Lady. By the mid 1850s he had accumulated a library of over a thousand valuable antiquarian books, and an extra-ordinary collection of jewelled finery, much of which was sent to him on loan by established dealers and only returned after a flood of threatening letters. In England he was a member of a rifle club, a hunting club, an archery club, and a horticultural club, as well as being a member of the Athenaeum Society and the Society of Antiquaries. During the course of his life he published a small handful of essays on ecclesiastical rings and the devotion of the Virgin in England, but that was the only work he ever set himself to do. Since he wrote to a friend declaring that he had given up drinking, gambling and debauching, he must at times have indulged in all three vices, although, in his own view, '. . . considering how I have been placed, and what I have had to put up with, it is well I have not done worse'.[3] There is even a mysterious reference to 'Little McDonnell', a young boy who was brought up for the Church and sent to Stonyhurst at Edmund's expense; presumably because he had reasons for feeling financially obliged to the child.

For Edmund the acquisition of money simply meant the possibility of borrowing more. In 1853 he inherited from his uncle Robert Carr a sum that was to be held in trust until such time as he married, and this enabled him to raise £3,000. In that same year his father gave him an annual settlement of £300 which he quickly transformed into a mortgage of £2,000. In 1856 Eliza paid off his earlier debts to his father and loaned him £2,000, and by 1859 this loan stood at £5,500. Until 1862 Edmund was regularly having to thank 'My good Aunts . . . for all their kindness in getting me out of my scrapes . . .' and he was also having to ask them kindly not to mention anything to his father.

In 1859, with his papal duties apparently over, Edmund determined to make his home in England. He was growing ever more anxious to 'settle down quietly and lead the life of an English Squire', and he was also beginning to anticipate his father's imminent death, commenting on various falls and accidents with a rather uneasy concern.

> My father is beginning to fail rather in his strength . . . His usual remedies were resorted to, and having lost about 60 ounces of blood and taken calomel wholesale, together with less rigorous measures and the unremitting attention of my aunts, I have the satisfaction of letting you know that he is so far recovered as to be meditating a journey to Scarborough.[4]

Marriage was also very much on his mind, and he was hoping to arrange to bring a wife back with him from the Continent. In a letter to Eliza in 1859 he wrote, 'You might meet with a Mrs EW this winter! . . . but as yet the prospects are only vague.' Further 'suggestions for a settlement' were drawn up with another matrimonial candidate in 1861, and then in 1862 he married Josephine, the second daughter of Sir John Ennis Bt, a Governor of the Bank of Ireland, a Chairman of the Midland Great Western Railway, and, according to Waterton, a dealer in blankets and a millionaire. Edmund's bride provided him with a dowry of £13,300, and released whatever was left of his first inheritance. With his new status he was able to make a much more thorough break with his own family, and Waterton was not even informed in advance about his plans: 'In money matters Edmund expects great things, and this is all I know. Being abroad at the time of the courtship, I was not consulted, and only told after it was arranged . . . so my consent or veto were rendered nugatory. It would not do to have the parties taking up their abode here.'[5]

Edmund acquired a house near Bury St Edmunds, and in June 1863 his first son, Charlie, was born. But although the child was the 'subject of genuine rejoicing and the delight and pride of his grandfather', particularly since he 'very quickly showed signs of an interest in natural history', relations between Waterton and his son deteriorated still further. It would seem that Waterton had agreed to accept compensation in return for allowing a railway line to cut across a portion of his land, and he had promised to give some of this money to Edmund. However Edmund arranged for the entire sum to be paid to him directly, as his father's marriage settlement, and this was done secretly and with the help of a 'pernicious London lawyer'. In a letter signed in the presence of a witness so that it stood as a legal document, Waterton released the full flood of his anger and despair:

> In giving instructions for your marriage settlement . . . you ignore altogether the understanding existing between us . . . I cannot describe how much I felt on first being acquainted with this. To say that I suffered for some time seriously in my bodily health is the least . . . More has occurred, sufficient to embitter my feelings, nay to estrange me altogether . . . I do not ask you to act as a *son*, but as a *man of honour.*[6]

Waterton went on to declare that he did not wish to see Edmund, or to communicate with him further until 'this annoyance is stopped'. In December 1863 he redrafted his will, and although Edmund was not as yet disinherited, his two aunts were made into joint executors, along with the family solicitor, and were given £10,000, a sum which Waterton did not possess, and which therefore stood as a mortgage right on Walton Hall.

It was during that same year, between the writing of the letter and the rewriting of the will, that Waterton began an important new friendship. To put it simply, he acquired a substitute son, 'one of the finest and most talented youths I ever saw', and someone who had all the qualities which mattered to him and which Edmund apparently lacked. Unexpectedly and uninvited, a very young man turned up at Walton Hall one morning, having made the journey on foot from Manchester. He was let in by the old butler, and given permission to go round the museum, although its creator was nowhere to be seen. When he was about to leave, the butler returned with a tray of food which was set down before him. Afterwards, as he was walking towards the park gate,

> I saw the Wanderer in the Wilds of Guiana. He is an old man of middle height. His hair is white, but his senses are more acute than those of a much younger man, and he does not stoop at all.

He was directing and helping a man clip the yew hedges. Having thanked him for the food he had sent me, I began asking various questions. We talked near a structure built for the accommodation of starlings and owls. I will now tell all that I can remember of what Mr Waterton told me.[7]

The young man was Norman Moore, later to become Sir Norman Moore, President of the Royal College of Physicians, and a doctor who treated some of the most important people of his time, including Charles Darwin whom he attended during his last illness. When he arrived at Walton Hall he was sixteen years old. He was living in Manchester with his mother, working as an apprentice in a cotton factory during the day and attending evening classes at a Working Man's Natural History Society. His father was an Anglo-Irish barrister, famous for his womanizing and his powers of oratory, who bore the dramatic name of Robert Ross Rowan Moore. His mother came from an established Irish Quaker family, his parents had been estranged since before his birth and he never once met his father.

Norman Moore visited Waterton on eight occasions during the next two years. Sometimes he could only stay a few days, sometimes for a few weeks. He knew that the old man might suddenly die if he had a slight accident or a bout of illness, and so with the urgent sense that each meeting might be the last, he spent as many hours as he could find in his company, asking questions, listening, studying Waterton's way of working and of observing nature, and following him everywhere with the patient devotion of a puppy. Together the two of them clambered into the old watergate to inspect the assortment of birds which had chosen to nest there. Together they went hedging and ditching, mending fences and bridges, dredging mud from a stream, plastering a crack in the branch of an old tree. Together they rowed across the lake to inspect the site of the grave.

At the close of almost every day that he spent at Walton Hall, Moore would put an entry in his journal. He was still very young and his writing has an innocent rush to it: quickly telling all before it is lost or forgotten, but nothing else that has been written about Waterton succeeds so well in following the old man through his days, and providing a sense of sitting with him in silence and understanding something of his nature and his particular qualities of kindness and humility. Over ten years later, Moore kept another detailed journal which he wrote for his wife during the long and enforced waiting time before they were allowed to marry. In these pages Waterton often entered his thoughts, and he tried to describe with the clarity of distance what that early friendship had meant to him:

> When I was coming he used to come out and meet me, and gave me his hands so kindly that I felt I loved him more each time he spoke. He used to call me Normando . . . He used to say to me, 'I hope when you grow old you manage to have a little land of your own, and you'll sit in the sun and now and then think of me.' I am not old yet, but I often, often think of him, and the more I think, the more glad I am that I knew him.[8]

During his first three visits to Walton Hall, Moore wrote his journal with the clear intention of providing a documentary record. Cautiously and with a formality which attempts to reflect the importance of everything he was putting into words, he described the house, the park, the 'two kind and stately ladies' who were Waterton's sisters-in-law, a 'very handsome young lady' called Lydia who was an Edmonstone cousin staying as a guest, the parrot, the cat, the telescope, the lake, the birds. He described the 'beautiful big blue china cups' in which tea was served, the red room with a four-poster bed in which he slept, and for page after page he meticulously itemized everything that was on show in the museum. He also made occasional uncertain pencil drawings, and kept a numbered note of Waterton's remarks and anecdotes,

> 11—If you want to catch a snake approach it very gently, slowly squat down, slowly bring forward your hand and seize it round the neck.
> 14—A surgeon is the noblest profession one could choose.
> 24—Do not go into the swamps of Guiana till you have been accustomed to the climate or you will die.
> 25—There are a great number of ants in Guiana.
> Violence in man always arouses violence in an animal.
> I have been living here for more than eighty years, and when I look back upon my life it seems immeasurably short.[9]

In July 1864 Moore was on his third visit to Walton Hall. He left to set out on a walking tour of Ireland.

> The night my father died, I slept on a windy mountain in the northwest of Ireland, called Long Salt. I was ignorant of his illness. I had lost my way and I was very tired, so I lay down in a hollow and

covered myself with pieces of turf to keep off the wind which swept furiously across the mountains. Fierce driving rain followed. But at last I fell asleep, and when I woke it was a clear starlit morning, I walked on thinking of the protecting care of God. My father had been dying that night.[10]

He was back with Waterton in October and, without wishing to make a forced interpretation, it would seem as if from this time onwards the closeness between the old man and the young man became much more open, and he was accepted as if he were a member of the family. In 1865 he was there again in January, February, April, and for several weeks from May to June. With each new meeting he was quick to remark if Mr Waterton seemed tired, or 'was looking well but suffering from occasional attacks of ague' or was bothered by the cold, and in all of his brief but vivid descriptions it was as if he were seeing everything through Waterton's own eyes,

5 November 1864
I found Mr Waterton sitting by the fire at the Grotto House. He welcomed me kindly and I sat down beside him. He said, 'I like to come here and talk to the Cock Robins and Magpies.' He said of later years the wood pigeons have become less numerous about Walton Hall. He told me the green woodpecker comes every night and sleeps in the starling tower at the Grotto. He told me that since I was last at Walton Hall, Sir Lionel Pilkington shot a bittern which was the last one to be seen near Walton. He told me that Sir William Pilkington shot the last raven in the country, on her nest which was in a low tree.

January 1865
Mr Waterton caught a Red Breast, and we cut a small piece off his tail in order that we might know him again.

7 April 1865
We watched the rooks feeding their young and the sandmartins going in and out of their holes. We talked of natural history, of Sterne and Guiana. After a while we went to the Grotto and after pulling up some brambles we sat in the upper temple and basked in the sun.
After dinner Mr Waterton and I ascended the old ruin. In the hole under the crucifix we found two jackdaw eggs.

10 April 1865

We went to the hollow tree near the water's edge. We were going to pull sticks out of it, when out flew two fine white owls. One perched on a tree close to us. They did not seem to be confused by the light. Further on a Canada goose flew out of the briar. In a willow near the fish canal we saw a pair of long-tailed titmice. We also saw a spotted woodpecker, which I got close to, and watched carefully for some minutes. We also saw some herons, woodpigeons, rooks, kestrels and several other birds.[11]

There is page after page of such simple descriptions: nine kestrels rising in an unlikely flock by the oak trees; four brown owls flying out of the wood in the early evening; 1,640 wild duck, 30 coots and 28 Canada geese within view of the drawing room window one morning; two hares playing on the hillside near a group of trees which Waterton called the Beatitudes; two wild swans rising steeply into the air. Moore was very aware of the fact that such concentrations of wild life were only possible because of Waterton's careful husbandry, and he told how many of the birds had lost their natural fear, and would watch him as if he were 'an intruder on their privacy' and would let him move quite close to them without once stirring. He also realized that this magical garden could easily be made to merge with the outside world, and each time he went walking in the surrounding countryside he was shocked by the silence, the stillness and the lack of wild life that was to be found on the other side of the high walls of the park.

Inevitably Waterton instructed his young disciple in the art of taxidermy. The journal for November 1864 includes a detailed account of the preparation of a toucan, 'Mr Waterton used to call them the Magpies of South America,' and by January 1865 Waterton felt that they were ready to take on some interesting carcass together, setting his heart on a gorilla, 'As I am now sure to be at home every day till July, methinks that if yourself and myself were to put our heads together, we might procure an old gorilla in spirits. I could wish for nothing more.'[12]

Thanks to the co-operation of the Manchester Museum, a large male gorilla was dully delivered to the doorstep in a barrel of rum. Although neither Waterton nor Moore ever explained its previous history, it was obvious that some considerable time had elapsed between the hour of its death and the hour of its arrival at Walton Hall. As soon as dinner was over the two of them, along with a certain Dr Wright, transferred the creature into a wooden trough and carried it triumphantly into the drawing room, where they set to work.

Mr Waterton told me that the gorilla skin was in a hopeless condition . . . The beast must have been a huge one. The colour of the hair was grise, whitest at the back. The head was immense, I could have put my head in it with ease. The eyes were small. But this otherwise fine specimen was a complete wreck.[13]

As Waterton explained in a letter, '. . . we laboured and laboured in vain at it . . . It stank horribly whilst nothing but the bones could be saved.'[14]

Waterton, who was in the habit of retiring to his room at eight o'clock and seeing no one until breakfast the following morning, was obviously affected by Moore's endless enthusiasm. The two of them could be found sitting together in the attic talking about natural history at midnight, at two in the morning and before the dawn. One entry in the journal mentions in a matter-of-fact way, 'This morning at two o'clock, Mr Waterton and I were standing on the staircase. We looked out to see if any waterfowl were left. The moon was shining full on the ice, but except for the Canada goose, we saw none of any kind.'[15]

Moore's eighth visit to Walton Hall was in May 1865. He had several weeks ahead of him during which he was preparing for some examinations. On 12 May he went up to Waterton's room at a quarter past six in the morning, and found him sitting by the fire reading from *Don Quixote*. 'He showed me a fine fungus which he is preparing and also a large toad from Bahia which he is painting.'[16] After lunch they went outside; a thick rain was falling and it was bitterly cold. They fed the cats in the saddle room, and then went to the grotto where they sat by a fire talking for most of the afternoon.

On the evening of 24 May Moore was still at Walton Hall. Having finished his mathematics studies he went up to Waterton's room at midnight:

He was sleeping, sitting by the fire, wrapped in his great Italian cloak, with his head resting on his wooden pillow on his little table. I stood by him, and in a few minutes he awoke. He then went to the Chapel for a few minutes, and when he came back we talked together for three quarters of an hour about the brown owl, and the nightjar, and many other things, natural history and otherwise.[17]

The following morning, 25 May 1865, Moore, a carpenter and Waterton set out to finish their work on some bridges at the far side of the park. They were on their way back and crossing over a small bridge, when Waterton caught his foot in a bramble and fell heavily on a log. He was greatly shaken and said 'he thought he was dying'. Yet he managed to walk unaided to the boat, walked from the landing place to the house, changed his clothes and sat in the downstairs room. A doctor was called in, and Doctor Cleaton, the Director of the Wakefield Lunatic Asylum, came by unexpectedly for a friendly visit, and stayed to examine the patient also. Waterton insisted on going upstairs, but although he wanted to reach his attic, he got no further than Eliza's sitting room, and there he lay down on a sofa. His sisters-in-law watched over him during the night and the next day he seemed better, although every time he felt his pulse he remarked, 'this is a bad business.'

The following night Moore and Lydia Edmonstone stayed up with the sick man. Moore wrote in his journal that he lay on his elbow, so that he might keep his eyes on Mr Waterton's face. Towards midnight it became clear that he was going to die, and when he was asked if he would like to be given the Last Sacrament he replied, 'By all means!' He sang the hymn of St Bernard and a few verses of the '*Dies Irae*', and gave his blessing to his grandson Charlie, to his baby granddaughter, to Eliza and Helen, to Lydia and to Norman Moore, and he left a message for Edmund who was hurrying back from Rome. Then he took the Sacrament and died.

'He died just as the rooks were beginning to caw and the swallows to chirp. He died as he always said he would, sitting up, and conscious to the last.'[18]

CHAPTER XXI

Coda

No enemy,
But winter and rough weather.[1]

Waterton was buried on his birthday, 3 June 1865. He had left careful instructions for his funeral. The entrance hall of the house was turned into a chapel where the Requiem Mass was held, with the museum exhibits hidden beneath folds of black drapery. Thirteen priests, four canons in purple cloaks, and a bishop in mitre and robes officiated at the ceremony. The coffin was placed in a little coal boat, and towed by a barge with a cross in its bows. The coal boat in turn pulled Waterton's own boat, *The Percy*, empty and draped in black. Members of the family and friends accompanied the procession in three more boats. Hundreds of mourners walked alongside the lake towards the two great oak trees and the stone cross. Only the sisters-in-law did not come. Instead they sat on a bench under a tree near the drawing room window, heard the singing voices grow fainter and watched the dark shapes receding into the distance. It was said that a flock of birds flew above the procession, and when the coffin was lowered into the earth a linnet began to sing, joining its brave voice with the chanting of the '*Benedictus*'.

And then, is it relevant to chronicle the slow chaos that followed? Certainly there is no purpose in trying to do so, if all that is left is a sense of sadness. When Waterton died, the world he had created fell apart; but that world was such a simple thing: easily made and easily lost. It was only a wall around an area of trees and water. It was only quiet and shelter and the possibility for wild creatures to live and die undisturbed by human beings. Such a world can be brought into existence, again and again.

213

Norman Moore tried as well as he could to hold the threads together. He tried to do everything he felt Waterton would have wanted from him: 'It is my most earnest wish to live as he lived, and in the end to die as he died.'[2] But this meant that he also had to learn how to care and not to care, and to realize that in many ways the case was hopeless. Nevertheless he did manage to obtain the complete bundle of letters written to George Ord, and to keep them away from Edmund, and while he was studying at Cambridge he produced a new edition of the *Essays* in which he enlarged on Waterton's *Autobiography* with his own *Life of the Author*. He also kept everything that came his way: the block of mahogany that had been used as a pillow; a marble portrait bust; the 'old birds' feet and so on from a drawer' which Helen realized she had no further use for, since Charlie Waterton did not seem to want them; an album of photographs, and all the letters exchanged between himself and the surviving but dwindling members of the family. Eliza and Helen would write to Moore on small stiff sheets of paper always bordered by the black band of mourning; Edmund wrote with his letter-headings embossed with a golden image of the otter with a trout in its mouth, and the old family motto, 'Better kinde frende than strange kyne'. And so it is, for the most part, from Norman Moore's collection that the end of the story can be assembled.

Edmund and his wife arrived at Walton Hall on the day before the funeral, and with them came 'great quantities of things from Rome: rings, medals, pictures, marbles and etc.' Within four days Edmund was filled with plans. He wanted to build a chapel of mourning behind his father's grave and presumably closely flanked by the two great oak trees, and he wanted to build another, larger chapel on the island near to the house. The plans for the second construction were drawn up and agreed upon, and Edmund got so far as to decide that his father's coffin must be moved to the new site; but the chapel never grew beyond two of its exterior walls and Waterton's weary bones were left undisturbed.

It would seem that just a few weeks before his fatal accident, Waterton had become aware of the full extent of his son's debts, and so he made a final attempt to safeguard his home and his park, realizing that 'anything not tightly tied up would be seized by the creditors'.[3] According to this, his last will, the house, the park, the farmlands, all monies, all furniture, books, silver, paintings, and the mortgaged sum of £10,000 were given to Eliza and Helen and, 'in case of the death of one of them before me, I give the same personal estate and real estate unto the survivor of them absolutely.'[4] The understanding was that

Eliza and Helen would provide Edmund with any money they felt he needed, and the estate in its entirety would eventually pass on to his eldest son Charlie.

At the graveside Edmund was heard to declare himself 'perfectly satisfied' with the will, and a few days later he and Josephine went to stay in a hotel in London. Norman Moore returned to his studies, and shortly afterwards received a letter from the two sisters, asking him cautiously if he thought they could plant some flowers on their dear brother's grave, 'It will be easy enough to take them up again, if Edmund does not like them.'[5]

In August 1865 the sheriffs came to the house to seize whatever goods they could find belonging to Edmund, and Eliza intervened and bought back everything on his behalf. It would seem that by now Edmund had already begun to prepare his legal case against his aunts, disputing their right to have inherited anything from his father, and they, preferring not to have a confrontation, offered to leave Walton Hall if he in turn would keep it intact and unchanged, 'for his father's sake'. And so in September they bought themselves a house in Scarborough, and their endless, restless wanderings from place to place had begun.

In the spring of 1866 Edmund's lawyer had the certain knowledge that the sisters would not challenge the case against them in a court of law. When Eliza was forced to make a statement, explaining her position as '. . . an active woman of business, who had for many years great influence over my father and over her sister',[6] all that she would say was, 'The Plaintiffs have ample material in their possession for shewing Charles Waterton's reasons for making his will, but they are unwilling, out of regard for the defendant, Edmund Waterton, to do so.'[7]

And so it was as good as settled, and Edmund and Josephine moved into their ancestral home which Edmund had officially renamed Walton Castle. He was henceforth to be known as the twenty-eighth Lord of Walton, and his wife put it about in polite circles that she was to be 'introduced at the drawing room as the Lady of Walton Castle'. According to one local witness, a doctor from Wakefield:

They had a brief career of pride and folly and extravagances. They brought carriages and furniture and debts . . . and assumed a baronial style of living. The butler and cook served up 'banquets in the Italian style', but the bailiffs were constantly in the house as well as on the grounds.[8]

While he was temporarily at Walton Hall, Edmund was able to make some money to pay for his pleasures by arranging shooting parties, and by inviting wood dealers, 'bravoes from Wakefield and Barnsley', to come and 'contend for mastery' in the park. 'The water birds were shot off without mercy. The game shared the same fate. The trees where the herons incubated were felled by the remorseless woodman, and the herons which were not shot, flew away and did not return.'[9]

Eliza and Helen visited in June 1867, and 'found the place sadly changed for the worse'. They asked Edmund for permission to put a fence of iron railings around Waterton's grave, and this permission was granted.

In 1868 Edmund received legal confirmation that he was the owner of everything that had once been his father's. He immediately rented out the farming land and the park, and initiated a plan to sell off building plots; offering one of these prime sites to his aunts, free of charge and with all the necessary building stones. He arranged for the whole area to be carefully examined to see if any coal was to be found, and indeed one seam was discovered, although nothing was done to prove whether it was workable. He also decided to get rid of the museum of natural curiosities, apart from a few cases which he wished to keep for himself. He therefore presented the almost entire collection on loan to Ushaw College, formerly Tudhoe, the school that Waterton had hated so vehemently because the masters had not allowed him to follow his 'ruling passion' of hunting for birds and birds' eggs. Eliza wrote to inform Norman Moore of this latest news:

> You will be grieved to hear that everything on the dear old staircase is to be dismantled, The Natural History has gone to Ushaw, and we have taken a room in Wakefield for the paintings.
>
> The gardener and other servants are leaving . . . All these changes are a sad grief to us. Polly [the parrot] has gone to Canon Browne, to take care of till we have got a home for him, darling Whity [Waterton's favourite cat], has been sent to a dear friend of ours . . .[10]

In spite of his inheritance, Edmund was still deep in debt, and was forced to declare himself bankrupt and go to live with his family on the Continent. It was said that he 'lives in one place until lack of credit forces him to move on',[11] and quite often he ended up in whatever house his aunts happened to be occupying, whether in Brussels, Bruges or Ostend.

Eliza wrote to Norman Moore from Ostend, 'We have Edmund and all his family staying with us; the latter for some months, but we hope that they are leaving soon . . .'[12]

At Walton Hall Edmund at first installed a distant relation, who was known in the village as the Baroness, and was rarely seen and even more rarely spoken to. She acted as a sort of housekeeper, and inhabited the almost empty rooms in the deserted building with a servant girl to help her and an old grey pony to take her into the village and to church on Sundays. She was there until 1871 when the house was let to a Mr Hailstone, a retired solicitor, who was much liked for his gentle ways and who did his best to keep the park in order and to encourage some of the birds to return.

Not surprisingly, Edmund in his exile became increasingly drawn to the idea of selling his entire estate and, as it happened, there was a man living in Walton village who was extremely interested in buying it. At this point the story of how Waterton's peaceable kingdom was dismantled and lost takes such a strange and ironic turn that it is as if one can hear the distant sound of harsh laughter. The prospective buyer was none other than Edward Simpson, the eldest son of Waterton's soap-boiling neighbour, whose stinking effluents had once flowed into the little Drain Beck River.

Simpson was by now a 'gentleman of quite considerable means'. He lived at Thornhill House in Walton village, employed 300 men and boys at his Calder Soap Works, and his product was bought by royalty and sold as far afield as South Africa and India. His father had died in 1871, but the wounds from that battle between the old world and the new were still as fresh as ever. 'Charles Waterton tried hard to ruin my Father, and nothing would have delighted my Father more than for his son to buy Waterton's estate.'[13] Simpson's step in realizing this ambition was to contact his land agent, explaining the information he had received, and what his own position was: 'The Mortgagees will sell some part of the estate of Walton Hall, and I am ready to buy what they will sell; but I want the whole.'[14] He then arranged for friends on the Continent to take a good look at Edmund, and in this way he learnt that he was '. . . living in one place until lack of credit forces him to move on . . . vain and anxious for more income wherewith to adorn his person and amuse his fancy. He formerly lived in Ostend where he had a house furnished with lots of curiosities, he bought anything he fancied, quite irrespective of the cost.'[15]

Simpson's name was not mentioned when Edmund was first approached, but even when he realized who it was who wished to take over Walton Hall, he was prepared to go ahead with the sale. He managed to produce a very enthusiastic document on the likelihood of finding a rich coal seam in the park, and the estate was sold in 1877 for the phenomenal sum of £114,000. He was staying with his aunt Helen at the time (Eliza had died in 1870), although he never spoke to her directly on the subject, but she learnt what was happening from some other source, and wrote at once to Norman Moore.

> I have had sad news confirmed this morning. The dear old estate has been passed into the hands of Simpson of Walton Village. I cannot but feel this unkindness, I cannot encounter Edmund at present . . . Oh what a blessing the dear old Squire and my sister have been spared this grief. My cup of sorrow is brimful and overflowing.[16]

At last able to pay off his debts, Edmund returned to England. He bought a house near Market Deeping in Lincolnshire, and promptly renamed it Deeping Waterton, confidently explaining to Moore, 'I take possession of a new Lincolnshire home next week. I believe there is every possibility that it will turn out to have been old Waterton property.'[17] He became quite friendly with Simpson, and went to stay as a guest in his house in the village and even offered him the painting of 'The Old Squire on the crocodile, and multifarious beasts and birds with the Hall and the Park',[18] for the sum of one hundred guineas, and when Simpson protested that the price was too high, he gave it to him as a gift.

Helen, without her sister and with 'old age creeping on apace', kept in regular contact with Moore, and an element of humour and unexpected gentleness would sometimes creep into her letters. Once Edmund was established in his new way of life she remarked, 'Poor fellow, I fear his sorrows are only beginning.' She proved right, for no sooner was he safe from financial worries than he was overwhelmed by physical ills: headaches, dizziness, and his 'old enemy, hysteria' which crept ever closer to him. He married twice, had eight children and died in 1887.

It was not until 1889, after the death of Mr Hailstone, that Edward Simpson was able to occupy Walton Hall. He at once adopted the 'squireship' of the village, and was said to have taken his new role very seriously. There was much entertaining and travelling and many servants.

In 1891, Mrs Pitte-Byrne, the lady who had stayed as a guest at Walton Hall some thirty years previously, decided to go and look again at the house and the park. She had no idea of what had happened to the place, and was under the impression that the present owner, whoever that might be, would be glad to meet a friend of Waterton and to hear stories about him. When she wrote about the occasion later, she had by then discovered that a certain Mr and Mrs Soap-Boiler were in residence, but she never realized that Waterton had also made acquaintance with the family.

Mrs Pitte-Byrne knocked at the door, explained her reasons for coming and presented her visiting card to a young servant. The card was taken in and promptly returned to her, folded in half: 'Mrs Soap-Boiler was evidently indifferent to Waterton's friends, and did not want to hear about him.'[19] She asked the servant if she might walk around the park and about the fate of the huge elm tree by the lake which Waterton had mended each time it was attacked by lightning or high winds: 'What, that rotten, split-up old tree, quite a disfigurement to the place! That we cut down when we first come!'[20]

She walked around the edge of the lake, to the place where Waterton lay buried. The oak trees were still there.

The cross remained straight, but the letters of his epitaph were so thickly overgrown with moss, that they could scarcely be deciphered by anyone not previously acquainted with the words, and so could never tell the visitor whose weary bones were lying near the cross.[21]

NOTES

INTRODUCTION

1. Lewis Carroll, *Alice in Wonderland* (Macmillan Publishers, Ltd 1865)
2. George Harley, *The Life of a London Physician*, ed. Mrs Alec Tweedie, p. 263 (Scientific Press Ltd, London 1899)
3. A. D. Bartlett, *Life Among the Wild Beasts of the Zoo* (London 1900)
4. Sir James Menteath, *Some Account of Walton Hall* (Loudon's *Magazine of Natural History*, p. 30, 1834)
5. George Ord, in letter to Waterton 25 March 1838 (American Philosophical Society Library). 'There is something peculiar in your way of writing, which tickles the reader and prevents satiety. Your *Wanderings* are getting into notice at this side of the Atlantic and Captain Waterton plays a considerable part in a book of immense popularity here—*Peter Parley*. We have this year an almanac which is graced with a report of your combat with a Coulacanara snake.'
6. Theodore Roosevelt, quoted in Allan J. Jenkins, *The Naturalists, Pioneers of Natural History*, p. 73 (Hamish Hamilton 1978)
7. Percy Hetherington Fitzgerald, *Notebooks* (Stonyhurst College)
8. Charles Darwin in letter to Lyell (1845), *Darwin Life and Letters*, Vol. I, p. 343–4
9. Norman Douglas, *Experiments*, p. 192–3 (1925)
10. Edith Sitwell, *English Eccentrics*, p. 226 (Penguin 1980)
11. Graham Greene, essay on Eric Gill, 1941, quoted in Frank Hills, *Charles Waterton: An Eccentric?* 20th Century Advocate Press, Melbourne 1972)

CHAPTER I: BROWN RATS AND BLACK RATS

1. Charles Waterton, *Essays on Natural History*, Vol. I, The Rat, p. 214 (Longmans 1838)
2. Charles Waterton, *Natural History Essays with a Life of the Author*, ed.

Norman Moore, *The Monkey Family*, p. 192 (Frederick Warne Ltd 1870)
3. In the possession of the family of Sir Alan Moore
4. Letter dated 18 January 1758

CHAPTER II: ASPECTS OF AN EDUCATION

1. Charles Waterton, *Natural History Essays with a Life of the Author*, op. cit., *Life of the Author*, p. 15
2. Waterton in letter to Rev. A. Brooke, 1 December 1861, *Reminiscences of Charles Waterton the Naturalist* by Rev. J. Brooke (Thomas Birch 1877)
3. Waterton in letter to Francis T. Buckland, 4 April 1856 (David Attenborough Collection)
4. Charles Waterton, *Natural History Essays with a Life of the Author*, op. cit., Waterton in letter to George Waterton, 26 March 1862, *Life of the Author*, p. 16
5. Stonyhurst French Grammar Book
6. Waterton in letter to Eliza and Helen, 27 December 1859 (Moore Collection)
7. Charles Dickens, *The Old Curiosity Shop*, Chapter 45
8. Daniel Defoe, *A Tour Through the Whole Island of Great Britain, 1724–7*, Vol. II
9. Charles Waterton, *Essays on Natural History*, op. cit., Vol. I, *The Raven*, p. 286
10. *Ibid.*, *The Kingfisher*, p. 376
11. *Ibid.*, *Autobiography*, p. xxiv
12. Father Clifford in letter to Waterton, 23 April 1804 (American Philosophical Society Library)
13. Dr John Dalton, 1766–1844 *see* Angus Smith, *Memoir of John Dalton and History of the Atomic Theory* (1856)
14. Charles Waterton, *Essays on Natural History*, op. cit., Vol. III, *The Fox*, p. 246
15. *Ibid.*, p. 251

CHAPTER III: MALAGA AND THE BLACK VOMIT

1. Charles Waterton, *Essays on Natural History*, op. cit., Vol. I, *Autobiography*, p. xxxiv
2. *Ibid.*, p. xxxvi
3. *Ibid.*, p. xxxvii
4. *Ibid.*, p. xxxix
5. Father Clifford in letter to Waterton 23 April 1804 (American Philosophical Society Library)
6. *Ibid.*

CHAPTER IV: BRITISH GUIANA

1. Waterton in conversation noted in Norman Moore's *Notebooks*, 1864 (Moore Collection)
2. Waterton in letter to John Wells, Mayor of Nottingham, 28 April 1839 (British Museum, Natural History Archives)
3. Charles Waterton, *Essays on Natural History*, *op cit.*, p. 9
4. '70,000 negroes in the colony to a million in money invested for every 100 of them', William Hilhouse, *Agriculture in 1829* (*Timehri*, p. 29, December 1897, Georgetown)
5. George Pinckard, *Notes on the West Indies*, Vol. II, p. 171 (London 1806)
6. Henry Bolingbroke, *Voyage to the Demerary*, p. 26 (London 1809)
7. *Georgetown Gazette* (1818)
8. Richard Schomburgk, *Travels in British Guiana, 1840–44*, trans. Walter E. Roth, Vol. I, p. 55 (Georgetown 1922)
9. M. N. Menezes, *British Policy towards the Amerindians in Guyana 1803–1873* (Oxford Clarendon Press 1977)
10. Charles Waterton, *Wanderings in South America*, p. 175 (Century Publishing Co. 1984)
11. Charles Waterton, *Essays on Natural History*, *op. cit.*, Vol. I, *Autobiography*, p. xlii–xliii
12. Waterton in letter to William Swainson, 18 August 1828 (The Linnean Society, Swainson Correspondence)
13. Charles Waterton, *Essays on Natural History*, *op. cit.*, Vol. I, *Autobiography*, p. 1
14. Waterton in letter to Pope Pius VII, December 1817, Account of the State of Religion (Moore Collection)
15. George Pinckard, *op. cit.*, Vol. III, p. 280
16. *Ibid.*, p. 46
17. *Notes & Records of the Royal Society of London*, Vol 33, August 1978 (*Darwin's Negro Bird Stuffer*). This was John, whom Waterton 'tried to show the proper way to do birds'. He was employed in the Glasgow and then the Edinburgh Museum and there in 1825 he gave lessons to Charles Darwin. 'A negro lived in Edinburgh, who had travelled with Waterton and gained his livelihood by stuffing birds, which he did excellently: He gave me lessons for payment, and I often used to sit with him; for he was a very pleasant and intelligent man.' (*Autobiography*, October 1825–April 1827)
18. Henry Bolingbroke, *op. cit.*, p. 26
19. Charles Edmonstone's report to Governor Bentinck, 18 January 1810 (*Timehri*, p. 33, June 1890, Georgetown)
20. *Ibid.*, p. 50
21. M. N. Menezes, *op. cit.*, p. 54

CHAPTER V: A SEARCH FOR EL DORADO

1. Nicholas Guppy, *A Young Man's Journey* (John Murray 1973)
2. Charles Waterton, *Wanderings in South America, op. cit.*, p. 88
3. *Ibid.*, p. 104
4. *Ibid.*, p. 90
5. Waterton in letter to Robert Bakewell (Loudon's *Magazine of Natural History*, p. 394, 1833
6. Waterton in letter to Pope Pius VII, December 1817, Account of The State of Religion (Moore Collection)
7. Charles Waterton, *Wanderings in South America, op. cit.*, p. 125
8. *Guiana Chronicle* (1822)
9. Waterton in conversation noted in Norman Moore's *Notebooks*, 1864 (Moore Collection)
10. In the possession of Wakefield Museum
11. Charles Waterton, *Wanderings in South America, op. cit.*, p. 96
12. Waterton in letter to William Swainson, 7 August 1828 (The Linnean Society, Swainson Correspondence)
13. Charles Waterton, *Wanderings in South America, op. cit.*, p. 118–19
14. *Ibid.*, p. 109
15. *Ibid.*, p. 93
16. *Ibid.*
17. Waterton's instructions for those in swampy countries, 24 June 1838 (Moore Collection)
18. Charles Waterton, *Wanderings in South America, op. cit.*, p. 91
19. *Ibid.*, p. 101 and 108
20. *Ibid.*, p. 109
21. *Ibid.*, p. 107
22. Nicholas Guppy, *op. cit.*
23. Charles Waterton, *Wanderings in South America, op. cit.*, p. 117
24. *Ibid.*, p. 147
25. Waterton in letter to Robert Bakewell (Loudon's *Magazine of Natural History*, p. 394, 1833)
26. *Ibid.*
27. Charles Waterton, *Wanderings in South America, op. cit.*, p. 149

CHAPTER VI: THE PARK

1. Waterton in letter to Rev. Charles Wright, 11 January 1814 (Stonyhurst College Collection)
2. Charles Waterton, *Wanderings in South America, op. cit.*, p. 142
3. Waterton in letter to John Wells, Mayor of Nottingham, 28 April 1839 (British Museum, Natural History Archives)
4. Charles Waterton, *Essays on Natural History, op. cit.*, Vol. I, *Autobiography*, p. lxiv

5. *Ibid.*, Vol. I. *Autobiography*, p. lxvi
6. *Ibid.*, Vol. I. *Autobiography*, p. lxvi–ii
7. *Ibid.*, Vol. I, *The Heron*, p. 184
8. W. H. Allen, *The Naturalist in Britain*, p. 142–3 (Allen Lane 1976)
9. In Waterton's area Walton Green and Walton Common were enclosed in 1799, in 1844 he was lamenting the loss of Heath Common, the last stretch of open land in the district
10. T. Halliday, *Vanishing Birds: Their Natural History & Conservation*, p. 86 (Sidgwick & Jackson 1978)
11. Charles Waterton, *Essays on Natural History, op. cit.*, Vol. I, *The Barn Owl*, p. 10
12. *Ibid.*, Vol. I, *The Kingfisher*, p. 166
13. *Ibid.*, Vol. I, *The Tawny Owl*, p. 178
14. *Ibid.*, *The Magpie*, p. 233
15. *Ibid.*, Vol. I, *The Tawny Owl*, p. 172
16. *Ibid.*, Vol. I, *The Windhover Hawk*, p. 257
17. *Ibid.*, Vol. I, *The Heron*, p. 185
18. *Ibid.*, Vol. I, *The Carrion Crow*, p. 89–90
19. *Ibid.*, *The Weasel*
20. *Ibid.*, Vol. I, *The Magpie*, p. 319
21. *Ibid.*, Vol. III, *The Fox*, p. 234
22. *Ibid.*, Vol. I, *The Tawny Owl*, p. 175

CHAPTER VII: CURARE

1. As tuborcaine, it is still used as a muscle relaxant, especially for abdominal operations and to diminish trauma during ECT therapy
2. Charles Waterton, *Wanderings in South America, op. cit.*, p. 128–9
3. Gordon Watson, *Charles Waterton Traveller and Naturalist*, p. 14 (Wakefield Museum Catalogue 1982)
4. Samples were tested at the Department of Anaesthesia and Pharmacy, Leeds University, 1985
5. Waterton in letter to Duke of Northumberland, 3 June 1839 (Northumberland Collection, Percy Letters & Papers, Vol. 69)
6. Waterton in letter to George Harley, 8 June 1856 (Royal College of Surgeons Archives)
7. Waterton's 'Directions concerning the Wourali poison, contained in this box, 26 March 1838' (American Philosophical Society Library)
8. Charles Waterton, *Wanderings in South America, op. cit.*, p. 140–1
9. Edward Bancroft, *Essay on the Natural History of Guiana* (London 1769)
10. Hakluyt Society, ed. R. Schomburgk (1868)
11. Charles Waterton, *Natural History Essays with a Life of the Author, op. cit.*, *Life of the Author* p. 48–9

12. Richard Schomburgk, *op. cit*
13. Charles Waterton, *Natural History Essays with a Life of the Author*, *op. cit.*, *Life of the Author*, p. 48–9
14. Sir Benjamin Collis Brodie, *Croonian Lecture, Philosophical Transactions of the Royal Society of London*, Part I (1811)
15. Sir Benjamin Collis Brodie, *Physiological Researches*, p. 142 (London 1851)
16. Sir Joseph Banks, quoted in letter from Waterton to John Wells, Mayor of Nottingham, 28 April 1839 (British Museum, Natural History Archives)
17. Charles Waterton, *Wanderings in South America*, *op. cit.*, p. 143–4
18. *Ibid.*, p. 151
19. Charles Waterton, *Natural History Essays with a Life of the Author*, *op. cit.*, *Life of the Author*, p. 48
20. *Ibid.*, p. 67
21. Waterton in letter to an unknown correspondent 1842 (Wilson Collection)
22. Waterton in letter to George Ord, 13 May 1838 (Moore Collection)
23. *Nottingham Journal* (12 April 1839)
24. Waterton in letter to George Ord, 24 April 1839 (Moore Collection)
25. Waterton in letter to Francis Sibson, 3 July 1855 (The Royal Institution of Cornwall, Truro, Enys Autograph Collection)
26. Waterton, 8 June 1856 (Royal College of Surgeons Archives)
27. Charles Waterton, *Essays on Natural History*, *op. cit.*, Vol. III, *The Dog Tribe*, p. 182

CHAPTER VIII: THE SECOND WANDERING

1. Sir Joseph Banks in letter to Waterton, 10 March 1816 (British Museum Manuscript Collection)
2. Toméde Sousa, *The Expulsion of the Jesuits from Latin America*, ed. Magnus Mörner, p. 189 (A. Knopf, New York 1965)
3. John McLeod, *Narrative of a Voyage* (John Murray 1817)
4. Maria Graham, *Journal of a Voyage to Brazil* (Longmans 1824)
5. Charles Waterton, *Wanderings in South America*, *op. cit.*, p. 159
6. Henry Koster, *Travels in Brazil*, p. 7 (London 1816)
7. L. F. de Tollenare quoted in *Children of God's Fire, a Documentary History of Black Slavery in Brazil*, ed. & trans. Robert Edgar Conrad, p. 65 (Princetown University Press 1983)
8. Charles Waterton, *Wanderings in South America*, *op. cit.*, p. 167
9. *Ibid.*, p. 174
10. *Ibid.*, p. 175–6
11. *Ibid.*, p. 174

CHAPTER IX: THE HOUSE ON MIBIRI CREEK

1. Charles Waterton, *Essays on Natural History, op. cit.*, Vol. I, *Auto-biography*, p. xxi
2. *Ibid.*, Vol. II, *The Ivy*, p. 68
3. Charles Waterton, *Wanderings in South America, op. cit.*, p. 214
4. *Ibid.*, p. 209
5. *Ibid.*, p. 210
6. *Ibid.*, p. 236
7. *Ibid.*, p. 213
8. *Ibid.*, p. 237
9. *Ibid.*, p. 226
10. *Ibid.*, p. 212
11. *Ibid.*, p. 234
12. *Ibid.*, p. 225
13. *Ibid.*, p. 256
14. *Ibid.*, p. 260
15. *Ibid.*, p. 268
16. *Ibid.*, p. 270
17. *Ibid.*, p. 273
18. *Ibid.*, p. 274
19. *Ibid.*, p. 275
20. In the possession of Wakefield Museum
21. Charles Waterton, *Wanderings in South America, op. cit.*, p. 279

CHAPTER X: THE TAX INSPECTOR AND THE NONDESCRIPT

1. Waterton in letter to Maxwell, late 1840s (Moore Collection)
2. *Ibid.*
3. Charles Waterton, *Wanderings in South America, op cit.*, p. 280
4. *Ibid.*, p. 281
5. *Ibid.*, p. 282
6. *Ibid.*, p. 324
7. *Ibid.*
8. *Timehri*, Vol. X, p. 252–3, December 1896 (Georgetown)
9. *Ibid.*
10. Charles Waterton, *Natural History Essays with a Life of the Author, op. cit.*, Waterton in letter to a bookmaker, 28 June 1863, p. 523–4
11. Waterton in conversation noted in Norman Moore's *Notebooks*, 1864 (Moore Collection)
12. Charles Waterton, *Wanderings in South America, op. cit.*, p. 324
13. *Edinburgh Review*, p. xliii (1826)
14. William Swainson, *Lardner's Cabinet Encyclopedia*
15. Charles Waterton, *Essays on Natural History, op. cit.*, Vol. I, *Auto-biography*, p. ixxv

CHAPTER XI: AMERICA, ITS BIRDS AND ITS BIRD MEN

1. Letter to William Bartram, *see* Joseph Kastner, *A Species of Eternity*, p. 165 (A. Knopf 1977)
2. *Ibid.*, p. 186
3. *Ibid.*, p. 165
4. *Dickens on America and the Americans*, ed. Michael Slater (Harvester Press 1979)
5. Charles Waterton, *Wanderings in South America*, op. cit., p. 305
6. *Miss Lawson's Recollections of Ornithologists* in *The Auk*, Vol. XXXIV, p. 281 (Boston 1917)
7. Charles Waterton, *America*, op. cit., p. 294
8. *Ibid.*
9. Waterton in letter to Rev. Joseph Dunn, 9 April 1825 (North Yorkshire County Museum, York)
10. Dickens in letter to Forster, 24 February 1842
11. Dickens in letter to Forster, 25 March 1842
12. *Indiana As Seen by Early Travellers*, ed. Harlow Lindley, *see* Kastner, *op. cit.*
13. Charles Waterton, *Wanderings in South America*, op. cit., p. 291
14. Bénédict Henry Révoil: *Shooting & Fishing in N. America*, Vol. I, p. xi (1865)
15. J. J. Audubon, *Ornithological Biography*, *see* E. W. Teale, *Audubon's Wildlife*, p. 52 (Thames and Hudson 1965)
16. Charles Waterton, *Wanderings in South America*, op. cit., p. 303
17. Letter from Benjamin Franklin, Bénédict Henry Révoil, *op. cit.*, p. 1–2
18. J. J. Audubon, *op. cit.*, p. 165
19. J. J. Audubon, *The Birds of America*, double Elephant Folio (London 1827–38); *Ornithological Biography*, five volumes (Edinburgh 1831–9); *The Viviparous Quadrupeds of North America*, two volumes (New York 1845–48)
20. Waterton in letter to George Ord, 16 February 1832 (Moore Collection) 'When I was in Philadelphia [1824], no scientific man mentioned him, the only place was at Dr. Meases' who invited him to tea, in order that I may see his drawings.'
21. Audubon, portrait by his son, John Woodhouse Audubon, *c.* 1842 (New York Historical Society)
   Waterton, portrait by Charles Wilson Peale 1824 (National Portrait Gallery, London)
22. E. W. Teale, *Audubon's Wildlife*, p. 165 (Thames and Hudson 1965)
23. John Chancellor, *Audubon*, p. 34 (Weidenfeld & Nicolson 1978)
24. *Ibid.*, p. 61–2
25. Francis H. Herrick, *Audubon*, Vol. I, p. 222
26. Alice Ford, *John James Audubon*, p. 279–80 (University of Oklahoma Press 1964)
27. John Chancellor, *op. cit.*, p. 88

28. *Ibid.*, p. 134
29. J. J. Audubon, *Ornithological Biography*, *The Passenger Pigeon*
30. Charles Waterton, *Natural History Essays with a Life of the Author*, *op. cit.*, *The Passenger Pigeon*, p. 354
31. Audubon in letter to his son Victor, 24 December 1833
32. Loudon's *Magazine of Natural History*, p. 309–72 (1833)

CHAPTER XII: A BRIEF MARRIAGE

1. 'If it had not been for you I might now have been married in the Oronoque with 20,000 head of cattle to my fortune; but you made up to the old woman and she would have nothing to say to me.' Waterton in letter to C. Edmonstone, 16 August 1825 (Moore Collection)
2. Richard Aldington, *The Strange Life of Charles Waterton*, p. 127 (Evans Brothers Ltd 1949)
3. Waterton in letter to Charles Edmonstone, 17 January 1827 (Moore Collection)
4. Norman Moore's *Notebooks*, 1864 (Moore Collection)
5. Edmonstone family letters, esp. Eliza to Anne, 23 June 1829 (Jim Daniel Collection)
6. American Philosophical Society Library
7. Anne Edmonstone to Eliza, 20 April 1829 (Jim Daniel Collection)
8. Eliza in letter to Anne, 23 June 1829 (Jim Daniel Collection)
9. Anne Waterton in letter to Eliza (American Philosophical Society Library)
10. Anne in letter to Helen (American Philosophical Society Library)
11. Rev. J. G. Norris in letter to Sister Marian Nyren at the English Convent, 27 April 1830 (Jim Daniel Collection)
12. *Random Recollections of a Visit to Walton Hall* by W. M. K., *Gentleman's Magazine* (January 1848)
13. Waterton in letter to George Ord, June 1830 (Moore Collection)
14. Marian Nyren in letter to Eliza, 25 June 1830 (Jim Daniel Collection)

CHAPTER XIII: THE TWO YOUNG LADIES

1. Waterton in letter to Eliza and Helen, 29 January 1855 (American Philosophical Society Library)
2. Darwin in letter to Lyell, *op. cit.*
3. Waterton in letter to Eliza, October 1861 (Moore Collection)
4. Waterton in letter to John Gordon, 9 May 1832 (American Philosophical Society Library)
5. Waterton in letter to Norman Moore, 1864 (Moore Collection)
6. Marian Nyren in letter to Eliza, 25 June 1830 (Jim Daniel Collection)
7. Waterton's Notebook (Wakefield Museum Collection)
8. Charles Waterton, *Essays on Natural History*, *op. cit.*, Vol. I, *The Barn Owl*, p. 7

9. *Ibid.*, Vol. I, *The Cormorant*, p. 160
10. From the Wakefield Lunatic Asylum by arrangement with Dr John Davis Cleaton, Medical Director from 1858–66, and a good friend of Waterton
11. Waterton in letter to George Ord, June 1830 (Moore Collection)
12. Richard Aldington, *op. cit.*
13. The collection of the Staircase at Walton Hall, Catalogue, 1842 (Moore Collection)
14. Waterton in letter to George Ord, 20 December 1831 (Moore Collection)
15. Loudon's *Magazine of Natural History*, p. 488 (1832)
16. Charles Waterton, *Essays on Natural History*, *op. cit.*, Vol. I, *The Guillemot*, p. 156
17. *Ibid.*, p. 157
18. *Ibid.*, p. 159
19. Waterton's *Remarks on Rennie's Edition of Montagu's Ornithological Dictionary* (Loudon's *Magazine of Natural History*, p. 517, 1831)
20. Loudon's *Magazine of Natural History*, p. 517 (1836)
21. Waterton's *The question of the office of the gland upon the rump of birds* (Loudon's *Magazine of Natural History*, p. 268, 1836)
22. Letter from Rev. F. O. Morris (Loudon's *Magazine of Natural History*, p. 271, 1836)
23. *Some account of Walton Hall* (Loudon's *Magazine of Natural History*, p. 31, 1834)
24. Charles Waterton, *Essays on Natural History*, *op. cit.*, Vol. I, *The Barn Owl*, p. 16

CHAPTER XIV: SENTIMENTAL JOURNEYS

1. John Murray, *Handbook for Travellers on the Continent*, p. 120 (London 1854)
2. Charles Waterton, *Essays on Natural History*, *op. cit.*, Vol. III, *Aix la Chapelle*, p. 144
3. Waterton in letter to Rev. Joseph Hunt, 16 March 1834 (American Philosophical Society Library)
4. Waterton's European Journal, 1844 (Wakefield Museum Collection)
5. Mariana Starke, *Travels in Europe for the use of Travellers on the Continent and in Sicily*, p. 325 (1829 Edition)
6. Waterton in letter to George Ord, 1 July 1839 (Moore Collection)
7. Eliza in letter to Elizabeth Gray, 3 November 1839 (Jim Daniel Collection)
8. Waterton's European Journal, *op. cit.*
9. *Ibid.*
10. *Ibid.*

11. Charles Waterton, *Essays on Natural History*, *op. cit.*, Vol. III, *Aix la Chapelle*, p. 132
12. Waterton's European Journal, *op. cit.*
13. *Ibid.*
14. *Ibid.*
15. Charles Waterton, *Essays on Natural History*, *op. cit.*, Vol. II, *Autobiography*, p. lxvi–lxvii
16. *Ibid.*, p. lxvii
17. Waterton in letter to George Ord, 4 August 1840 (Moore Collection)
18. Charles Waterton, *Essays on Natural History*, *op. cit.*, Vol. II, *Autobiography*, p. lxxiv
19. Waterton in letter to Prof. Richard Owen, 19 March 1851 (British Museum Natural History Archive, Richard Owen letters)
20. Charles Waterton, *Essays on Natural History*, *op. cit.*, Vol. II, *Autobiography*, p. lxix
21. *Ibid.*, p. lxxxii–lxxxiii
22. *Ibid.*, p. xci
23. Waterton's European Journal, *op. cit.*
24. *Ibid.*

CHAPTER XV: THE SOAPWORKS

1. *Parliamentary Papers, Health, General*. Royal Commission Report No. 614, 1854–62, Vol. 8, *Noxious Vapours*, p. 783–4 (HMSO 1878)
2. *Ibid.*, p. 827
3. *Ibid.*, p. 784
4. *Ibid.*, p. 875
5. *Rivers Commission Report*, Vol. I, p. 17 (1867)
6. *Parliamentary Papers*, *op. cit.*, p. 835
7. *Gardener's Chronicle* (18 August 1849)
8. *Ibid.* (25 August 1849)
9. *Ibid.* (18 November 1848)
10. Waterton in letter to George Ord, 27 July 1849 (Moore Collection)
11. Waterton in letter to *Wakefield Examiner* (1 September 1849)
12. John Middleton in letter to Edward Simpson, 18 February 1847 (John Goodchild Collection)
13. *Gardener's & Farmer's Journal* (1 September 1849)
14. Joseph Wilcock in letter to *Wakefield & West Riding Examiner* (12 October 1849)
15. Waterton in letter to Eliza, 1 August 1848 (American Philosophical Society Library)
16. Waterton in letter to *Wakefield & West Riding Examiner* (14 August 1849)
17. Waterton in letter to George Ord, May 1847 (Moore Collection)
18. *Ibid.*, 22 August 1847

19. Waterton in letter to Mr Brett, 28 May 1848
20. Waterton's evidence prepared for Robert Pashley, 12 July 1849 (Stony-hurst Collection)
21. Waterton in letter to Robert Pashley, 26 February 1849 (Stonyhurst Collection)
22. John Middleton in letter to Edward Simpson, 17 July 1849 (John Goodchild Collection)
23. Waterton in letter to Robert Pashley, 3 April 1852 (Stonyhurst Collection)

CHAPTER XVI: FATHER AND SON

1. Charles Waterton, *Essays on Natural History, op. cit.,* Vol. II, *Autobiography,* p. cxxvi
2. *Ibid.,* p. cxxvii
3. Percy Hetherington Fitzgerald, *Stonyhurst Memories,* p. 43–6
4. *Ibid.*
5. Waterton in letter to Eliza, 29 December 1852 (American Philosophical Society Library)
6. Edmund Waterton in letter to George Ord, October 1854 (Moore Collection)
7. Waterton in letter to Edmund, 21 June 1863 (North Yorkshire County Library Museum)
8. Julia Pitte-Byrne, *Social Hours with Celebrities,* p. 45 (1898)
9. *Ibid.,* p. 44
10. *Ibid.,* p. 45
11. Waterton in letter to George Ord, 1856 (Moore Collection)
12. Percy Hetherington Fitzgerald, *Memoirs of an Author* (Richard Bentley & Son 1895)
13. *Ibid.*
14. Julia Pitte-Byrne, *op. cit.,* p. 108
15. *Ibid.,* p. 74
16. Charles Waterton, *Essays on Natural History, op. cit.,* Vol. III, *Autobiography,* p. xxxv
17. *Ibid.,* p. xxxvi
18. *Ibid.,* p. xxxviii
19. Edmund's doctor in letter to Norman Moore, 19 July 1887 (Moore Collection)

CHAPTER XVII: A WAY OF LIFE

1. Charles Waterton, *Essays on Natural History, op. cit.,* Vol. II, *The Ivy,* p. 68–9
2. *Ibid., The Yew,* p. 60–1

3. *Ibid., The Holly*, p. 36
4. *Ibid.*, Vol. I, *The Starling*, p. 83
5. Waterton's Notebook, *op. cit.*, 24 May 1862
6. Charles Waterton, *Essays on Natural History, op. cit.*, Vol. III, *Snakes*, p. 279
7. *Ibid.*, Vol. I, *The Jay*, p. 227–8
8. *Ibid., The Carrion Crow*, p. 96
9. Waterton's Notebook, *op. cit.*, 14 October 1852
10. Charles Waterton, *Natural History Essays with a Life of the Author, op. cit., The Heron*, p. 385
11. *Ibid., The Weasel*, p. 230
12. Waterton's Notebook, *op. cit.*, 21 April 1849
13. Charles Waterton, *Essays on Natural History, op. cit.*, Vol. II, *On Beauty in the Animal Creation*, p. 158–9
14. Waterton's Notebook, *op. cit.*, 21 April 1849
15. Waterton in letter to George Ord, 4 July 1833 (Moore Collection)
16. Charles Waterton, *Essays on Natural History, op. cit.*, Vol. I, *The Magpie*, p. 235–6

CHAPTER XVIII: OTHER PEOPLE

1. Waterton in conversation noted in Norman Moore's *Notebooks*, 1865 (Moore Collection)
2. *Ibid.*
3. George Harley, *op. cit.*, p. 264
4. *Ibid.*, p. 265–6
5. *Ibid.*, p. 269
6. *Ibid.*, p. 277
7. Charles Darwin in letter to Lyell, 1845, *Darwin Life and Letters*, Vol. I, p. 343–4
8. W. M. Thackeray, *The Newcomes* (1854–5)
9. Richard Owen in letter to Waterton, 18 October 1850 (Royal College of Surgeons Collection)
10. Waterton in letter to Richard Owen, 19 May 1851 (Royal College of Surgeons Collection)
11. *Ibid.*
12. Waterton in letter to George Ord, 31 May 1851 (Moore Collection)
13. Paul Belloni du Chaillu, *Explorations & Adventures in Equatorial Africa* (1861)
14. Waterton in letter to George Ord, 27 June 1861 (Moore Collection)
15. George Ord in letter to Waterton, 27 March 1838 (American Philosophical Society Library)
16. *Ibid.*, 26 July 1858
17. *Ibid.*, 4 March 1860
18. Waterton in letter to George Ord, 7 November 1854 (Moore Collection)

19. *Ibid.*, 11 September 1862
20. *Miss Lawson's Recollections of Ornithologists, op. cit.*, p. 280
21. Waterton in letter to Eliza, 11 September 1858
22. Waterton in letter to George Ord (Moore Collection)
23. *Ibid.*, February 1864
24. *Ibid*, 21 February 1863
25. *Ibid.*, 18 April 1852
26. *Ibid.*, 11 January 1861
27. George Ord in letter to Waterton, 1835 (American Philosophical Society Library)
28. Lydia Edmonstone in letter to George Ord, 1865 (Moore Collection)
29. Waterton in letter to Eliza, 1850 (Moore Collection)
30. Richard Hobson, *Charles Waterton, His Home, Habits and Handiwork*, p. 142 (Whitaker & Sons, Ltd, London, 2nd Edition, 1867)
31. *Ibid.*, p.194
32. *Ibid.*, p. 66
33. *Ibid.*, Preface, p. vi
34. Waterton in letter to his publisher, 6 August 1862 (Moore Collection)
35. Edmund in letter to family solicitor, 1865 (Moore Collection)
36. Richard Hobson, *op. cit.*, *Preface*, p. ix
37. *Ibid.*, *List of Contents*, p. xiii–xxx
38. *Westminster Gazette* (1866)

CHAPTER XIX: STRANGE CREATURES

1. Frank Buckland, *Curiosities of Natural History*, p. 143 (Hodder & Stoughton 1946)
2. Wilfrid Blunt, *The Ark in the Park: The Zoo in the Nineteenth Century*, p. 136 (Thames & Hudson 1976)
3. Waterton in letter to George Ord, 26 April 1854 (Moore Collection)
4. *A Brazilian in Bloomsbury* (*Household Words* 1853)
5. Charles Waterton, *Essays on Natural History, op. cit.*, Vol. III, *A New History of the Monkey Family*, p. 11
6. *Ibid.*, p. 53
7. *Ibid.*, p. 54
8. *Ibid.*, p. 55
9. *Ibid.*, p. 58
10. Richard Hobson, *op. cit.*, p. 74
11. Waterton in letter to George Ord, 18 June 1852 (Moore Collection)
12. Waterton in letter to Rev. J. J. Wood, 8 April 1863 (Wellcome Institute Collection)
13. Charles Waterton, *Essays on Natural History, op. cit.*, Vol. III, *A New History of the Monkey Family*, p. 64–5
14. *Ibid.*, p. 66–7
15. Waterton in letters to unnamed ladies, 1863 (Moore Collection)

16. Charles Waterton, *Natural History Essays with a Life of the Author*, *op. cit.*, Waterton in letter to Alfred Ellis, 3 April 1861, p. 615–16
17. Waterton in letter to Hon. Stanhope Hawke, 16 January 1863 (American Philosophical Society Library)
18. Waterton in letter to George Ord, 12 June 1853 (Moore Collection)
19. *Ibid.*, 4 November 1852
20. *Ibid.*
21. Charles Waterton, *Essays on Natural History*, *op. cit.*, Vol. III, *Snakes*, p. 286
22. Richard Hobson, *op. cit.*, p. 71
23. *Ibid.*, p. 73
24. Charles Waterton, *Essays on Natural History*, *op. cit.*, Vol. III, *A New History of the Monkey Family*, p. 38

CHAPTER XX: THERE IS A REMEDY FOR EVERYTHING BUT DEATH

1. Charles Waterton, *Essays on Natural History*, *op. cit.*, Vol. III, *Aix-la-Chapelle*, p. 144
2. *Ibid.*, p. 142–3
3. Edmund in letter to Robert Pashley, 1860s
4. *Ibid.*
5. Waterton in letter to George Ord, 11 April 1863 (Moore Collection)
6. Waterton in letter to Edmund, 8 September 1863 (American Philosophical Society Library)
7. Norman Moore's *Notebooks*, September 1863 (Moore Collection)
8. Norman Moore, A New Journal to Stella, Vol. II, 28 January 1877 (Moore Collection)
9. Norman Moore's *Notebooks*, 1863 (Moore Collection)
10. Norman Moore, A New Journal to Stella, Vol. IV, 1876–78 (Moore Collection)
11. Norman Moore's *Notebooks*, 1863 (Moore Collection)
12. Waterton in letter to Norman Moore, 14 January 1865 (Moore Collection)
13. Norman Moore's *Notebooks*, 4–14 February 1865 (Moore Collection)
14. Waterton in letter to unknown correspondent, 27 February 1865 (Moore Collection)
15. Norman Moore's *Notebooks*, 8 February 1865 (Moore Collection)
16. *Ibid.*, May 1865
17. *Ibid.*, 24 May 1865
18. Norman Moore in letter to Mr Hereford, 27 May 1865 (Moore Collection)

CHAPTER XXI: CODA

1. William Shakespeare, *As You Like It*, Act II, Scene V
2. Norman Moore in letter to his mother, 1 June 1865 (Moore Collection)
3. Lydia Edmonstone in letter to George Ord, June 1865 (Moore Collection
4. Waterton's last will, 15 May 1865 (Wakefield Library Collection)
5. Eliza in letter to Norman Moore, 22 June 1865 (Moore Collection)
6. Chancery Document, 1866 (Wakefield Library Collection)
7. *Ibid.*
8. Papers sent to Philip Gosse by a Wakefield man whose grandfather knew Waterton, 1941 (Brotherton Collection, Leeds)
9. Letter from a Naturalist (Rotherham) to *The Times*, 1867 (Fitzwilliam Archive, Cambridge)
10. Eliza in letter to Norman Moore, 9 December 1868 (Moore Collection)
11. Letter from unknown correspondent to Edward Simpson (John Goodchild Collection)
12. Eliza in letter to Norman Moore, Ostend, 14 August 1870 (Moore Collection)
13. Letter from Edward Simpson to unknown correspondent *c.* 1876 (John Goodchild Collection)
14. *Ibid.*
15. *Ibid.*
16. Helen Edmonstone in letter to Norman Moore, 5 April 1877 (Moore Collection)
17. Edmund in letter to Norman Moore, 10 December 1879 (Moore Collection)
18. Edmund in letter to Edward Simpson, *c.* 1879 (John Goodchild Collection)
19. Julia Pitte-Byrne, *op. cit.*, p. 114
20. *Ibid.*
21. *Ibid.*, p. 117

SELECT BIBLIOGRAPHY

Aldington, Richard, *The Strange Life of Charles Waterton* (Evans Brothers 1949)

Allen, David Elliston, *The Naturalist in Britain: A Social History* (Allen Lane 1976)

Barber, Lynn, *The Heyday of Natural History* (Jonathan Cape 1980)

Blunt, Wilfrid, *The Ark in the Park: The Zoo in the Nineteenth Century* (Hamish Hamilton 1976)

Chancellor, John P., *Audubon: A Biography* (Thames and Hudson 1978)

Dance, Peter, *Animal Fakes and Frauds* (Sampson Low 1976)

Durrell, Gerald, *Three Singles to Adventure* (Rupert Hart Davis 1954)

Gosse, Philip, *The Squire of Walton Hall* (Cassell 1940)

Gunther, A. E. A., *A Century of Zoology at the British Museum* (Dawsons 1975)

Halliday, T., *Vanishing Birds. Their Natural History and Conservation* (Sidgwick & Jackson 1978)

Hobson, Richard, *Charles Waterton, His Home, Habits and Handiwork* (Whitaker & Sons, Ltd 1867)

Irwin, R. A., *Letters of Charles Waterton* (Rocliff 1955)

Jenkins, Alan C., *The Naturalists, Pioneers of Natural History* (Hamish Hamilton 1978)

Kastner, Joseph, *A Species of Eternity* (Alfred Knopf, New York 1977)

Keay, John, *Eccentric Travellers* (John Murray 1982)

Kingzett, C. T., *History of the Alkali Trade* (London 1877)

Lloyd, Clare, *The Travelling Naturalists* (Croom Helm Ltd 1985)

Rodway, James, *History of British Guiana from the year 1668 to the present time* (3 volumes) (J. Thomson, Georgetown 1894)

Sitwell, Edith, *English Eccentrics* (Penguin Books 1980)

Teale, Edwin Way, *Audubon's Wildlife* (Thames and Hudson 1965)

Waterton, Charles, *Essays on Natural History* (3 volumes) (Longmans 1838)

Waterton, Charles, *Natural History Essays with a Life of the Author*, ed. Norman Moore (Frederick Warne Ltd 1870)

Waterton, Charles, *Wanderings in South America*, ed. J. G. Wood (Century Publishing Co. 1984)

INDEX